CHOOSING
YOUR RV
HOME BASE

D1495400

Published by:

Roundabout Publications
PO Box 19235
Lenexa, KS 66285

800-455-2207

www.TravelBooksUSA.com
www.RoundaboutPublications.com

Published by:

Roundabout Publications
PO Box 19235
Lenexa, KS 66285

Phone:800-455-2207
Internet: www.TravelBooksUSA.com

Library of Congress Control Number: 2013958067

ISBN-10: 1-885464-49-5
ISBN-13: 978-1-885464-49-1

Contents

Introduction

The full-time RV lifestyle comes with many wonderful benefits, including the freedom to travel anywhere in this great country. That freedom, however, doesn't include escaping the realities of paying taxes and other legal matters such as registering a vehicle or obtaining a driver's license. Without proper planning, these common issues can become a challenge for the full-time RVer.

While it's possible to have a driver's license from one state, your vehicle registered in another state, and "live" somewhere else, this practice is not advised. Without a clearly established home base or domicile, it is possible that you could become liable for taxes in more than one state.

To avoid any potential complications, your best option is to establish a home base. This should be the state where your vehicle is registered, where you obtain your driver's license, register to vote, have your bank account, acquire your insurance and all the other necessities of life. This will also be the state in which you pay your taxes.

Choosing a home base can be an important decision. There are many factors that must be considered. Simply selecting a state that has the lowest (or no) state income tax is not always your best option. For example, a state with high income taxes may have a lower sales tax rate or vehicle registration fee. Some states rely heavily on property taxes for their revenue so they may have a lower income tax rate. This book provides a wealth of information to help you narrow your home base search.

It is recommended you use this book in combination with further research tailored to your specific needs. This can be a time-consuming process but the savings can be significant.

The full-time RV lifestyle gives you the unique opportunity to choose any state to call "home." Although you can legally only have one domicile at any time, your home base decision does not need to be permanent. As your personal situation changes, so can your domicile if it's to your advantage.

How to Use This Book

Choosing Your RV Home Base presents information in two useful formats. The first section shows all the information for each state. The second section shows the information topics in chart form. This allows you to easily compare specific information with all the other states.

Due to the nature of this information (taxes, fees, regulations, etc.) the rules can and do change. Before reaching any final decision, it is best to confirm the information provided.

Following is an explanation of all the *information topics* covered for each state and in the charts.

Terms / Definition

Ad Valorem Tax - "Ad valorem" is frequently used to refer to property values by county tax assessors. An *ad valorem* tax is a tax with a rate given as a proportion to an items value. It is commonly imposed on an annual basis for real estate, vehicles, and other *real* or *personal property*.

Median - The *median* is the numerical value separating the higher half of a data sample from the lower half. Half the numbers are above the *median* and half are below.

Per Capita - *Per Capita* is commonly used in statistics in place of saying "for each person" or "per person."

STATE AND LOCAL TAXES

State Sales Tax (%) 4	
Exempt: prescription drugs.	
Local Sales Taxes (up to an additional %) 8.5	
Inheritance Tax .... No	
Estate Tax .... No	

STATE AND LOCAL TAXES

State Sales Tax

Only five states do not collect sales tax (AK, DE, MT, NH, and OR). A few states have a single statewide rate but most allow local governments to add to the base tax rate. The state sales tax can range from a low of 2.9% (CO) to a high of 7.5% (CA).

Local Sales Taxes

In Alabama, the highest, local rates can add up to an additional 8.5%. Mississippi comes in with the lowest local rate at 0.25%. Arizona has the top spot with a combined state and local sales tax rate of 12.7%. Twelve states plus the District of Columbia have no local sales tax.

Inheritance Tax

An *Inheritance Tax* is charged against the shares of certain beneficiaries who inherit an estate. At the current time, only 6 states have an inheritance tax (IA, KY, MD, NE, NJ, and PA). Note that Maryland and New Jersey have both an *Inheritance Tax* and an *Estate Tax*. If this is a factor for you, check with the state for specifics; rules and limits vary with each state.

Estate Tax

An *Estate Tax* is charged against the entire estate regardless of who inherits the estate. At present, 15 states plus the District of Columbia have an estate tax. For each state you will find the exemption amount and the top tax rate. The tax in Tennessee will be phased out by 2016. Note that Maryland and New Jersey have both an *Inheritance Tax* and an *Estate Tax*. If this will be an issue for you, check with the state for specifics; rules and limits change and vary with each state. Also note that the Federal Estate Tax rate for 2013 is 40% on estates valued over $5.25 million.

PERSONAL INCOME TAXES

State Income Tax (%) ....3 - 4.9
   2 income brackets - Lowest $15,000; Highest $30,000.

Personal Exemption $ (single / joint) ...... 2,250 / 4,500

Standard Deduction $ (single / joint)...... 3,000 / 6,000
   Additional $850 if age 65 or over.

Federal Income Tax Paid - Deduction Allowed ..... None

Social Security Income - Tax Exempt......................Limits
   Exempt if federal adjusted gross income is $75,000 or less.

Retired Military Pay - Tax Exempt .... Yes

State & Local Government Pensions - Tax Exempt .Limits
   Full exemption for Kansas state pensions, none for out-of-state pensions.

Federal Civil Service Pensions - Tax Exempt .... Yes

Railroad Retirement - Tax Exempt .... Yes

Private Pension - Tax Exempt .... No

PERSONAL INCOME TAXES

State Income Tax

All states except for Alaska, Florida, Nevada, South Dakota, Texas, Washington, and Wyoming collect state income tax. Tennessee and New Hampshire tax only interest and dividend income. Seven states (CO, IL, IN, MA, MI, PA, and UT) have a flat tax rate, others use a graduated scale based on income. In addition, county or city level income taxes may be imposed in 14 states.

Tax rates are shown along with the number and range of the income brackets. The tax brackets are for single taxpayers or married people filing separate returns. Some states will increase or double the bracket widths for joint filers to avoid a marriage penalty. Some states will adjust the dollar values each year to the rate of inflation.

Personal Exemption and Standard Deduction

Shown are the deduction amounts for both "single filers" and "married, filing a joint return." Some states will adjust the dollar values each year to the rate of inflation.

Federal Income Tax Paid

This indicates which states allow a deduction for any taxes paid on your federal return.

Retirement Income

The rest of this section covers six types of pension and retirement income and the tax exempt status for each. A "Yes," "No," or "Limits" answer is provided for each retirement income type.

A general explanation for "Limits" is found either below the pension type or at the end with a common note that relates to all. Limits are usually based on age, income, or a maximum amount that can be deducted.

Most states that have an income tax exempt at least part of pension income. Rules vary by state and by type of pension (and there are exceptions to the rules). The information provided here is very general, be sure to get all the specific details for your type of retirement income before reaching any conclusions.

VEHICLES

Registration Fees .... 2 Years
> Passenger vehicles (under 10,000 lbs), $86.
>
> Camper and travel trailer, $81. Add $6.75 for each additional foot over 10 feet. (No vehicle over 45 feet can be registered.)
>
> Motor homes 6 - 14 feet, $54.
> Motor homes 15 feet, $163.50. Add $7.50 for each additional foot. (No vehicle over 45 feet can be registered.)

Annual Vehicle Tax .... No
> No property tax on vehicles.

State Emissions Test Required .... Yes
> Every 2 years. Within and near the Medford or Portland-Metro areas only. Diesel powered vehicles 8,501 lbs or more are exempt. Web Site: www.deq. state.or.us/aq/vip

Vehicle Safety Inspection Required .... No

Mandatory Minimum Liability Insurance 25/50/20
> Personal Injury Protection, Uninsured and Underinsured Motorists coverage is also required.

VEHICLES

Every state will have some basic fees when you first register a vehicle. Some are a one-time fee and include charges for a title transfer, license plate, plus a myriad of other miscellaneous fees that vary by state. Since these fees are due in every state and the difference between the states is relatively small, they are not included in this guide. As a general rule you can expect to pay about $40 to $100 to cover these expenses.

Registration Fee & Annual Vehicle Tax

The registration fee and annual vehicle tax varies substantially between the states. The basic registration fee is usually higher in states that do not have some form of a vehicle tax. If applicable, the vehicle tax is usually due at the time of registration.

The annual vehicle tax that is imposed by 29 states is basically a personal property tax although they may call it by another name. The fee is usually prorated the first time you register and annually thereafter.

Some states use a simple flat fee while others use a more complicated method which usually takes into account the age, weight, type and value of the vehicle. Where possible, these fees are included. Some rates vary depending on the county you live in or other factors that make it impossible to list the total. Some states provide a "Rate Calculator" at their web site.

These fees and taxes can add up. Once you have narrowed your home base search, you are strongly encouraged to contact the state for estimates on these annual vehicle expenses. Better safe than sorry.

State Emissions Test

There are currently 32 states (includes the District of Columbia) with an emissions test program. A few are required on a statewide basis but most only require testing in the major metro areas. The rules vary greatly by state and there are usually many exceptions to the rules including type, weight, and age of vehicle. Diesel-powered vehicles are often exempt. Fees for emissions test are generally inexpensive but there can be exceptions. There is also the obvious added expense for repairs if your vehicle fails to pass.

Vehicle Safety Inspection

Twenty states (includes the District of Columbia) currently require a vehicle safety inspection to verify the vehicle is road worthy. This inspection is usually required every one or two years. There is a minimal charge for the inspection.

In most states you will also need to have the vehicle inspected if moving in from another state. This generally is to verify the vehicle identification number. This is usually done free of charge and only when the vehicle is being registered for the first time.

Mandatory Liability Insurance

All states require that you have insurance or proof of financial responsibility before you are allowed to license and register a vehicle. Each state has established minimums that are indicated here.

The actual wording used by each state to define the limits vary. For comparison reasons we have adopted a "general definition" to represent each part of the insurance requirements. Use this as a guide for comparison purposes only.

As an example, the state minimums are represented as: 15/30/10. The general definition used for each number is as follows:

- The first number, 15 ($15,000) is what insurance will pay out *per person* injured in an accident.

- The second number, 30 ($30,000) is tied into the first and reflects the total injury payout *per accident*.

- The third number, 10 (10,000) refers solely to property damage and how much *per accident* the insurance will cover.

In addition to liability insurance, some states require other forms of coverage like Personal Injury Protection, Uninsured Motorist or other forms of "no-fault" coverage.

Note: The only accurate way to determine what your insurance will cost is to speak with an insurance agency in the area you are considering. No matter what type of insurance (health, life, vehicle, etc.) you will want to check the rates for all your insurance needs. The rates do vary greatly by state and location within the state as well as for the type of insurance.

COST OF LIVING INDICATORS

Rank: 1 highest; 51 lowest

Cost of Living - average statewide (rank)	03
Fuel - $ per gallon, Dec. 2013 (diesel / gas)	4.16 / 3.63

The following "Tax Collections" are all Per Capita

State Individual Income Tax (rank / $)	01 / 1,850
Local Individual Income Tax (rank / $)	03 / 425
State General Sales Tax (rank / $)	36 / 592
Local General Sales Tax (rank / $)	03 / 635
State Property Tax (rank / $)	33 / 0
Local Property Tax (rank / $)	04 / 2,321
State - All Tax Collections (rank / $)	09 / 3,472
Local - All Tax Collections (rank / $)	02 / 3,924
State & Local - All Tax Collections (rank / $)	03 / 7,396

COST OF LIVING INDICATORS

In this section you will find values represented in terms of dollars ($) or a rank of 1 through 51 (includes the District of Columbia). The data will help give you a broad overview of economic conditions and should be used for general reference only.

Cost of Living - average statewide

The ranking provided can give you some insight on the average overall costs associated with living in one state compared to another. Obviously many factors can contribute to your living expenses and each individual situation will be different.

Fuel - average price per gallon

Shown is the average statewide price for both gasoline and diesel fuel. This was in December, 2013, when oil was in the range of $100 per barrel. As a general rule, the price at the pump increases .25 cents for every $10 increase in the per barrel price. The averages for all states ranged from $3.61 in Oklahoma to $4.85 in Hawaii for diesel and $2.94 in Missouri to $3.95 in Hawaii for gasoline.

State & Local Individual Income Tax Collections

Here you will find the states rank and per capita

amount for individual income taxes. Numbers for both state and overall local collections are provided. Of the 43 states with this tax New York collects the most at $1,850. Tennessee with only $29 is the lowest. Only 13 states (counting the District of Columbia) have local governments which collect this tax and the District of Columbia tops the list with $2,073. Kansas is the lowest with $1 per capita collected.

State & Local General Sales Tax Collections

Here you will find the states rank and per capita amount for general sales taxes. Numbers for both state and overall local collections are provided. On the state level Hawaii ranks #1 with $1,793 collected. Colorado collects the least per capita with $419. Five states (AK, DE, MT, NH, and OR) do not have this tax. On the local level there are 17 states with no local taxes. The District of Columbia collects the most at $1,394 and the least amount collected per capita is $34 in Vermont.

State & Local Property Tax Collections

Property taxes can be a major expense in some states. As with all taxes, rules and rates vary widely by state and even within a state. For the 36 state governments with this tax, Massachusetts has the lowest per capita amount ($1) and Vermont is the highest ($1,526). On the local level Arkansas is the lowest with about $289 collected and the highest is from New Jersey with $2,878.

State & Local - All Tax Collections

Use this to compare by state the overall average burden of taxes. This represents income taxes, property taxes, sales taxes, fuel taxes, plus all other taxes paid by individuals and businesses. Your actual taxes will, of course, vary with your property value, where you live within the state, and your total amount and source of income, among other factors. Alaska has the highest combined per capita amount at $9,969 and Alabama at $2,878 collects the smallest amount.

STATE TAX COLLECTIONS

Rank: 1 highest; 50 lowest
Rank and % of total taxes collected from:

Property Tax	21 / 0.42
Sales & Gross Receipts	31 / 43.76
Motor Vehicle & Driver License	38 / 2.14
Individual Income Tax	05 / 49.12
Corporate Income Tax	39 / 3.56
Other Taxes	50 / 1.00

The following tax collections are Per Capita

Total Tax Collections - Ind. & Biz (rank / $)	49 / 1,671
Total Tax Collections - Ind. only (rank / $)	43 / 1,595

STATE TAX COLLECTIONS

Revenue from taxes is probably the one source of state income that effects our wallet the most, at least in a direct manner. The following shows the percentage of income, by source, for state tax collections. The District of Columbia is not included in this section.

Property Tax

Property tax is primarily a local government tax. See "Cost of Living" section for numbers on local property taxes. Property taxes at the state government level account for less than 2% of the total tax revenues for 22 of the 36 states with the tax. Vermont is the highest with 34.41% of their tax revenue coming from property tax. Florida is the lowest at 0.0004%.

Sales & Gross Receipts

This income group includes general sales tax, gross receipts tax, and excise taxes added to items like fuel, alcoholic beverages, and tobacco products. The percent of total revenue collected ranges from 3.52% (Alaska) to 82.64% (Florida).

Motor Vehicle & Driver License

Fees paid for a driver license and vehicle tags are a small part of each state's total tax revenue. The percentages range from 0.83% in Alaska to 7.71% in Oklahoma.

Individual Income Tax

The individual income tax can be a large source of revenue for many of the 43 states with this tax. The total tax revenue percentage ranges from 1.52% for Tennessee to 66.97% in Oregon. Seven states (AK, FL, NV, SD, TX, WA, and WY) have no individual income tax.

Corporate Income Tax

Although consumers do not pay the Corporate Income Tax directly, it is a cost of doing business for the company and is reflected in the prices paid for their products and services. Ohio comes in with the lowest percentage of total tax revenue at 0.45%, New Hampshire is the highest at 23.63%. Four states (NV, TX, WA, and WY) have no corporate income tax.

Other Taxes

Most of the revenue generated with "Other Taxes" are paid by businesses for license fees and severance taxes. Taxes paid by individuals include hunting & fishing license, death and gift taxes. Tax revenue percentages range from 1% to 83.19%. Although 42 states are under 15%, the remaining eight states range from 16.62% in Nevada to 83.19% in Alaska.

Total Tax Collections - Per Capita

There are two references given for *Per Capita* information. The first, **Individual & Business** (*Ind. & Biz*) shows the rank and dollar amount for taxes paid by both individuals and businesses. The next one, **Individual Only** (*Ind. only*) shows the same information but only includes the taxes paid by individuals. The most extreme example is Alaska which ranks the highest per capita with *Individual & Business* taxes, but is the lowest per capita with taxes paid by *Individuals Only*.

STATE FACTS & NUMBERS

Rank: 1 highest; 51 lowest

State Revenue - Per Capita (rank / $) .... 12 / 8,788
State & Local Rev. - Per Capita (rank / $) ..... 06 / 13,653
Personal Income - Per Capita (rank / $) ...... 13 / 46,477
Median Household Income (rank / $) .... 12 / 58,328
Median House Value (rank / $) .... 03 / 358,800
Total Area - Square Miles (rank / count) ... 03 / 163,695
Land Area - Square Miles (rank / count) ... 03 / 155,779
Water Area - Square Miles (rank / count) ..... 06 / 7,916
Number of Counties: 58
Name for Residents: Californians
Capital City: Sacramento
Nickname: The Golden State
State Motto: Eureka (I have found it)
State Bird: California Valley Quail
State Flower: California Poppy
State Tree: California Redwood
State Song: I Love You, California

STATE FACTS & NUMBERS

This section provides miscellaneous information on the state and select state symbols. It is interesting to note that state mottoes are said to reflect the character and beliefs of the citizens when the motto was adopted. They can help us gain insight into the history of a state. Following are some of the items found in this section, the rest are self-explanatory.

State Revenue - Per Capita

Includes total revenue from all sources including money the state receives from the federal government. Texas has the lowest amount per person at $5,114. Alaska tops the chart at $20,399.

State & Local Revenue - Per Capita

Includes the combined total revenue of state and local governments. With local revenue factored in Alabama now has the lowest amount per person at $8,432. Alaska still takes the top spot with $25,216 per capita.

Personal Income - Per Capita

When you take all the personal income and divide it by the state population, Mississippi shows the lowest amount per capita with $33,657. The District of Columbia beats out its closest rival by more than $15,000 with a total amount of $74,773.

Median Household Income

U.S. median household income is $51,371. The states ranged from $37,095 in Mississippi to $71,122 in Maryland.

Median House Value

The median home value for the U.S. is $174,600, down $17,300 from the last report period. The states ranged in value from $98,300 in West Virginia to $503,100 in Hawaii. As in all states, homes in rural areas are usually less expensive than in metro areas.

RESOURCES

Arizona State Government
Phone: 602-542-4900
Web Site: www.az.gov

Arizona Department of Revenue
Phone: 602-255-3381
Web Site: www.azdor.gov

Arizona Motor Vehicle Division
Phone: 602-255-0072
Web Site: www.azdot.gov/mvd

Arizona Office of Tourism
Phone: 866-275-5816
Web Site: www.arizonaguide.com

Voting Information
Phone: 602-542-4285 or 877-843-8683
Web Site: www.azsos.gov/election/

RESOURCES

Provides official state sources for more in-depth information.

POPULATION

Rank: 1 highest; 51 lowest

State Population (rank / count)	04 / 19,317,568
Population Per Square Mile (rank / count)	09 / 294
Male Population (rank / %)	35 / 48.88
Female Population (rank / %)	17 / 51.12
Sex Ratio & Population Median Age	95.6 / 40.7
(Sex Raio = the # of males per 100 females)	
Population % by age (under 18 / 18-44)	21.3 / 34.4
Population % by age (45-64 / 65+)	27.0 / 17.3

POPULATION

Here you will find the total estimated population for the state plus sex and age statistics.

Alabama

STATE AND LOCAL TAXES

State Sales Tax (%) 4
  Exempt: prescription drugs.

Local Sales Taxes (up to an additional %) 8.5
Inheritance Tax .... No
Estate Tax... No

PERSONAL INCOME TAXES

State Income Tax (%) ....2 - 5
  3 income brackets - Lowest $500; Highest $3,000. Any
  city and/or county income taxes are additional.

Personal Exemption $ (single / joint) ....1,500 / 3,000
Standard Deduction $ (single / joint)............2,500 / 7,500
  Deduction amount is gradually reduced as adjusted
  gross income goes above $20,000.

Federal Income Tax Paid - Deduction Allowed ....Full
Social Security Income - Tax Exempt ....Yes
Retired Military Pay - Tax Exempt ....Yes
State & Local Government Pensions - Tax Exempt ....Yes
Federal Civil Service Pensions - Tax Exempt ....Yes
Railroad Retirement - Tax Exempt ....Yes
Private Pension - Tax Exempt ....Limits
  Exempt for qualified plans.

VEHICLES

Registration Fees .... 1 Year
  Passenger cars and pickups to 8,000 lbs GVW, $23.
  Travel trailers, $12.
  Motor home fees are based on GVW:
  0 - 8,000 lbs, $23.
  8,001 - 12,000 lbs, $50.
  12,001 - 18,000 lbs, $100.
  18,001 - 26,000 lbs, $175.
  26,001 - 33,000 lbs, $275.
  33,001 - 42,000 lbs, $500.
  Over 42,000 lbs, varies.

Annual Vehicle Tax ....Yes
  Annual property tax on vehicles.

State Emissions Test Required .... No
Vehicle Safety Inspection Required .... No
Mandatory Minimum Liability Insurance 25/50/25

COST OF LIVING INDICATORS

  Rank: 1 highest; 51 lowest

Cost of Living - average statewide (rank) 36
Fuel - $ per gallon, Dec. 2013 (diesel / gas)......3.76 / 3.15
The following "Tax Collections" are all Per Capita
State Individual Income Tax (rank / $)...................37 / 580
Local Individual Income Tax (rank / $)................... 12 / 23
State General Sales Tax (rank / $).....................43 / 451
Local General Sales Tax (rank / $).....................08 / 373
State Property Tax (rank / $) .... 15 / 66
Local Property Tax (rank / $) ....50 / 471
State - All Tax Collections (rank / $).....................42 / 1,791
Local - All Tax Collections (rank / $)....................44 / 1,087
State & Local - All Tax Collections (rank / $) ......51 / 2,878

STATE TAX COLLECTIONS

  Rank: 1 highest; 50 lowest
  Rank and % of total taxes collected from:

Property Tax...12 / 3.59
Sales & Gross Receipts ....17 / 51.10
Motor Vehicle & Driver License................................34 / 2.46
Individual Income Tax..............................28 / 33.33
Corporate Income Tax................................31 / 4.56
Other Taxes ....26 / 4.93
The following tax collections are Per Capita
Total Tax Collections - Ind. & Biz (rank / $) ....42 / 1,877
Total Tax Collections - Ind. only (rank / $) ....40 / 1,699

STATE FACTS & NUMBERS

  Rank: 1 highest; 51 lowest

State Revenue - Per Capita (rank / $) ....49 / 5,277
State & Local Rev. - Per Capita (rank / $).............51 / 8,432
Personal Income - Per Capita (rank / $) ....43 / 35,926
Median Household Income (rank / $) ....48 / 41,574
Median House Value (rank / $)........................44 / 123,400
Total Area - Square Miles (rank / count) ....30 / 52,420
Land Area - Square Miles (rank / count) ....28 / 50,645
Water Area - Square Miles (rank / count) ....23 / 1,775
Number of Counties... 67
Name for Residents.................................Alabamans
Capital City.......................................Montgomery
Nickname ....Heart of Dixie
State Motto................. We Dare Defend Our Rights
State Bird ....Yellowhammer
State Flower..Camellia
State Tree.........................Southern Longleaf Pine
State Song... Alabama

POPULATION

Rank: 1 highest; 51 lowest

State Population (rank / count) .... 23 / 4,822,023
Population Per Square Mile (rank / count) .... 26 / 92
Male Population (rank / %)....................................45 / 48.54
Female Population (rank / %)................................07 / 51.46
Sex Ratio & Population Median Age..................94.3 / 37.9
  (Sex Ratio = the # of males per 100 females)

Population % by age (under 18 / 18-44) ....23.7 / 35.7
Population % by age (45-64 / 65+) ....26.8 / 13.8

RESOURCES

Alabama State Government
Phone: 334-242-7100
Web Site: www.alabama.gov

Alabama Department of Revenue
Phone: 334-242-1170
Web Site: www.ador.alabama.gov

Alabama Dept. of Public Safety (Driver License)
Phone: 334-242-4400 or 334-242-4371
Web Site: http://dps.alabama.gov

Alabama Motor Vehicles Division
Phone: 334-242-9000
Web Site: www.revenue.alabama.gov/motorvehicle/

Alabama Office of Tourism
Phone: 800-Alabama
Web Site: www.tourism.alabama.gov

Voting Information
Phone: 334-242-7210 or 800-274-8683
Web Site: www.alabamavotes.gov

Alabama

STATE AND LOCAL TAXES

State Sales Tax (%)... None
Local Sales Taxes (up to an additional %) 7.5
Inheritance Tax .... No
Estate Tax.. No

PERSONAL INCOME TAXES

State Income Tax (%) .... None
Personal Exemption $ (single / joint) .... n/a
Standard Deduction $ (single / joint)............................... n/a
Federal Income Tax Paid - Deduction Allowed .... n/a
Social Security Income - Tax Exempt................................. n/a
Retired Military Pay - Tax Exempt .... n/a
State & Local Government Pensions - Tax Exempt .... n/a
Federal Civil Service Pensions - Tax Exempt .... n/a
Railroad Retirement - Tax Exempt .... n/a
Private Pension - Tax Exempt .... n/a

VEHICLES

Registration Fees .... 2 Years
  Passenger vehicles and motor homes, $100.
  Trucks and cargo vans under 10,000 lbs, $100.
  Trailers, $30.

Annual Vehicle Tax ....Yes
  Some municipalities and boroughs levy a Motor Vehicle
  Registration Tax.

State Emissions Test Required .... No
Vehicle Safety Inspection Required .... No
Mandatory Minimum Liability Insurance 50/100/25

COST OF LIVING INDICATORS

Rank: 1 highest; 51 lowest

Cost of Living - average statewide (rank) 04
Fuel - $ per gallon, Dec. 2013 (diesel / gas)......4.07 / 3.68
The following "Tax Collections" are all Per Capita
State Individual Income Tax (rank / $)........................44 / 0
Local Individual Income Tax (rank / $).........................14 / 0
State General Sales Tax (rank / $)....................................46 / 0
Local General Sales Tax (rank / $)...........................05 / 457
State Property Tax (rank / $) ....06 / 252
Local Property Tax (rank / $) ....09 / 1,789
State - All Tax Collections (rank / $).....................01 / 7,571
Local - All Tax Collections (rank / $).....................05 / 2,399
State & Local - All Tax Collections (rank / $) ......01 / 9,969

STATE TAX COLLECTIONS

Rank: 1 highest; 50 lowest

Rank and % of total taxes collected from:

Property Tax...14 / 3.06
Sales & Gross Receipts ....50 / 3.52
Motor Vehicle & Driver License...............................50 / 0.83
Individual Income Tax...44 / 0.00
Corporate Income Tax..04 / 9.41
Other Taxes ....01 / 83.19

The following tax collections are Per Capita

Total Tax Collections - Ind. & Biz (rank / $) ....01 / 9,638
Total Tax Collections - Ind. only (rank / $) ....50 / 714

STATE FACTS & NUMBERS

Rank: 1 highest; 51 lowest

State Revenue - Per Capita (rank / $) ....01 / 20,399
State & Local Rev. - Per Capita (rank / $)..........01 / 25,216
Personal Income - Per Capita (rank / $) ....09 / 49,436
Median Household Income (rank / $) ....03 / 67,712
Median House Value (rank / $)........................12 / 241,400
Total Area - Square Miles (rank / count) ....01 / 665,384
Land Area - Square Miles (rank / count)........01 / 570,641
Water Area - Square Miles (rank / count) ....01 / 94,743
Number of Counties..27
Name for Residents...Alaskans
Capital City..Juneau
Nickname ....The Last Frontier
State Motto... North To The Future
State Bird ....Willow Ptarmigan
State Flower.. Forget-Me-Not
State Tree.. Sitka Spruce
State Song.. Alaska's Flag

POPULATION

Rank: 1 highest; 51 lowest

State Population (rank / count) ....47 / 731,449
Population Per Square Mile (rank / count) ....51 / 1
Male Population (rank / %).....................................01 / 52.04
Female Population (rank / %)................................51 / 47.96
Sex Ratio & Population Median Age...............108.5 / 33.8
   (Sex Ratio = the # of males per 100 females)
Population % by age (under 18 / 18-44) ....26.4 / 38.2
Population % by age (45-64 / 65+) ....27.7 / 7.7

RESOURCES

Alaska State Government
Phone: 907-465-2200
Web Site: www.alaska.gov

Alaska Department of Revenue
Phone: Tax Division 907-269-6620 (Anchorage) or
   907-465-2320 (Juneau)
Web Site: www.dor.alaska.gov

Alaska Division of Motor Vehicles
Phone: 907-269-5551 or 855-269-5551 (in -state)
Web Site: www.state.ak.us/dmv

Alaska Office of Tourism
Phone: 800-862-5275
Web Site: www.travelalaska.com

Voting Information
Phone: 907-465-4611 or 866-952-8683
Web Site: www.elections.alaska.gov/

Arizona

STATE AND LOCAL TAXES

State Sales Tax (%) 5.6
Exempt: food and prescription drugs.

Local Sales Taxes (up to an additional %) 7.1
Inheritance Tax .... No
Estate Tax .... No

PERSONAL INCOME TAXES

State Income Tax (%) .... 2.59 - 4.54
5 income brackets - Lowest $10,000; Highest $150,000.

Personal Exemption $ (single / joint) .... 2,100 / 4,200
Standard Deduction $ (single / joint) .... 4,833 / 9,665
Federal Income Tax Paid - Deduction Allowed .... None
Social Security Income - Tax Exempt .... Yes
Retired Military Pay - Tax Exempt .... Limits
Up to $2,500 exempt.

State & Local Government Pensions - Tax Exempt .. Limits
Up to $2,500 exempt.

Federal Civil Service Pensions - Tax Exempt .... Limits
Up to $2,500 exempt.

Railroad Retirement - Tax Exempt .... Yes
Private Pension - Tax Exempt .... No

VEHICLES

Registration Fees .... 1 Year
Basic fee, $13.50. The VLT tax described below will be in addition to the basic fee.

Annual Vehicle Tax .... Yes
An annual vehicle license tax (VLT) assessed in place of property tax. VLT is based on an assessed value of 60% of the manufacturer's base retail price reduced by 16.25% for each year since the vehicle was first registered in Arizona. The rate is calculated as $2.80 (new vehicles) or $2.89 (used vehicles) for each $100 of the assessed value.

Example: A new vehicle that costs $25,000, the first year assessed value is $15,000 and the VLT would be $420. The second year VLT would be $363.06.

State Emissions Test Required .... Yes
In metro Phoenix and Tucson emission test areas. Some exceptions. New vehicles (5 model years) are exempt. Web Site: www.myazcar.com

Vehicle Safety Inspection Required .... No
Mandatory Minimum Liability Insurance 15/30/10

COST OF LIVING INDICATORS

Rank: 1 highest; 51 lowest

Cost of Living - average statewide (rank) 18
Fuel - $ per gallon, Dec. 2013 (diesel / gas) ...... 3.77 / 3.15
The following "Tax Collections" are all Per Capita
State Individual Income Tax (rank / $) .... 41 / 437
Local Individual Income Tax (rank / $) .... 14 / 0
State General Sales Tax (rank / $) .... 16 / 896
Local General Sales Tax (rank / $) .... 09 / 358
State Property Tax (rank / $) .... 13 / 116
Local Property Tax (rank / $) .... 35 / 968
State - All Tax Collections (rank / $) .... 40 / 1,872
Local - All Tax Collections (rank / $) .... 31 / 1,433
State & Local - All Tax Collections (rank / $) ...... 41 / 3,305

STATE TAX COLLECTIONS

Rank: 1 highest; 50 lowest
Rank and % of total taxes collected from:

Property Tax .... 08 / 5.82
Sales & Gross Receipts .... 09 / 62.17
Motor Vehicle & Driver License .... 49 / 1.36
Individual Income Tax .... 37 / 23.85
Corporate Income Tax .... 26 / 4.99
Other Taxes .... 47 / 1.81
The following tax collections are Per Capita
Total Tax Collections - Ind. & Biz (rank / $) .... 39 / 1,980
Total Tax Collections - Ind. only (rank / $) .... 38 / 1,845

STATE FACTS & NUMBERS

Rank: 1 highest; 51 lowest

State Revenue - Per Capita (rank / $) .... 45 / 5,803
State & Local Rev. - Per Capita (rank / $) .... 45 / 8,961
Personal Income - Per Capita (rank / $) .... 42 / 36,243
Median Household Income (rank / $) .... 31 / 47,826
Median House Value (rank / $) .... 29 / 158,100
Total Area - Square Miles (rank / count) .... 06 / 113,990
Land Area - Square Miles (rank / count) .... 06 / 113,594
Water Area - Square Miles (rank / count) .... 48 / 396
Number of Counties 15
Name for Residents .... Arizonans
Capital City .... Phoenix
Nickname .... Grand Canyon State
State Motto .... God Enriches
State Bird .... Cactus Wren
State Flower .... Saguaro Cactus Blossom
State Tree .... Palo Verde
State Song .... Arizona March Song

POPULATION

Rank: 1 highest; 51 lowest

State Population (rank / count) .... 15 / 6,553,255
Population Per Square Mile (rank / count) .... 34 / 57
Male Population (rank / %)..13 / 49.68
Female Population (rank / %)................................39 / 50.32
Sex Ratio & Population Median Age..................98.7 / 35.9
    (Sex Ratio = the # of males per 100 females)

Population % by age (under 18 / 18-44) ....25.5 / 36.2
Population % by age (45-64 / 65+) ....24.5 / 13.8

RESOURCES

Arizona State Government
Phone: 602-542-4900
Web Site: www.az.gov

Arizona Department of Revenue
Phone: 602-255-3381
Web Site: www.azdor.gov

Arizona Motor Vehicle Division
Phone: 602-255-0072
Web Site: www.azdot.gov/mvd

Arizona Office of Tourism
Phone: 866-275-5816
Web Site: www.arizonaguide.com

Voting Information
Phone: 602-542-4285 or 877-843-8683
Web Site: www.azsos.gov/election/

Arkansas

STATE AND LOCAL TAXES

State Sales Tax (%)..6.5
    Prescription drugs exempt. Food is taxed at 1.5%.

Local Sales Taxes (up to an additional %) 5.5
Inheritance Tax .... No
Estate Tax.. No

PERSONAL INCOME TAXES

State Income Tax (%) ....1 - 7
    6 income brackets - Lowest $4,099; Highest $34,000. Any
    city and/or county income taxes are additional.

Personal Exemption $ (single / joint) .... 23 / 46
    Amount is a tax credit.

Standard Deduction $ (single / joint)............2,000 / 4,000
Federal Income Tax Paid - Deduction Allowed .... None
Social Security Income - Tax Exempt................................Yes
Retired Military Pay - Tax Exempt .... Limits
State & Local Government Pensions - Tax Exempt .. Limits
Federal Civil Service Pensions - Tax Exempt ....Limits
Railroad Retirement - Tax Exempt ....Yes
Private Pension - Tax Exempt ....Limits

> *Note: Limits include a maximum combined exemption*
> *of $6,000 from all retirement income sources other than*
> *Social Security and Railroad Retirement.*

VEHICLES

Registration Fees .... 1 Year
    Passenger cars, trucks, vans, and motor homes. Rate is
    based on vehicle weight, $20 - $33.

Annual Vehicle Tax ....Yes
    Annual property tax on vehicles.

State Emissions Test Required .... No
Vehicle Safety Inspection Required .... No
Mandatory Minimum Liability Insurance 25/50/25
    Personal Injury Protection is also required.

COST OF LIVING INDICATORS

Rank: 1 highest; 51 lowest

Cost of Living - average statewide (rank) 43
Fuel - $ per gallon, Dec. 2013 (diesel / gas)......3.73 / 3.05
The following "Tax Collections" are all Per Capita
State Individual Income Tax (rank / $)...................28 / 770
Local Individual Income Tax (rank / $)........................14 / 0

State General Sales Tax (rank / $) .... 12 / 928
Local General Sales Tax (rank / $) .... 15 / 310
State Property Tax (rank / $) .... 03 / 326
Local Property Tax (rank / $) .... 51 / 289
State - All Tax Collections (rank / $) .... 16 / 2,697
Local - All Tax Collections (rank / $) .... 51 / 677
State & Local - All Tax Collections (rank / $) ...... 39 / 3,374

STATE TAX COLLECTIONS

Rank: 1 highest; 50 lowest
Rank and % of total taxes collected from:

Property Tax .... 04 / 12.17
Sales & Gross Receipts .... 23 / 48.06
Motor Vehicle & Driver License .... 40 / 2.07
Individual Income Tax .... 33 / 28.98
Corporate Income Tax .... 28 / 4.87
Other Taxes .... 34 / 3.84
The following tax collections are Per Capita
Total Tax Collections - Ind. & Biz (rank / $) .... 17 / 2,810
Total Tax Collections - Ind. only (rank / $) .... 12 / 2,565

STATE FACTS & NUMBERS

Rank: 1 highest; 51 lowest

State Revenue - Per Capita (rank / $) .... 24 / 7,726
State & Local Rev. - Per Capita (rank / $) .... 37 / 9,440
Personal Income - Per Capita (rank / $) .... 46 / 35,437
Median Household Income (rank / $) .... 50 / 40,112
Median House Value (rank / $) .... 49 / 106,900
Total Area - Square Miles (rank / count) .... 29 / 53,179
Land Area - Square Miles (rank / count) .... 27 / 52,035
Water Area - Square Miles (rank / count) .... 31 / 1,143
Number of Counties 75
Name for Residents .... Arkansans
Capital City .... Little Rock
Nickname .... The Natural State
State Motto .... The People Rule
State Bird .... Mockingbird
State Flower .... Apple Blossom
State Tree .... Pine Tree
State Songs .... Arkansas / Oh, Arkansas

POPULATION

Rank: 1 highest; 51 lowest

State Population (rank / count) .... 32 / 2,949,131
Population Per Square Mile (rank / count) .... 35 / 55
Male Population (rank / %) .... 28 / 49.10
Female Population (rank / %) .... 24 / 50.90

Sex Ratio & Population Median Age .... 96.5 / 37.4
(Sex Ratio = the # of males per 100 females)
Population % by age (under 18 / 18-44) .... 24.4 / 35.2
Population % by age (45-64 / 65+) .... 26.0 / 14.4

RESOURCES

Arkansas State Government
Phone: 501-682-3000
Web Site: www.arkansas.gov

Arkansas Department of Finance and Administration
Phone: 501-682-1100
Web Site: www.arkansas.gov/dfa

Arkansas Office of Motor Vehicle
Phone: 501-682-4692
Web Site: www.dfa.arkansas.gov/offices/motorVehicle/
Pages/default.aspx

Arkansas Office of Tourism
Phone: 501-682-7777
Web Site: www.arkansas.com

Moving to Arkansas, A Tax Guide For New Residents
Web Site: www.arkansas.gov/dfa/income_tax/
documents/moving_2_arkansas.pdf

Voting Information
Phone: 501-682-1010
Web Site: www.sos.arkansas.gov/elections

California

STATE AND LOCAL TAXES

State Sales Tax (%) 7.5
Exempt: food and prescription drugs.

Local Sales Taxes (up to an additional %) 2.5
Inheritance Tax .... No
Estate Tax .... No

PERSONAL INCOME TAXES

State Income Tax (%) .... 1 - 12.3
9 income brackets - Lowest $7,455; Highest $500,000.

Personal Exemption $ (single / joint) .... 104 / 208
Amount is a tax credit. Tax credit is gradually eliminated starting with adjusted gross income of $169,730 for single filers and $339,464 for joint filers.

Standard Deduction $ (single / joint) .... 3,841 / 7,682
Federal Income Tax Paid - Deduction Allowed .... None
Social Security Income - Tax Exempt .... Yes
Retired Military Pay - Tax Exempt .... No
State & Local Government Pensions - Tax Exempt .... No
Federal Civil Service Pensions - Tax Exempt .... No
Railroad Retirement - Tax Exempt .... Yes
Private Pension - Tax Exempt .... No

VEHICLES

Registration Fees .... 1 Year
$46 plus. Fees vary. An exact amount can only be calculated when you submit your application. Some fees are due on every vehicle, assessment of other fees is based on type of vehicle and county of residence.

To estimate registration fees you can use the "Vehicle Registration Fee Calculator" at www.dmv.ca.gov/ FeeCalculatorWeb/index.jsp

In addition to registration fees, a Nonresident Service Fee of $17 is charged for any vehicle previously registered out-of-state.

Annual Vehicle Tax .... Yes
An annual Vehicle License Fee (VLF) is assessed in lieu of property tax. The VLF is based on the purchase price or the value of the vehicle when acquired. The VLF decreases with each renewal for the first 11 years.

State Emissions Test Required .... Yes
Every two years in 40 counties (only some "Zip Codes" within 6 of the counties). Diesel powdered vehicles manufactured prior to 1998 or with a GVWR of more than 14,000 lbs are exempt.
Web Site: www.dmv.ca.gov/vr/smogfaq.htm

Vehicle Safety Inspection Required .... No
Mandatory Minimum Liability Insurance 15/30/5

COST OF LIVING INDICATORS

Rank: 1 highest; 51 lowest

Cost of Living - average statewide (rank) 07
Fuel - $ per gallon, Dec. 2013 (diesel / gas) ...... 4.07 / 3.58
The following "Tax Collections" are all Per Capita
State Individual Income Tax (rank / $) .... 06 / 1,328
Local Individual Income Tax (rank / $) .... 14 / 0
State General Sales Tax (rank / $) .... 20 / 815
Local General Sales Tax (rank / $) .... 18 / 239
State Property Tax (rank / $) .... 14 / 84
Local Property Tax (rank / $) .... 21 / 1,322
State - All Tax Collections (rank / $) .... 11 / 3,068
Local - All Tax Collections (rank / $) .... 16 / 1,801
State & Local - All Tax Collections (rank / $) ..... 12 / 4,869

STATE TAX COLLECTIONS

Rank: 1 highest; 50 lowest
Rank and % of total taxes collected from:

Property Tax .... 15 / 1.85
Sales & Gross Receipts .... 42 / 34.37
Motor Vehicle & Driver License .... 15 / 3.41
Individual Income Tax .... 06 / 48.97
Corporate Income Tax .... 07 / 7.07
Other Taxes .... 28 / 4.32
The following tax collections are Per Capita
Total Tax Collections - Ind. & Biz (rank / $) .... 12 / 2,954
Total Tax Collections - Ind. only (rank / $) .... 10 / 2,617

STATE FACTS & NUMBERS

Rank: 1 highest; 51 lowest

State Revenue - Per Capita (rank / $) .... 12 / 8,788
State & Local Rev. - Per Capita (rank / $) .... 06 / 13,653
Personal Income - Per Capita (rank / $) .... 13 / 46,477
Median Household Income (rank / $) .... 12 / 58,328
Median House Value (rank / $) .... 03 / 358,800
Total Area - Square Miles (rank / count) .... 03 / 163,695
Land Area - Square Miles (rank / count) .... 03 / 155,779
Water Area - Square Miles (rank / count) .... 06 / 7,916
Number of Counties 58
Name for Residents .... Californians
Capital City .... Sacramento

Nickname ....The Golden State
State Motto...Eureka (I have found it)
State Bird ....California Valley Quail
State Flower..California Poppy
State Tree.....................................California Redwood
State Song..................................I Love You, California

POPULATION

Rank: 1 highest; 51 lowest

State Population (rank / count) ....01 / 38,041,430
Population Per Square Mile (rank / count) ....12 / 232
Male Population (rank / %)......................................12 / 49.71
Female Population (rank / %)................................40 / 50.29
Sex Ratio & Population Median Age..................98.8 / 35.2
(Sex Ratio = the # of males per 100 females)
Population % by age (under 18 / 18-44) ....25.0 / 38.7
Population % by age (45-64 / 65+) ....24.9 / 11.4

RESOURCES

California State Government
Phone: 916-657-9900 or 800-807-6755
Web Site: www.ca.gov

California Franchise Tax Board
Phone: 800-852-5711
Web Site: www.ftb.ca.gov

California Office of Motor Vehicles
Phone: 800-777-0133
Web Site: www.dmv.ca.gov

California Office of Tourism
Phone: 916-444-4429 or 877-225-4367
Web Site: www.visitcalifornia.com

Voting Information
Phone: 916-653-6814 or 800-345-8683
Web Site: www.sos.ca.gov/elections/

Colorado

STATE AND LOCAL TAXES

State Sales Tax (%)...2.9
Exempt: food and prescription drugs.

Local Sales Taxes (up to an additional %) 7
Inheritance Tax .... No
Estate Tax... No

PERSONAL INCOME TAXES

State Income Tax (%) 4.63
Flat rate, no income brackets.

Personal Exemption $ (single / joint) ....3,900 / 7,800
Standard Deduction $ (single / joint)........................... None
Federal Income Tax Paid - Deduction Allowed .... None
Social Security Income - Tax Exempt ....Yes
Retired Military Pay - Tax Exempt .... Limits
State & Local Government Pensions - Tax Exempt .. Limits
Federal Civil Service Pensions - Tax Exempt .... Limits
Railroad Retirement - Tax Exempt ....Yes
Private Pension - Tax Exempt .... Limits

Note: Limits include a maximum combined exemption of $20,000 ($24,000 if 65 or older) from all retirement income sources other than Social Security and Railroad Retirement.

VEHICLES

Registration Fees .... 1 Year
Fees are based on the empty weight and type of vehicle. Additional fees may be collected based on county of residence.

Some county web sites will help calculate the fees, visit www.ccionline.org for a list of Colorado counties. If the fees are not available on the county web site you will need to go to the county motor vehicle office.

Annual Vehicle Tax ....Yes
An annual "Ownership Tax" is assessed in lieu of property tax. These taxes are based on the model year and the original taxable value when the vehicle was new.

State Emissions Test Required ....Yes
In some counties, especially around Denver. Requirements for gasoline and diesel powered vehicles vary by county. Web Site: www.aircarecolorado.com

Vehicle Safety Inspection Required .... No
Mandatory Minimum Liability Insurance 25/50/15

COST OF LIVING INDICATORS

Rank: 1 highest; 51 lowest

Cost of Living - average statewide (rank) 21
Fuel - $ per gallon, Dec. 2013 (diesel / gas) ......3.74 / 3.13
The following "Tax Collections" are all Per Capita
State Individual Income Tax (rank / $) .... 21 / 875
Local Individual Income Tax (rank / $) .... 14 / 0
State General Sales Tax (rank / $) .... 45 / 419
Local General Sales Tax (rank / $) .... 04 / 588
State Property Tax (rank / $) .... 33 / 0
Local Property Tax (rank / $) .... 13 / 1,604
State - All Tax Collections (rank / $) .... 41 / 1,825
Local - All Tax Collections (rank / $) .... 06 / 2,376
State & Local - All Tax Collections (rank / $) ......21 / 4,201

STATE TAX COLLECTIONS

Rank: 1 highest; 50 lowest
Rank and % of total taxes collected from:

Property Tax .... 37 / 0.00
Sales & Gross Receipts .... 38 / 39.91
Motor Vehicle & Driver License .... 07 / 4.75
Individual Income Tax .... 08 / 47.56
Corporate Income Tax .... 29 / 4.80
Other Taxes .... 42 / 2.98
The following tax collections are Per Capita
Total Tax Collections - Ind. & Biz (rank / $) ....40 / 1,976
Total Tax Collections - Ind. only (rank / $) ....39 / 1,822

STATE FACTS & NUMBERS

Rank: 1 highest; 51 lowest

State Revenue - Per Capita (rank / $) ....46 / 5,684
State & Local Rev. - Per Capita (rank / $) ....28 / 10,220
Personal Income - Per Capita (rank / $) .... 17 / 45,775
Median Household Income (rank / $) .... 15 / 56,765
Median House Value (rank / $) ....15 / 235,000
Total Area - Square Miles (rank / count) ....08 / 104,094
Land Area - Square Miles (rank / count) ....08 / 103,642
Water Area - Square Miles (rank / count) .... 44 / 452
Number of Counties 64
Name for Residents .... Coloradans
Capital City ....Denver
Nickname ....Centennial State
State Motto ....Nothing Without Providence
State Bird ....Lark Bunting
State Flower .... Rocky Mountain Columbine
State Tree ....Colorado Blue Spruce
State Song ....Where The Columbines Grow

POPULATION

Rank: 1 highest; 51 lowest

State Population (rank / count) .... 22 / 5,187,582
Population Per Square Mile (rank / count) .... 38 / 50
Male Population (rank / %) ....07 / 50.12
Female Population (rank / %) ....45 / 49.88
Sex Ratio & Population Median Age .... 100.5 / 36.1
     (Sex Ratio = the # of males per 100 females)
Population % by age (under 18 / 18-44) ....24.4 / 38.1
Population % by age (45-64 / 65+) ....26.7 / 10.8

RESOURCES

Colorado State Government
Phone: 800-970-3468
Web Site: www.colorado.gov

Colorado Department of Revenue
Phone: 303-238-7378
Web Site: www.colorado.gov/revenue

Colorado Division of Motor Vehicles
Phone: 303-205-5600 or 303-205-5607
Web Site: www.colorado.gov/revenue/dmv

Colorado Office of Tourism
Phone: 800-265-6723
Web Site: www.colorado.com

Voting Information
Phone: 303-894-2200 or 855-428-3555
Web Site: www.sos.state.co.us/pubs/elections/main.htm

Connecticut

STATE AND LOCAL TAXES

State Sales Tax (%) 6.35
  Exempt: food and prescription drugs.

Local Sales Taxes (up to an additional %) .... None
Inheritance Tax .... No
Estate Tax ....Yes
  12% on estates valued over $2 million.

PERSONAL INCOME TAXES

State Income Tax (%) .... 3 - 6.7
  6 income brackets - Lowest, $10,000; Highest, over $250,000.

Personal Exemption $ (single / joint) ....13,000 / 24,000
  There is a $1,000 reduction in the exemption amount for every $1,000 of state adjusted gross income over 27,000.

Standard Deduction $ (single / joint)............................ None
Federal Income Tax Paid - Deduction Allowed .... None
Social Security Income - Tax Exempt............................Limits
  Exempt for individual taxpayers with federal adjusted gross income of less than $50,000. Married, joint return $60,000.

Retired Military Pay - Tax Exempt ....Limits
  50% is tax exempt.

State & Local Government Pensions - Tax Exempt .... No
Federal Civil Service Pensions - Tax Exempt .... No
Railroad Retirement - Tax Exempt ....Yes
Private Pension - Tax Exempt .... No

VEHICLES

Registration Fees .... 2 Years
  Passenger vehicle and pick up truck (under 8,500 lbs GVWR), $80 - $88.
  Trucks and sport utility vehicles are based on the GVWR of the vehicle:
  less than 5,000 lbs, $94 - $130.
  5,001 - 8,000 lbs, $153.20 - $199.60.
  8,001 - 10,000 lbs, $222.80 - $246.
  10,001 - 12,500 lbs, $269.20 - $315.60.
  Camper, $75.

Annual Vehicle Tax ....Yes
  Annual property tax on vehicles.

State Emissions Test Required ....Yes
  Statewide, every two years. Vehicles with a GVWR of

more than 10,000 lbs are exempt. New vehicles (4 model years) are exempt. Web Site: www.ctemissions.com

Vehicle Safety Inspection Required ....Yes
  Some exceptions.

Mandatory Minimum Liability Insurance 20/40/10

COST OF LIVING INDICATORS

  Rank: 1 highest; 51 lowest

Cost of Living - average statewide (rank) 05
Fuel - $ per gallon, Dec. 2013 (diesel / gas)......4.17 / 3.64
The following "Tax Collections" are all Per Capita
State Individual Income Tax (rank / $).................02 / 1,802
Local Individual Income Tax (rank / $)................ 14 / 0
State General Sales Tax (rank / $) .... 15 / 906
Local General Sales Tax (rank / $)................................ 35 / 0
State Property Tax (rank / $) .... 33 / 0
Local Property Tax (rank / $) ....03 / 2,571
State - All Tax Collections (rank / $).....................05 / 3,735
Local - All Tax Collections (rank / $)....................04 / 2,605
State & Local - All Tax Collections (rank / $) ......06 / 6,340

STATE TAX COLLECTIONS

  Rank: 1 highest; 50 lowest
  Rank and % of total taxes collected from:

Property Tax...37 / 0.00
Sales & Gross Receipts ....34 / 43.30
Motor Vehicle & Driver License................................47 / 1.64
Individual Income Tax...07 / 47.80
Corporate Income Tax..35 / 4.05
Other Taxes ....39 / 3.20
The following tax collections are Per Capita
Total Tax Collections - Ind. & Biz (rank / $) ....05 / 4,295
Total Tax Collections - Ind. only (rank / $) ....02 / 4,032

STATE FACTS & NUMBERS

  Rank: 1 highest; 51 lowest

State Revenue - Per Capita (rank / $) ....17 / 8,051
State & Local Rev. - Per Capita (rank / $) ....14 / 11,740
Personal Income - Per Capita (rank / $) ....02 / 59,687
Median Household Income (rank / $) ....04 / 67,276
Median House Value (rank / $)........................08 / 278,600
Total Area - Square Miles (rank / count) ....48 / 5,543
Land Area - Square Miles (rank / count)............48 / 4,842
Water Area - Square Miles (rank / count) ....38 / 701
Number of Counties 8
Name for Residents...Connecticuters
Capital City...Hartford

Nickname ....Constitution State
State Motto................... He Who Transplanted Still Sustains
State Bird...American Robin
State Flower... Mountain Laurel
State Tree... White Oak
State Song...Yankee Doodle

POPULATION

Rank: 1 highest; 51 lowest

State Population (rank / count) .... 29 / 3,590,347
Population Per Square Mile (rank / count) ....04 / 648
Male Population (rank / %).....................................42 / 48.67
Female Population (rank / %)................................10 / 51.33
Sex Ratio & Population Median Age...................94.8 / 40.0
(Sex Ratio = the # of males per 100 females)

Population % by age (under 18 / 18-44) ....22.9 / 34.5
Population % by age (45-64 / 65+) ....28.5 / 14.1

RESOURCES

Connecticut State Government
Phone: 860-622-2200 or 888-703-5410
Web Site: www.ct.gov

Connecticut Department of Revenue Services
Phone: 860-297-5962
Web Site: www.ct.gov/drs

Connecticut Department of Motor Vehicles
Phone: 860-263-5700
Web Site: www.ct.gov/dmv

Connecticut Office of Tourism
Phone: 800-288-4748
Web Site: www.ctvisit.com

Voting Information
Phone: 860-509-6100 or 800-540-3764
Web Site: www.ct.gov/sots/site/

Delaware

STATE AND LOCAL TAXES

State Sales Tax (%) .... None
Local Sales Taxes (up to an additional %) .... None
Inheritance Tax .... No
Estate Tax..Yes
16% on estates valued over $5.34 million.

PERSONAL INCOME TAXES

State Income Tax (%) .... 2.2 - 6.75
6 income brackets - Lowest $5,000; Highest $60,000. Any
city and/or county income taxes are additional.

Personal Exemption $ (single / joint) ....110 / 220
Amount is a tax credit. Additional $110 if age 60 or over.

Standard Deduction $ (single / joint)............3,250 / 6,500
Federal Income Tax Paid - Deduction Allowed .... None
Social Security Income - Tax Exempt...................................Yes
Retired Military Pay - Tax Exempt ....Limits
State & Local Government Pensions - Tax Exempt ..Limits
Federal Civil Service Pensions - Tax Exempt ....Limits
Railroad Retirement - Tax Exempt ....Yes
Private Pension - Tax Exempt ....Limits

Note: Limits include a maximum combined exemption
of $2,000 ($12,500 if 60 or older) from all retirement
income sources other than Social Security and Railroad
Retirement.

VEHICLES

Registration Fees .... 1 Year
Cars, light duty trucks and vans 5,000 lbs or less: $40.
Motor homes and travel trailers for the first 5,000 lbs,
$40. Additional $6.40 per 1,000 lbs above 5,000 lbs.

Annual Vehicle Tax .... No
No property tax on vehicles.

State Emissions Test Required ....Yes
Annual, new vehicles (5 model years) are exempt.
Web Site: www.dmv.de.gov/services/vehicle_services/
other/ve_other_general.shtml

Vehicle Safety Inspection Required ....Yes
Annual, some exceptions.

Mandatory Minimum Liability Insurance 15/30/10
Personal Injury Protection is also required.

COST OF LIVING INDICATORS

Rank: 1 highest; 51 lowest

Cost of Living - average statewide (rank) 15
Fuel - $ per gallon, Dec. 2013 (diesel / gas) ......3.81 / 3.36
The following "Tax Collections" are all Per Capita
State Individual Income Tax (rank / $) ....07 / 1,284
Local Individual Income Tax (rank / $) .... 08 / 56
State General Sales Tax (rank / $) ....46 / 0
Local General Sales Tax (rank / $) ....35 / 0
State Property Tax (rank / $) ....33 / 0
Local Property Tax (rank / $) ....45 / 726
State - All Tax Collections (rank / $) ....06 / 3,556
Local - All Tax Collections (rank / $) ....49 / 884
State & Local - All Tax Collections (rank / $) ......18 / 4,440

STATE TAX COLLECTIONS

Rank: 1 highest; 50 lowest
Rank and % of total taxes collected from:

Property Tax...37 / 0.00
Sales & Gross Receipts ....49 / 14.61
Motor Vehicle & Driver License................................46 / 1.64
Individual Income Tax..17 / 39.03
Corporate Income Tax..06 / 7.81
Other Taxes ....04 / 36.91
The following tax collections are Per Capita
Total Tax Collections - Ind. & Biz (rank / $) ....08 / 3,664
Total Tax Collections - Ind. only (rank / $) ....30 / 2,039

STATE FACTS & NUMBERS

Rank: 1 highest; 51 lowest

State Revenue - Per Capita (rank / $) ....07 / 10,195
State & Local Rev. - Per Capita (rank / $) ....08 / 12,214
Personal Income - Per Capita (rank / $) ....23 / 44,224
Median Household Income (rank / $) ....11 / 58,415
Median House Value (rank / $).........................14 / 235,900
Total Area - Square Miles (rank / count) ....49 / 2,489
Land Area - Square Miles (rank / count) ....49 / 1,949
Water Area - Square Miles (rank / count) ....40 / 540
Number of Counties 3
Name for Residents...Delawareans
Capital City..Dover
Nickname ....First State / Diamond State
State Motto................................Liberty and Independence
State Bird ....Blue Hen Chicken
State Flower....................................Peach Blossom
State Tree.. American Holly
State Song.......................................Our Delaware

POPULATION

Rank: 1 highest; 51 lowest

State Population (rank / count) ....45 / 917,092
Population Per Square Mile (rank / count) ....07 / 368
Male Population (rank / %)....................................46 / 48.44
Female Population (rank / %).................................06 / 51.56
Sex Ratio & Population Median Age...................93.9 / 38.8
(Sex Ratio = the # of males per 100 females)
Population % by age (under 18 / 18-44) ....22.9 / 35.5
Population % by age (45-64 / 65+) ....27.2 / 14.4

RESOURCES

Delaware State Government
Phone: 800-273-9500 (out-of-state) or
        800-464-4357 (in-state)
Web Site: www.delaware.gov

Delaware Division of Revenue
Phone: 302-577-8200
Web Site: www.revenue.delaware.gov

Delaware Division of Motor Vehicles
Phone: 302-434-3200
Web Site: www.dmv.de.gov

Delaware Office of Tourism
Phone: 866-284-7483
Web Site: www.visitdelaware.com

Voting Information
Phone: 302-739-4277
Web Site: www.elections.delaware.gov/

District of Columbia

STATE AND LOCAL TAXES

State Sales Tax (%) 5.75
  Exempt: food and prescription drugs.

Local Sales Taxes (up to an additional %) .... None
Inheritance Tax .... No
Estate Tax ....Yes
  16% on estates valued over $1 million.

PERSONAL INCOME TAXES

State Income Tax (%) ....4 - 8.95
  4 income brackets - Lowest $10,000; Highest $350,000.

Personal Exemption $ (single / joint) ....1,675 / 3,350
Standard Deduction $ (single / joint)...........2,000 / 4,000
Federal Income Tax Paid - Deduction Allowed .... None
Social Security Income - Tax Exempt ....Yes
Retired Military Pay - Tax Exempt .... Limits
State & Local Government Pensions - Tax Exempt .. Limits
Federal Civil Service Pensions - Tax Exempt .... Limits
Railroad Retirement - Tax Exempt ....Yes
Private Pension - Tax Exempt .... No

  *Note: Limits include a maximum combined exemption
  of $3,000 (for taxpayers 62 or older) from all retirement
  income sources other than Social Security and Railroad
  Retirement.*

VEHICLES

Registration Fees .... 1 Year
  Passenger Class A vehicles, rate based on weight:
  3,499 lbs or less, $72.
  3,500 - 4,999 lbs, $115.
  5,000 lbs or more, $155.

  Trailer Class C vehicle, rate based on weight:
  1,499 lbs or less, $50.
  1,500 - 3,499 lbs, $125.
  3,500 - 4,999 lbs, $250.
  5,000 - 6,999 lbs, $400.
  7,000 - 10,999 lbs, $500.
  11,000 - 11,999 lbs, $550.
  For each additional 1,000 lbs over 11,000 lbs, $50.

Annual Vehicle Tax .... No
  No excise tax on most vehicles.

State Emissions Test Required ....Yes

  Every two years. New vehicles are exempt.
  *Web Site: www.dmv.dc.gov/service/vehicle-inspection-
  landing-page*

Vehicle Safety Inspection Required ....Yes
  Every two years.

Mandatory Minimum Liability Insurance 25/50/10
  Uninsured Motorist coverage is also required.

COST OF LIVING INDICATORS

  Rank: 1 highest; 51 lowest

Cost of Living - average statewide (rank) 02
Fuel - $ per gallon, Dec. 2013 (diesel / gas)......3.95 / 3.51
The following "Tax Collections" are all Per Capita
State Individual Income Tax (rank / $)........................44 / 0
Local Individual Income Tax (rank / $)...............01 / 2,073
State General Sales Tax (rank / $) ....46 / 0
Local General Sales Tax (rank / $)......................01 / 1,394
State Property Tax (rank / $) ....33 / 0
Local Property Tax (rank / $) ....02 / 2,779
State - All Tax Collections (rank / $).............................51 / 0
Local - All Tax Collections (rank / $)...................01 / 8,491
State & Local - All Tax Collections (rank / $) ......02 / 8,491

STATE FACTS & NUMBERS

  Rank: 1 highest; 51 lowest

State Revenue - Per Capita (rank / $) ....02 / 20,366
State & Local Rev. - Per Capita (rank / $) ....02 / 20,366
Personal Income - Per Capita (rank / $) ....01 / 74,773
Median Household Income (rank / $) ....05 / 66,583
Median House Value (rank / $)........................02 / 436,000
Total Area - Square Miles (rank / count) .... 51 / 68
Land Area - Square Miles (rank / count) .... 51 / 61
Water Area - Square Miles (rank / count) ....51 / 7
Number of Counties 0
Name for Residents.....................................Washingtonians
Capital City..Washington D.C.
Nickname .... D.C.
State Motto...Justice For All
State Bird .... Wood Thrush
State Flower.......................... American Beauty Rose
State Tree...Scarlet Oak
State Song.......................The Star-Spangled Banner

POPULATION

  Rank: 1 highest; 51 lowest

State Population (rank / count) ....49 / 632,323
Population Per Square Mile (rank / count) ....01 / 9,299

Male Population (rank / %)....................................51 / 47.23
Female Population (rank / %)...............................01 / 52.77
Sex Ratio & Population Median Age..................89.5 / 33.8
   (Sex Ratio = the # of males per 100 females)
Population % by age (under 18 / 18-44) ....16.8 / 48.6
Population % by age (45-64 / 65+) ....23.2 / 11.4

RESOURCES

District of Columbia Government
Phone: 202-737-4404
Web Site: www.dc.gov

Washington DC Office of Tax and Revenue
Phone: 202-727-4829
Web Site: www.otr.cfo.dc.gov

Washington DC Department of Motor Vehicles
Phone: 202-737-4404
Web Site: www.dmv.dc.gov

Washington DC Office of Tourism
Phone: 202-789-7000
Web Site: www.washington.org

Voting Information
Phone: 202-727-2525 or 866-328-6837
Web Site: www.dcboee.org/home.asp

Florida

STATE AND LOCAL TAXES

State Sales Tax (%) 6
   Exempt: food and prescription drugs.
Local Sales Taxes (up to an additional %) 1.5
Inheritance Tax.. No
Estate Tax.. No

PERSONAL INCOME TAXES

State Income Tax (%) .... None
Personal Exemption $ (single / joint) .... n/a
Standard Deduction $ (single / joint)............................. n/a
Federal Income Tax Paid - Deduction Allowed .... n/a
Social Security Income - Tax Exempt................................ n/a
Retired Military Pay - Tax Exempt .... n/a
State & Local Government Pensions - Tax Exempt .... n/a
Federal Civil Service Pensions - Tax Exempt .... n/a
Railroad Retirement - Tax Exempt .... n/a
Private Pension - Tax Exempt .... n/a

VEHICLES

Registration Fees .... 1 Year
   For automobiles, trucks, campers, and motor homes.
   Base fee varies with type of vehicle, length, and weight,
   $13.50 - $47.50. Miscellaneous "Statutory Fees" and "Tax
   Collector Fees" can be an additional $30.

Annual Vehicle Tax .... No
   No property tax on vehicles.

State Emissions Test Required .... No
Vehicle Safety Inspection Required .... No
Mandatory Minimum Liability Insurance 10/20/10
   Personal Injury Protection is also required.

COST OF LIVING INDICATORS

   Rank: 1 highest; 51 lowest

Cost of Living - average statewide (rank) 24
Fuel - $ per gallon, Dec. 2013 (diesel / gas)......3.94 / 3.40
The following "Tax Collections" are all Per Capita
State Individual Income Tax (rank / $)..........................44 / 0
Local Individual Income Tax (rank / $).........................14 / 0
State General Sales Tax (rank / $) ....06 / 1,002
Local General Sales Tax (rank / $)..............................29 / 92
State Property Tax (rank / $) ....33 / 0
Local Property Tax (rank / $) ....19 / 1,343
State - All Tax Collections (rank / $).....................45 / 1,685

Local - All Tax Collections (rank / $)......................23 / 1,693
State & Local - All Tax Collections (rank / $) ......38 / 3,378

STATE TAX COLLECTIONS

Rank: 1 highest; 50 lowest
Rank and % of total taxes collected from:

Property Tax...36 / 0.0004
Sales & Gross Receipts ....01 / 82.63
Motor Vehicle & Driver License...............05 / 5.02
Individual Income Tax.................................44 / 0.00
Corporate Income Tax................................12 / 6.07
Other Taxes ....19 / 6.28
The following tax collections are Per Capita
Total Tax Collections - Ind. & Biz (rank / $) ....47 / 1,708
Total Tax Collections - Ind. only (rank / $) ....47 / 1,497

STATE FACTS & NUMBERS

Rank: 1 highest; 51 lowest

State Revenue - Per Capita (rank / $) ....47 / 5,496
State & Local Rev. - Per Capita (rank / $).............39 / 9,379
Personal Income - Per Capita (rank / $) ....28 / 41,012
Median Household Income (rank / $) ....41 / 45,040
Median House Value (rank / $)........................30 / 154,900
Total Area - Square Miles (rank / count) ....22 / 65,758
Land Area - Square Miles (rank / count)..........26 / 53,625
Water Area - Square Miles (rank / count) ....03 / 12,133
Number of Counties 67
Name for Residents..Floridians
Capital City...Tallahassee
Nickname ....The Sunshine State
State Motto...In God We Trust
State Bird .... Mockingbird
State Flower.. Orange Blossom
State Tree..Palmetto Palm
State Song... Swanee River

POPULATION

Rank: 1 highest; 51 lowest

State Population (rank / count) ....04 / 19,317,568
Population Per Square Mile (rank / count) ....09 / 294
Male Population (rank / %)....................................35 / 48.88
Female Population (rank / %)................................17 / 51.12
Sex Ratio & Population Median Age...................95.6 / 40.7
      (Sex Ratio = the # of males per 100 females)
Population % by age (under 18 / 18-44) ....21.3 / 34.4
Population % by age (45-64 / 65+) ....27.0 / 17.3

RESOURCES

Florida State Government
Phone: 850-488-1234 or 866-693-6748
Web Site: www.myflorida.com

Florida Department of Revenue
Phone: 800-352-3671
Web Site: www.myflorida.com/dor

Florida Dept. of Highway Safety and Motor Vehicles
Phone: 850-617-2000
Web Site: www.flhsmv.gov

Florida Office of Tourism
Phone: 888-735-2872
Web Site: www.visitflorida.com

Voting Information
Phone: 850-245-6200 or 866-308-6739
Web Site: http://election.dos.state.fl.us/

Georgia

STATE AND LOCAL TAXES

State Sales Tax (%)...4
  Prescription drugs exempt. Food is subject to local taxes.

Local Sales Taxes (up to an additional %) 4
Inheritance Tax .... No
Estate Tax .... No

PERSONAL INCOME TAXES

State Income Tax (%) ....1 - 6
  6 income brackets - Lowest $750; Highest $7,000. ($1,000 to $10,000 for joint filers.)

Personal Exemption $ (single / joint) ....2,700 / 5,400
Standard Deduction $ (single / joint).............2,300 / 3,000
  Additional $1,300 if age 65 or over.

Federal Income Tax Paid - Deduction Allowed .... None
Social Security Income - Tax Exempt ....Yes
Retired Military Pay - Tax Exempt .... Limits
State & Local Government Pensions - Tax Exempt .. Limits
Federal Civil Service Pensions - Tax Exempt .... Limits
Railroad Retirement - Tax Exempt ....Yes
Private Pension - Tax Exempt .... Limits

  Note: Limits include a maximum combined exemption of $65,000 (for taxpayers 65 or older) from all retirement income sources other than Social Security and Railroad Retirement.

VEHICLES

Registration Fees .... 1 Year
  Passenger vehicle and trucks 14,000 lbs or less, $20.

Annual Vehicle Tax .... No
  Vehicles purchased on or after March 1, 2013 are subject to the new Title Ad Valorem Tax, a one-time tax based on the value of the vehicle. This replaces sales and use tax and the annual ad valorem tax.

State Emissions Test Required ....Yes
  Annual. Vehicles up to 8,500 lbs in 13 metro-Atlanta counties only. RVs, motor homes, and diesel powered vehicles are exempt. New vehicles (3 model years) are exempt. Web Site: www.cleanairforce.com

Vehicle Safety Inspection Required .... No
Mandatory Minimum Liability Insurance 25/50/25

COST OF LIVING INDICATORS
  Rank: 1 highest; 51 lowest

Cost of Living - average statewide (rank) 37
Fuel - $ per gallon, Dec. 2013 (diesel / gas)......3.81 / 3.24
The following "Tax Collections" are all Per Capita
State Individual Income Tax (rank / $)...................26 / 772
Local Individual Income Tax (rank / $).........................14 / 0
State General Sales Tax (rank / $)..........................41 / 512
Local General Sales Tax (rank / $)...........................10 / 349
State Property Tax (rank / $) ....22 / 8
Local Property Tax (rank / $).............................30 / 1,036
State - All Tax Collections (rank / $).....................50 / 1,613
Local - All Tax Collections (rank / $)....................29 / 1,525
State & Local - All Tax Collections (rank / $) ......46 / 3,138

STATE TAX COLLECTIONS
  Rank: 1 highest; 50 lowest
  Rank and % of total taxes collected from:

Property Tax..21 / 0.42
Sales & Gross Receipts ....31 / 43.76
Motor Vehicle & Driver License...............................38 / 2.14
Individual Income Tax..05 / 49.12
Corporate Income Tax...39 / 3.56
Other Taxes ....50 / 1.00
The following tax collections are Per Capita
Total Tax Collections - Ind. & Biz (rank / $) ....49 / 1,671
Total Tax Collections - Ind. only (rank / $) ....43 / 1,595

STATE FACTS & NUMBERS
  Rank: 1 highest; 51 lowest

State Revenue - Per Capita (rank / $) ....50 / 5,272
State & Local Rev. - Per Capita (rank / $) ....50 / 8,576
Personal Income - Per Capita (rank / $) ....41 / 37,449
Median Household Income (rank / $) ....32 / 47,209
Median House Value (rank / $).........................32 / 149,300
Total Area - Square Miles (rank / count) ....24 / 59,425
Land Area - Square Miles (rank / count) ....21 / 57,513
Water Area - Square Miles (rank / count) ....22 / 1,912
Number of Counties...159
Name for Residents...Georgians
Capital City...Atlanta
Nickname ....Empire State of the South / Peach State
State Motto....................Wisdom, Justice, and Moderation
State Bird ....Brown Thrasher
State Flower.. Cherokee Rose
State Tree...Live Oak
State Song................................Georgia On My Mind

POPULATION

Rank: 1 highest; 51 lowest

State Population (rank / count) .... 08 / 9,919,945
Population Per Square Mile (rank / count) .... 17 / 167
Male Population (rank / %) .... 37 / 48.82
Female Population (rank / %) .... 15 / 51.18
Sex Ratio & Population Median Age .... 95.4 / 35.3
   (Sex Ratio = the # of males per 100 females)

Population % by age (under 18 / 18-44) .... 25.7 / 38.2
Population % by age (45-64 / 65+) .... 25.4 / 10.7

RESOURCES

Georgia State Government
Phone: 678-436-7442 or 800-436-7442
Web Site: www.georgia.gov

Georgia Department of Revenue
Phone: 877-423-6711
Web Site: www.etax.dor.ga.gov

Georgia Motor Vehicle Division (Tags & Registration)
Phone: 855-406-5221
Web Site: http://motor.etax.dor.ga.gov

Georgia Department of Driver Services (Driver License)
Phone: 678-413-8400 or 877-835-5337
Web Site: www.dds.ga.gov

Georgia Office of Tourism
Phone: 800-847-4842
Web Site: www.exploregeorgia.org

Voting Information
Phone: 404-656-2871
Web Site: www.sos.ga.gov/elections/

Hawaii

STATE AND LOCAL TAXES

State Sales Tax (%) 4
   Hawaii has a gross receipts tax of 0.15% to 4%, depending on the business activity. Common consumer transactions are at the 4% level. Exempt: prescription drugs.

Local Sales Taxes (up to an additional %) 0.5
Inheritance Tax .... No
Estate Tax .... Yes
   16% on estates valued over $5.34 million.

PERSONAL INCOME TAXES

State Income Tax (%) .... 1.4 - 11
   12 income brackets - Lowest $2,400; Highest $200,000.

Personal Exemption $ (single / joint) .... 1,040 / 2,080
Standard Deduction $ (single / joint) .... 2,200 / 4,400
Federal Income Tax Paid - Deduction Allowed .... None
Social Security Income - Tax Exempt .... Yes
Retired Military Pay - Tax Exempt .... Yes
State & Local Government Pensions - Tax Exempt .... Yes
Federal Civil Service Pensions - Tax Exempt .... Yes
Railroad Retirement - Tax Exempt .... Yes
Private Pension - Tax Exempt .... Yes

VEHICLES

Registration Fees .... 1 Year
   Hawaii has different rules and fees for each county government. Base fees are $30 plus. Additional fees are based on vehicle weight and usage.

   The annual state tax rates "per pound" are as follows:
   Up to 4,000 lbs, 0.75 cents.
   4,000 to 7,000 lbs, 1 cent.
   7,000 to 10,000 lbs, 1.25 cents.
   For vehicles weighing over 10,000 lbs, $150 flat fee.

   City and county taxes can add an additional 1 to 2 cents per pound.

Annual Vehicle Tax .... Yes
   Fees are included in vehicle registration. No property tax on vehicles.

State Emissions Test Required .... No
Vehicle Safety Inspection Required .... Yes
   Annual.

Mandatory Minimum Liability Insurance 20/40/10
   Personal Injury Protection is also required.

COST OF LIVING INDICATORS

Rank: 1 highest; 51 lowest

Cost of Living - average statewide (rank) 01
Fuel - $ per gallon, Dec. 2013 (diesel / gas)......4.85 / 3.95
The following "Tax Collections" are all Per Capita
State Individual Income Tax (rank / $)..................... 19 / 896
Local Individual Income Tax (rank / $)........................ 14 / 0
State General Sales Tax (rank / $)........................01 / 1,793
Local General Sales Tax (rank / $)............................. 35 / 0
State Property Tax (rank / $) .... 33 / 0
Local Property Tax (rank / $) .... 37 / 951
State - All Tax Collections (rank / $)...................08 / 3,489
Local - All Tax Collections (rank / $)....................38 / 1,232
State & Local - All Tax Collections (rank / $) ......14 / 4,721

STATE TAX COLLECTIONS

Rank: 1 highest; 50 lowest
Rank and % of total taxes collected from:

Property Tax...37 / 0.00
Sales & Gross Receipts ....07 / 64.93
Motor Vehicle & Driver License............................ 13 / 3.75
Individual Income Tax.......................................35 / 27.93
Corporate Income Tax...45 / 1.45
Other Taxes .... 46 / 1/94
The following tax collections are Per Capita
Total Tax Collections - Ind. & Biz (rank / $) ....06 / 3,962
Total Tax Collections - Ind. only (rank / $) ....03 / 3,838

STATE FACTS & NUMBERS

Rank: 1 highest; 51 lowest

State Revenue - Per Capita (rank / $) ....09 / 9,288
State & Local Rev. - Per Capita (rank / $).......... 17 / 11,462
Personal Income - Per Capita (rank / $) ....21 / 44,767
Median Household Income (rank / $) ....06 / 66,259
Median House Value (rank / $)........................01 / 503,100
Total Area - Square Miles (rank / count) ....43 / 10,932
Land Area - Square Miles (rank / count) ....47 / 6,423
Water Area - Square Miles (rank / count) ....13 / 4,509
Number of Counties 5
Name for Residents.......................................Hawaiians
Capital City.. Honolulu
Nickname ....Aloha State
State Motto........... The Life Of The Land Is Perpetuated In
    Righteouness
State Bird ....Hawaiian Goose
State Flower..............................Pua Aloalo (Hibiscus)
State Tree.............................Kukui (Candlenut)
State Song............................ Hawaii Ponoi (Hawaii's Own)

POPULATION

Rank: 1 highest; 51 lowest

State Population (rank / count) ....40 / 1,392,313
Population Per Square Mile (rank / count) ....21 / 127
Male Population (rank / %)....................................09 / 50.08
Female Population (rank / %)...............................43 / 49.92
Sex Ratio & Population Median Age................ 100.3 / 38.6
    (Sex Ratio = the # of males per 100 females)
Population % by age (under 18 / 18-44) ....22.3 / 36.2
Population % by age (45-64 / 65+) ....27.2 / 14.3

RESOURCES

Hawaii State Government
Phone: 808-586-2211
Web Site: www.ehawaii.gov

Hawaii Department of Taxation
Phone: 808-587-4242
Web Site: www.hawaii.gov/tax

Hawaii Department of Motor Vehicles
Hawaii does not have a statewide Department of Motor
Vehicles. Vehicle registration is managed by each
county government.

City & County of Honolulu
Phone: 808-768-4385
Web Site: www.honolulu.gov/csd/vehicle/mvehicle.htm

County of Maui
Phone: 808-270-7363
Web Site: www.co.maui.hi.us/index.aspx?NID=1328

County of Hawaii
Phone: 808-961-8223
Web Site: www.hawaiicounty.gov/finance-vrl/

County of Kauai
Phone: 808-241-4242 (Driver License) or
    808-241-4256 (Tags & Registration)
Web Site: www.kauai.gov

Hawaii Office of Tourism
Phone: 800-464-2924
Web Site: www.gohawaii.com

Voting Information
Phone: 808-453-8683
Web Site: http://hawaii.gov/elections

Idaho

STATE AND LOCAL TAXES

State Sales Tax (%) 6
   Exempt: prescription drugs.

Local Sales Taxes (up to an additional %) 3
Inheritance Tax .... No
Estate Tax .... No

PERSONAL INCOME TAXES

State Income Tax (%) .... 1.6 - 7.4
   7 income brackets - Lowest $1,380; Highest $10,350.

Personal Exemption $ (single / joint) ....3,900 / 7,800
Standard Deduction $ (single / joint) .... 5,950 / 11,900
Federal Income Tax Paid - Deduction Allowed .... None
Social Security Income - Tax Exempt ....Yes
Retired Military Pay - Tax Exempt .... Limits
State & Local Government Pensions - Tax Exempt .. Limits
   Limited to some public safety officer's benefits.

Federal Civil Service Pensions - Tax Exempt .... Limits
Railroad Retirement - Tax Exempt ....Yes
Private Pension - Tax Exempt .... No

Note: Limits include a maximum combined exemption of $27,876 (for taxpayers 65 or older) from all retirement income including Social Security and Railroad Retirement.

VEHICLES

Registration Fees .... 1 Year
   The total cost varies with vehicle age and county of residence. Basic fee for passenger cars and motorhomes, $35 - $60. RV trailers, $9.

   In addition to the basic fee, motorhomes and RV trailers require a recreational vehicle sticker which cost $8.50 for the first $1,000 of market value, plus $5.00 for each additional $1,000 of market value.

Annual Vehicle Tax ....Yes
   Fees are included in vehicle registration. No property tax on vehicles.

State Emissions Test Required ....Yes
   In Ada County only. Motorhomes and vehicles under 1,500 lbs GVWR are exempt.
   Web Site: www.emissiontest.org

Vehicle Safety Inspection Required .... No
Mandatory Minimum Liability Insurance 25/50/15

COST OF LIVING INDICATORS

   Rank: 1 highest; 51 lowest

Cost of Living - average statewide (rank) 44
Fuel - $ per gallon, Dec. 2013 (diesel / gas)......3.88 / 3.20
The following "Tax Collections" are all Per Capita
State Individual Income Tax (rank / $)...................31 / 733
Local Individual Income Tax (rank / $)...................... 14 / 0
State General Sales Tax (rank / $) ....24 / 744
Local General Sales Tax (rank / $) ....35 / 0
State Property Tax (rank / $) ....33 / 0
Local Property Tax (rank / $) ....40 / 857
State - All Tax Collections (rank / $).................36 / 2,044
Local - All Tax Collections (rank / $)....................48 / 908
State & Local - All Tax Collections (rank / $) ......49 / 2,953

STATE TAX COLLECTIONS

   Rank: 1 highest; 50 lowest
   Rank and % of total taxes collected from:

Property Tax...37 / 0.00
Sales & Gross Receipts ....20 / 49.33
Motor Vehicle & Driver License....................10 / 4.13
Individual Income Tax.................................25 / 35.96
Corporate Income Tax.................................15 / 5.59
Other Taxes...25 / 4.99
The following tax collections are Per Capita
Total Tax Collections - Ind. & Biz (rank / $) ....37 / 2,115
Total Tax Collections - Ind. only (rank / $) ....35 / 1,891

STATE FACTS & NUMBERS

   Rank: 1 highest; 51 lowest

State Revenue - Per Capita (rank / $)...................33 / 6,565
State & Local Rev. - Per Capita (rank / $).............46 / 8,834
Personal Income - Per Capita (rank / $) ....50 / 34,481
Median Household Income (rank / $) ....37 / 45,489
Median House Value (rank / $)....................27 / 160,000
Total Area - Square Miles (rank / count) ....14 / 83,569
Land Area - Square Miles (rank / count) ....11 / 82,643
Water Area - Square Miles (rank / count) ....33 / 926
Number of Counties... 44
Name for Residents..Idahoans
Capital City... Boise
Nickname .... Gem State
State Motto...It Is Perpetual
State Bird ....Mountain Bluebird
State Flower...Syringa
State Tree......................... Western White Pine
State Song.........................Here We Have Idaho

Illinois

POPULATION

Rank: 1 highest; 51 lowest

State Population (rank / count) .... 39 / 1,595,728
Population Per Square Mile (rank / count) .... 45 / 19
Male Population (rank / %)................................08 / 50.10
Female Population (rank / %)................................44 / 49.90
Sex Ratio & Population Median Age................ 100.4 / 34.6
   (Sex Ratio = the # of males per 100 females)
Population % by age (under 18 / 18-44) ....27.4 / 35.4
Population % by age (45-64 / 65+) ....24.8 / 12.4

RESOURCES

Idaho State Government
Phone: 800-926-2588
Web Site: www.idaho.gov

Idaho State Tax Commission
Phone: 208-334-7660 or 800-972-7660
Web Site: www.tax.idaho.gov

Idaho Division of Motor Vehicles
Phone: 208-334-8735 (Driver License) or
       208-334-8663 (Tags & Registration)
Web Site: www.itd.idaho.gov/dmv

Idaho Office of Tourism
Phone: 208-334-2470 or 800-847-4843
Web Site: www.visitidaho.org

Voting Information
Phone: 208-334-2852
Web Site: www.idahovotes.gov/

STATE AND LOCAL TAXES

State Sales Tax (%)...6.25
   1% tax on qualifying food and prescription drugs.
Local Sales Taxes (up to an additional %) 4.25
Inheritance Tax .... No
Estate Tax..Yes
   16% on estates valued over $4 million.

PERSONAL INCOME TAXES

State Income Tax (%) 5
   Flat rate, no income brackets.
Personal Exemption $ (single / joint) ....2,000 / 4,000
Standard Deduction $ (single / joint)........................ None
Federal Income Tax Paid - Deduction Allowed .... None
Social Security Income - Tax Exempt...................Yes
Retired Military Pay - Tax Exempt ....Yes
State & Local Government Pensions - Tax Exempt........Yes
Federal Civil Service Pensions - Tax Exempt ....Yes
Railroad Retirement - Tax Exempt ....Yes
Private Pension - Tax Exempt ....Limits
   Exempt for qualified plans.

VEHICLES

Registration Fees .... 1 Year
   Passenger vehicles and trucks up to 8,000 lbs, $101.
   Recreational trailer, fee is based on weight:
   3,000 lbs or less, $18.
   3,001 - 8,000 lbs, $30.
   8,001 - 10,000 lbs, $38.
   10,001 lbs and over, $50.

   Recreational vehicle, fee is based on weight:
   8,000 lbs or less, $78.
   8,0001 - 10,000 lbs, $90.
   10,000 lbs and over, $102.

Annual Vehicle Tax .... No
   No property tax on vehicles.

State Emissions Test Required ....Yes
   Every two years. Vehicles registered in specific ZIP codes
   in Northeastern Illinois and Metro-East St. Louis areas are
   subject to testing. Diesel-powered vehicles are exempt.
   Web Site: www.epa.state.il.us/air/vim

Vehicle Safety Inspection Required .... No
Mandatory Minimum Liability Insurance 20/40/15
   Uninsured Motorist coverage is also required.

COST OF LIVING INDICATORS

Rank: 1 highest; 51 lowest

Cost of Living - average statewide (rank) 31
Fuel - $ per gallon, Dec. 2013 (diesel / gas)......3.89 / 3.29
The following "Tax Collections" are all Per Capita
State Individual Income Tax (rank / $)....................22 / 872
Local Individual Income Tax (rank / $)........................14 / 0
State General Sales Tax (rank / $)...........................38 / 576
Local General Sales Tax (rank / $)...........................26 / 130
State Property Tax (rank / $) ....25 / 5
Local Property Tax (rank / $) ....08 / 1,873
State - All Tax Collections (rank / $).....................22 / 2,377
Local - All Tax Collections (rank / $).....................08 / 2,248
State & Local - All Tax Collections (rank / $) ......15 / 4,625

STATE TAX COLLECTIONS

Rank: 1 highest; 50 lowest
Rank and % of total taxes collected from:

Property Tax...26 / 0.18
Sales & Gross Receipts ....40 / 39.23
Motor Vehicle & Driver License...............................08 / 4.73
Individual Income Tax...11 / 43.07
Corporate Income Tax...03 / 9.59
Other Taxes ....40 / 3.20
The following tax collections are Per Capita
Total Tax Collections - Ind. & Biz (rank / $) ....16 / 2,830
Total Tax Collections - Ind. only (rank / $) ....15 / 2,486

STATE FACTS & NUMBERS

Rank: 1 highest; 51 lowest

State Revenue - Per Capita (rank / $) ....40 / 6,267
State & Local Rev. - Per Capita (rank / $)..........27 / 10,379
Personal Income - Per Capita (rank / $) ....16 / 45,832
Median Household Income (rank / $) ....17 / 55,137
Median House Value (rank / $)..........................22 / 179,900
Total Area - Square Miles (rank / count) ....25 / 57,914
Land Area - Square Miles (rank / count)..........24 / 55,519
Water Area - Square Miles (rank / count) ....19 / 2,395
Number of Counties...102
Name for Residents...Illinoisan
Capital City...Springfield
Nickname ....Land of Lincoln
State Motto....................State Sovereignty, National Union
State Bird ....Cardinal
State Flower..Native Violet
State Tree.. White Oak
State Song... Illinois

POPULATION

Rank: 1 highest; 51 lowest

State Population (rank / count) ....05 / 12,875,255
Population Per Square Mile (rank / count) ....13 / 222
Male Population (rank / %).....................................31 / 49.04
Female Population (rank / %)................................21 / 50.96
Sex Ratio & Population Median Age..................96.2 / 36.6
   (Sex Ratio = the # of males per 100 females)
Population % by age (under 18 / 18-44) ....24.4 / 37.0
Population % by age (45-64 / 65+) ....26.1 / 12.5

RESOURCES

Illinois State Government
Phone: 217-782-2000
Web Site: www.illinois.gov

Illinois Department of Revenue
Phone: 217-782-3336 or 800-732-8866
Web Site: www.revenue.state.il.us

Illinois Driver Services Department
Phone: 217-785-3000 (out-of-state) or
   800-252-8980 (in-state)
Web Site: www.cyberdriveillinois.com

Illinois Office of Tourism
Phone: 800-226-6632
Web Site: www.enjoyillinois.com

Voting Information
Phone: 217-782-4141 (Springfield Office) or
   312-814-6440 (Chicago Office)
Web Site: www.elections.il.gov/InfoForVoters.aspx

Indiana

STATE AND LOCAL TAXES

State Sales Tax (%) 7
  Exempt: food and prescription drugs.

Local Sales Taxes (up to an additional %) .... None
Inheritance Tax .... No
Estate Tax .... No

PERSONAL INCOME TAXES

State Income Tax (%) 3.4
  Flat rate, no income brackets. Any city and/or county income taxes are additional.

Personal Exemption $ (single / joint) ....1,000 / 2,000
  Additional $1,000 if age 65 or over.

Standard Deduction $ (single / joint) .... None
Federal Income Tax Paid - Deduction Allowed .... None
Social Security Income - Tax Exempt ....Yes
Retired Military Pay - Tax Exempt .... Limits
  Up to $2,000 (if 60 or older) less Social Security and Railroad benefits received.

State & Local Government Pensions - Tax Exempt .... No
Federal Civil Service Pensions - Tax Exempt .... Limits
  Up to $2,000 (if 60 or older) less Social Security and Railroad benefits received.

Railroad Retirement - Tax Exempt ....Yes
Private Pension - Tax Exempt .... No

VEHICLES

Registration Fees .... 1 Year
  Passenger cars, $21.05.

  Truck fees are based on weight:
  7,000 lbs or less, $30.05.
  7,001 - 16,000, $50.05 - 144.75
  16,001 - 30,000, $144.75 - $304.75

  Recreational vehicle, $29.75

Annual Vehicle Tax ....Yes
  An annual excise tax is charged in lieu of property tax. Some counties also have a surtax or wheel tax. The excise tax varies with age, type, and value (manufacture's original retail price) of vehicle. Fees can range from $12 to over $500 for passenger cars and more than $2,000 for motor homes.

  Examples: For a 3 year old passenger vehicle with an original value of $15,000 the excise tax would be $156.

For a 3 year old RV with an original value of $70,000 the tax is $782.

A chart showing the Excise Tax Fees for passenger cars and recreational vehicles is available at the Bureau of Motor Vehicles web site.

Some counties charge a flat rate for the "surtax or wheel tax" anywhere from $10 to $25. Other counties charge a "%" fee. More information is available from the Bureau of Motor Vehicles web site.

State Emissions Test Required ....Yes
  Every two years. Lake and Porter counties only. Diesel powered and recreational vehicles are exempt. New vehicles (4 model years) are exempt.
  Web Site: www.cleanaircarcheck.com

Vehicle Safety Inspection Required .... No
Mandatory Minimum Liability Insurance 25/50/10

COST OF LIVING INDICATORS

  Rank: 1 highest; 51 lowest

Cost of Living - average statewide (rank) 48
Fuel - $ per gallon, Dec. 2013 (diesel / gas) ......3.88 / 3.27
The following "Tax Collections" are all Per Capita
State Individual Income Tax (rank / $) .... 32 / 701
Local Individual Income Tax (rank / $) .... 06 / 248
State General Sales Tax (rank / $) .... 09 / 959
Local General Sales Tax (rank / $) .... 35 / 0
State Property Tax (rank / $) .... 33 / 0
Local Property Tax (rank / $) .... 36 / 966
State - All Tax Collections (rank / $) .... 30 / 2,281
Local - All Tax Collections (rank / $) .... 36 / 1,261
State & Local - All Tax Collections (rank / $) ......33 / 3,542

STATE TAX COLLECTIONS

  Rank: 1 highest; 50 lowest
  Rank and % of total taxes collected from:

Property Tax .... 35 / 0.0011
Sales & Gross Receipts ....10 / 58.41
Motor Vehicle & Driver License .... 14 / 3.45
Individual Income Tax ....32 / 30.35
Corporate Income Tax .... 11 / 6.10
Other Taxes .... 48 / 1.70
The following tax collections are Per Capita
Total Tax Collections - Ind. & Biz (rank / $) ....28 / 2,402
Total Tax Collections - Ind. only (rank / $) ....24 / 2,242

STATE FACTS & NUMBERS

  Rank: 1 highest; 51 lowest

State Revenue - Per Capita (rank / $) ....43 / 5,950
State & Local Rev. - Per Capita (rank / $).............48 / 8,697
Personal Income - Per Capita (rank / $) ....39 / 38,119
Median Household Income (rank / $) ....33 / 46,974
Median House Value (rank / $)........................45 / 122,600
Total Area - Square Miles (rank / count) ....38 / 36,420
Land Area - Square Miles (rank / count) ....38 / 35,826
Water Area - Square Miles (rank / count) ....39 / 593
Number of Counties... 92
Name for Residents...Indianians
Capital City... Indianapolis
Nickname .... Hoosier State
State Motto................................The Crossroads of America
State Bird ....Cardinal
State Flower...Peony
State Tree...Tulip Tree
State Song............On The Banks Of The Wabash, Far Away

POPULATION

Rank: 1 highest; 51 lowest

State Population (rank / count) ....16 / 6,537,334
Population Per Square Mile (rank / count) ....16 / 179
Male Population (rank / %)......................................27 / 49.20
Female Population (rank / %).................................25 / 50.80
Sex Ratio & Population Median Age...................96.8 / 37.0
(Sex Ratio = the # of males per 100 females)

Population % by age (under 18 / 18-44) ....24.8 / 35.8
Population % by age (45-64 / 65+) ....26.5 / 12.9

RESOURCES

Indiana State Government
Phone: 317-233-0800 or 800-457-8283
Web Site: www.in.gov

Indiana Department of Revenue
Phone: 317-232-2240
Web Site: www.in.gov/dor

Indiana Bureau of Motor Vehicles
Phone: 888-692-6841
Web Site: www.in.gov/bmv

Indiana Office of Tourism
Phone: 800-677-9800
Web Site: www.visitindiana.com

Voting Information
Phone: 866-461-8683
Web Site: www.in.gov/sos/elections/2398.htm

Iowa

STATE AND LOCAL TAXES

State Sales Tax (%) 6
    Exempt: food and prescription drugs.

Local Sales Taxes (up to an additional %) 2
Inheritance Tax ....Yes
    *Ranges from 0% to 15% depending on the relationship
    of the recipient to the decedent.*

Estate Tax.. No

PERSONAL INCOME TAXES

State Income Tax (%) ....0.36 - 8.98
    *9 income brackets - Lowest $1,494; Highest $67,230. Any
    city and/or county income taxes are additional.*

Personal Exemption $ (single / joint) ....40 / 80
    Amount is a tax credit.

Standard Deduction $ (single / joint)............1,900 / 4,670
Federal Income Tax Paid - Deduction Allowed ....Full
Social Security Income - Tax Exempt...................................Yes
Retired Military Pay - Tax Exempt ....Limits
State & Local Government Pensions - Tax Exempt ..Limits
Federal Civil Service Pensions - Tax Exempt ....Limits
Railroad Retirement - Tax Exempt ....Yes
Private Pension - Tax Exempt ....Limits

*Note: Limits include a maximum combined exemption
of $6,000 (if 55 or older) from all retirement income
sources including Social Security benefits.*

VEHICLES

Registration Fees .... 1 Year
    *Automobiles, trucks and multipurpose vehicles (SUV)
    registration fee is based on the weight, list price and age
    of vehicle. The minimum fee is $50.*

    *The formula is calculated as follows: 40 cents per
    hundred pounds of vehicle weight, plus...*
    1% of list price on vehicles 1 to 7 years old
    3/4% of list price on vehicles 8 to 9 years old
    1/2% of list price on vehicles 10 to 11 years old
    Vehicles 12 model years old or more are a flat fee of $50.

    *Travel trailer fees are 30 cents per square foot of floor
    space for vehicles under 7 model years old and 75% of
    total thereafter.*

    *Motor home fees are based on list price, age, and type.
    Class A, 1 to 5 years old, list price $80,000 and more,*

$400. Six years or older $300.

Class A, 1 to 5 years old, list price $40,000 to $79,999, $200. Six years or older $150.

Class A, 1 to 5 years old, list price $20,000 to $39,999, $140. Six years or older $105.

Class A, 1 to 5 years old, list price less than $20,000, $120. Six years or older $85.

Class B, 1 to 5 years old, $90. Six years or older $65.

Class C, 1 to 5 years old, $110. Six years or older $80.00.

Annual Vehicle Tax ....Yes
Fees are included in vehicle registration. No property tax on vehicles.

State Emissions Test Required .... No
Vehicle Safety Inspection Required .... No
Mandatory Minimum Liability Insurance 20/40/15

COST OF LIVING INDICATORS

Rank: 1 highest; 51 lowest

Cost of Living - average statewide (rank) 40
Fuel - $ per gallon, Dec. 2013 (diesel / gas)......3.74 / 3.11
The following "Tax Collections" are all Per Capita
State Individual Income Tax (rank / $).................... 17 / 928
Local Individual Income Tax (rank / $)...................... 11 / 30
State General Sales Tax (rank / $) .... 26 / 726
Local General Sales Tax (rank / $) .... 19 / 218
State Property Tax (rank / $) ....33 / 0
Local Property Tax (rank / $) ....16 / 1,421
State - All Tax Collections (rank / $)....................24 / 2,354
Local - All Tax Collections (rank / $)....................20 / 1,761
State & Local - All Tax Collections (rank / $) ......23 / 4,115

STATE TAX COLLECTIONS

Rank: 1 highest; 50 lowest
Rank and % of total taxes collected from:

Property Tax...37 / 0.00
Sales & Gross Receipts ....27 / 45.10
Motor Vehicle & Driver License................................02 / 6.75
Individual Income Tax..20 / 38.68
Corporate Income Tax..19 / 5.44
Other Taxes ....30 / 4.02
The following tax collections are Per Capita
Total Tax Collections - Ind. & Biz (rank / $) ....23 / 2,548
Total Tax Collections - Ind. only (rank / $) ....19 / 2,333

STATE FACTS & NUMBERS

Rank: 1 highest; 51 lowest

State Revenue - Per Capita (rank / $)...................22 / 7,836
State & Local Rev. - Per Capita (rank / $)..........20 / 11,236
Personal Income - Per Capita (rank / $) ....24 / 43,935

Median Household Income (rank / $) .... 24 / 50,957
Median House Value (rank / $).........................43 / 124,300
Total Area - Square Miles (rank / count) .... 26 / 56,273
Land Area - Square Miles (rank / count) .... 23 / 55,857
Water Area - Square Miles (rank / count) .... 45 / 416
Number of Counties.. 99
Name for Residents...Iowans
Capital City...Des Moines
Nickname ....Hawkeye State
State Motto..... Our Liberties We Prize And Our Rights We
    Will Maintain
State Bird ....Eastern Goldfinch
State Flower..Wild Prairie Rose
State Tree.. Oak
State Song.. The Song of Iowa

POPULATION

Rank: 1 highest; 51 lowest

State Population (rank / count) .... 30 / 3,074,186
Population Per Square Mile (rank / count) .... 36 / 55
Male Population (rank / %).....................................19 / 49.51
Female Population (rank / %)................................33 / 50.49
Sex Ratio & Population Median Age.................98.1 / 38.1
    (Sex Ratio = the # of males per 100 females)

Population % by age (under 18 / 18-44) ....23.9 / 34.6
Population % by age (45-64 / 65+) ....26.7 / 14.8

RESOURCES

Iowa State Government
Phone: 515-281-5011
Web Site: www.iowa.gov

Iowa Department of Revenue
Phone: 515-281-3114
Web Site: www.iowa.gov/tax

Iowa Motor Vehicle Division
Phone: 515-244-9124 or 800-532-1121 (in-state)
Web Site: www.iowadot.gov/mvd and www.
iowataxandtags.gov

Iowa Office of Tourism
Phone: 515-725-3084 or 888-472-6035
Web Site: www.traveliowa.com

Voting Information
Phone: 515-281-5204
Web Site: www.sos.iowa.gov/elections/
voterinformation/index.html

Kansas

STATE AND LOCAL TAXES

State Sales Tax (%)...5.7
  Exempt: prescription drugs.

Local Sales Taxes (up to an additional %) 5

Inheritance Tax .... No

Estate Tax... No

PERSONAL INCOME TAXES

State Income Tax (%) .... 3 - 4.9
  2 income brackets - Lowest $15,000; Highest $30,000.

Personal Exemption $ (single / joint) ....2,250 / 4,500

Standard Deduction $ (single / joint)...........3,000 / 6,000
  Additional $850 if age 65 or over.

Federal Income Tax Paid - Deduction Allowed .... None

Social Security Income - Tax Exempt...........................Limits
  *Exempt if federal adjusted gross income is $75,000 or
  less.*

Retired Military Pay - Tax Exempt ....Yes

State & Local Government Pensions - Tax Exempt ..Limits
  *Full exemption for Kansas state pensions, none for out-
  of-state pensions.*

Federal Civil Service Pensions - Tax Exempt ....Yes

Railroad Retirement - Tax Exempt ....Yes

Private Pension - Tax Exempt .... No

VEHICLES

Registration Fees .... 1 Year
  *Basic fee for autos and trucks is $35 - $45, depending on
  weight of vehicle.*
  Basic fee for trailers is $24 - $44, depending on weight.

Annual Vehicle Tax ....Yes
  *Property tax due with vehicle registration. Rate varies by
  county.*

State Emissions Test Required .... No

Vehicle Safety Inspection Required .... No

Mandatory Minimum Liability Insurance 25/50/10
  *Personal Injury Protection, Uninsured and Underinsured
  Motorists coverage is also required.*

COST OF LIVING INDICATORS

  Rank: 1 highest; 51 lowest

Cost of Living - average statewide (rank) 38

Fuel - $ per gallon, Dec. 2013 (diesel / gas)......3.76 / 3.00

The following "Tax Collections" are all Per Capita

State Individual Income Tax (rank / $)................... 15 / 932

Local Individual Income Tax (rank / $)....................... 13 / 1

State General Sales Tax (rank / $) .... 18 / 862

Local General Sales Tax (rank / $) .... 17 / 276

State Property Tax (rank / $) .... 19 / 25

Local Property Tax (rank / $) ....20 / 1,332

State - All Tax Collections (rank / $)....................23 / 2,355

Local - All Tax Collections (rank / $)....................22 / 1,718

State & Local - All Tax Collections (rank / $) ......24 / 4,074

STATE TAX COLLECTIONS

  Rank: 1 highest; 50 lowest
  Rank and % of total taxes collected from:

Property Tax..19 / 1.00

Sales & Gross Receipts ....19 / 49.68

Motor Vehicle & Driver License..............................24 / 2.78

Individual Income Tax.....................................18 / 38.98

Corporate Income Tax.....................................34 / 4.28

Other Taxes ....37 / 3.27

The following tax collections are Per Capita

Total Tax Collections - Ind. & Biz (rank / $) ....21 / 2,571

Total Tax Collections - Ind. only (rank / $) ....18 / 2,377

STATE FACTS & NUMBERS

  Rank: 1 highest; 51 lowest

State Revenue - Per Capita (rank / $) ....37 / 6,439

State & Local Rev. - Per Capita (rank / $)..............32 / 9,897

Personal Income - Per Capita (rank / $) ....25 / 43,015

Median Household Income (rank / $)..........27 / 50,241

Median House Value (rank / $)........................40 / 128,500

Total Area - Square Miles (rank / count) .... 15 / 82,278

Land Area - Square Miles (rank / count) .... 13 / 81,759

Water Area - Square Miles (rank / count) ....42 / 520

Number of Counties 105

Name for Residents..Kansans

Capital City...Topeka

Nickname .... Sunflower State

State Motto.....................To The Stars Through Difficulties

State Bird ....Western Meadowlark

State Flower..Sunflower

State Tree..Cottonwood

State Song................................Home On The Range

POPULATION

  Rank: 1 highest; 51 lowest

State Population (rank / count) ....33 / 2,885,905

Population Per Square Mile (rank / count) .... 41 / 35

Male Population (rank / %)......................................17 / 49.61

Female Population (rank / %)................................35 / 50.39
Sex Ratio & Population Median Age..................98.4 / 36.0
    (Sex Ratio = the # of males per 100 females)

Population % by age (under 18 / 18-44) ....25.5 / 35.5
Population % by age (45-64 / 65+) ....25.8 / 13.2

RESOURCES

Kansas State Government
Phone: 785-296-0111
Web Site: www.kansas.gov

Kansas Department of Revenue
Phone: 785-368-8222
Web Site: www.ksrevenue.org

Kansas Division of Motor Vehicles
Phone: 785-296-3963 (Driver License) and 785-296-3621
(Tags & Registration)
Web Site: www.ksrevenue.org/vehicle.htm

Kansas Office of Tourism
Phone: 785-296-2009
Web Site: www.travelks.com

Voting Information
Phone: 785-296-4564
Web Site: www.kssos.org/elections/elections.html

Kentucky

STATE AND LOCAL TAXES

State Sales Tax (%)..6
    Exempt: food and prescription drugs.

Local Sales Taxes (up to an additional %) .... None
Inheritance Tax ....Yes
    Ranges from 0% to 16% depending on the relationship
    of the recipient to the decedent.

Estate Tax... No

PERSONAL INCOME TAXES

State Income Tax (%) ....2 - 6
    6 income brackets - Lowest $3,000; Highest $75,000. Any
    city and/or county income taxes are additional.

Personal Exemption $ (single / joint) .... 20 / 40
    Amount is a tax credit.

Standard Deduction $ (single / joint)............2,290 / 4,580
Federal Income Tax Paid - Deduction Allowed .... None
Social Security Income - Tax Exempt..................................Yes
Retired Military Pay - Tax Exempt ....Limits
State & Local Government Pensions - Tax Exempt .. Limits
Federal Civil Service Pensions - Tax Exempt .... Limits
Railroad Retirement - Tax Exempt ....Yes
Private Pension - Tax Exempt ....Limits

    Note: Limits include a maximum combined exemption
    of $41,110 from all retirement income sources other
    than Social Security and Railroad Retirement.

VEHICLES

Registration Fees .... 1 Year
    Basic fee, $15 plus. Other miscellaneous fees may apply,
    varies by county.

    Note: A Motor Vehicle Usage Tax of 6% of the vehicles
    value is collected when registering a vehicle for the first
    time in Kentucky. A credit equal to the amount paid in
    another state will be applied to the amount owed in
    Kentucky.

Annual Vehicle Tax ....Yes
    Property tax due with vehicle registration. Rate varies by
    county.

State Emissions Test Required .... No
Vehicle Safety Inspection Required .... No
Mandatory Minimum Liability Insurance 25/50/10
    Personal Injury Protection is also required.

COST OF LIVING INDICATORS

Rank: 1 highest; 51 lowest

Cost of Living - average statewide (rank) 50
Fuel - $ per gallon, Dec. 2013 (diesel / gas) ......3.86 / 3.28
The following "Tax Collections" are all Per Capita
State Individual Income Tax (rank / $) .... 25 / 780
Local Individual Income Tax (rank / $) .... 07 / 247
State General Sales Tax (rank / $) .... 31 / 661
Local General Sales Tax (rank / $) .... 35 / 0
State Property Tax (rank / $) .... 11 / 118
Local Property Tax (rank / $) .... 49 / 568
State - All Tax Collections (rank / $) .... 26 / 2,328
Local - All Tax Collections (rank / $) .... 45 / 995
State & Local - All Tax Collections (rank / $) ......40 / 3,323

STATE TAX COLLECTIONS

Rank: 1 highest; 50 lowest

Rank and % of total taxes collected from:

Property Tax...09 / 5.06
Sales & Gross Receipts ....22 / 48.07
Motor Vehicle & Driver License................................44 / 1.95
Individual Income Tax..27 / 33.53
Corporate Income Tax..18 / 5.49
Other Taxes ....21 / 5.89
The following tax collections are Per Capita
Total Tax Collections - Ind. & Biz (rank / $) ....29 / 2,391
Total Tax Collections - Ind. only (rank / $) ....27 / 2,128

STATE FACTS & NUMBERS

Rank: 1 highest; 51 lowest

State Revenue - Per Capita (rank / $) ....30 / 7,089
State & Local Rev. - Per Capita (rank / $).............42 / 9,311
Personal Income - Per Capita (rank / $) ....45 / 35,643
Median Household Income (rank / $) ....47 / 41,724
Median House Value (rank / $)........................46 / 120,800
Total Area - Square Miles (rank / count) ....37 / 40,408
Land Area - Square Miles (rank / count)..........37 / 39,486
Water Area - Square Miles (rank / count) ....34 / 921
Number of Counties...120
Name for Residents..Kentuckians
Capital City...Frankfort
Nickname ....Bluegrass State
State Motto......................United We Stand, Divided We Fall
State Bird ....Cardinal
State Flower...Goldenrod
State Tree... Tulip Poplar
State Song............ My Old Kentucky Home / Blue Moon of
    Kentucky

POPULATION

Rank: 1 highest; 51 lowest

State Population (rank / count) .... 26 / 4,380,415
Population Per Square Mile (rank / count) ....22 / 108
Male Population (rank / %)..................................26 / 49.20
Female Population (rank / %)................................26 / 50.80
Sex Ratio & Population Median Age..................96.8 / 38.1
    (Sex Ratio = the # of males per 100 females)
Population % by age (under 18 / 18-44) ....23.6 / 35.9
Population % by age (45-64 / 65+) ....27.2 / 13.3

RESOURCES

Kentucky State Government
Phone: 502-564-3130
Web Site: www.kentucky.gov

Kentucky Department of Revenue
Phone: 502-564-4581
Web Site: www.revenue.ky.gov

Kentucky Department of Vehicle Regulation
Phone: 502-564-1257
Web Site: www.transportation.ky.gov/Motor-Vehicle-Licensing/
Web Site: www.transportation.ky.gov/Driver-Licensing/

Kentucky Office of Tourism
Phone: 800-225-8747
Web Site: www.kytourism.com

Voting Information
Phone: 502-573-7100
Web Site: www.elect.ky.gov/

Louisiana

STATE AND LOCAL TAXES

State Sales Tax (%) 4
Prescription drugs exempt. Food is subject to local taxes.

Local Sales Taxes (up to an additional %) 6.75
Inheritance Tax .... No
Estate Tax .... No

PERSONAL INCOME TAXES

State Income Tax (%) ....2 - 6
3 income brackets - Lowest $12,500; Highest $50,000.

Personal Exemption $ (single / joint) ....4,500 / 9,000
Standard Deduction $ (single / joint)............................None
Included in personal exemption.

Federal Income Tax Paid - Deduction Allowed ....Full
Social Security Income - Tax Exempt ....Yes
Retired Military Pay - Tax Exempt ....Yes
State & Local Government Pensions - Tax Exempt ..Limits
Full exemption for Louisiana state pensions. For out-of-state pensions see Private Pension.

Federal Civil Service Pensions - Tax Exempt ....Yes
Railroad Retirement - Tax Exempt ....Yes
Private Pension - Tax Exempt ....Limits
Up to $6,000 exempt for taxpayers 65 or older.

VEHICLES

Registration Fees .... 2 Years
Autos, based on the value of the vehicle, $20 - $82.
Motor homes, $50.
Trucks, up to 6,000 lbs GVWR, $40. Fee is for 4 years.

New residents are subject to payment of a use tax of 4% based on the value of the vehicle. A maximum of 4% credit may be allowed for a similar tax paid in another state.

Annual Vehicle Tax .... No
No property tax on vehicles.

State Emissions Test Required ....Yes
Annual in the five-parish Baton Rouge area consisting of Ascension, East Baton Rouge, Iberville, Livingston, and West Baton Rouge parishes. Diesel powered and all other vehicles over 10,000 lbs GVWR are exempt.
Web Site: www.deq.louisiana.gov/portal/DIVISIONS/ Assessment/AirFieldServices/MotorVehicleInspectionPr ogram.aspx

Vehicle Safety Inspection Required ....Yes
Every two years.

Mandatory Minimum Liability Insurance 15/30/25

COST OF LIVING INDICATORS

Rank: 1 highest; 51 lowest

Cost of Living - average statewide (rank) 32
Fuel - $ per gallon, Dec. 2013 (diesel / gas)......3.69 / 3.11
The following "Tax Collections" are all Per Capita
State Individual Income Tax (rank / $)....................39 / 522
Local Individual Income Tax (rank / $)........................14 / 0
State General Sales Tax (rank / $) ....35 / 611
Local General Sales Tax (rank / $)..............................02 / 813
State Property Tax (rank / $) ....20 / 11
Local Property Tax (rank / $) ....44 / 757
State - All Tax Collections (rank / $).....................38 / 1,926
Local - All Tax Collections (rank / $)....................24 / 1,683
State & Local - All Tax Collections (rank / $) ......32 / 3,610

STATE TAX COLLECTIONS

Rank: 1 highest; 50 lowest
Rank and % of total taxes collected from:

Property Tax..20 / 0.57
Sales & Gross Receipts ....12 / 54.36
Motor Vehicle & Driver License................................48 / 1.60
Individual Income Tax....................................36 / 27.51
Corporate Income Tax....................................41 / 3.23
Other Taxes ....11 / 12.73
The following tax collections are Per Capita
Total Tax Collections - Ind. & Biz (rank / $) ....41 / 1,954
Total Tax Collections - Ind. only (rank / $) ....42 / 1,643

STATE FACTS & NUMBERS

Rank: 1 highest; 51 lowest

State Revenue - Per Capita (rank / $) ....25 / 7,383
State & Local Rev. - Per Capita (rank / $)..........23 / 10,678
Personal Income - Per Capita (rank / $) ....31 / 40,057
Median Household Income (rank / $) ....44 / 42,944
Median House Value (rank / $)........................33 / 138,800
Total Area - Square Miles (rank / count) ....31 / 52,378
Land Area - Square Miles (rank / count) ....33 / 43,204
Water Area - Square Miles (rank / count) ....05 / 9,174
Number of Counties.. 64
Name for Residents....................................Louisianans
Capital City.. Baton Rouge
Nickname ....Sportsman's Paradise
State Motto.......................... Union, Justice, and Confidence

State Bird ....Eastern Brown Pelican
State Flower .... Magnolia Blossom
State Tree ....Bald Cypress
State Song ....Give Me Louisiana

POPULATION

Rank: 1 highest; 51 lowest

State Population (rank / count) .... 25 / 4,601,893
Population Per Square Mile (rank / count) .... 27 / 89
Male Population (rank / %)......................................33 / 48.95
Female Population (rank / %)................................19 / 51.05
Sex Ratio & Population Median Age...................95.9 / 35.8
   (Sex Ratio = the # of males per 100 females)

Population % by age (under 18 / 18-44) ....24.7 / 36.8
Population % by age (45-64 / 65+) ....26.2 / 12.3

RESOURCES

Louisiana State Government
Phone: 800-256-7777
Web Site: www.louisiana.gov

Louisiana Department of Revenue
Phone: 225-219-0102
Web Site: www.rev.state.la.us

Louisiana Office of Motor Vehicles
Phone: 225-925-6146
Web Site: www.expresslane.org

Louisiana Office of Tourism
Phone: 800-994-8626
Web Site: www.louisianatravel.com

Voting Information
Phone: 255-922-0900 or 800-883-2805
Web Site: www.sos.la.gov/ElectionsAndVoting/

Maine

STATE AND LOCAL TAXES

State Sales Tax (%) 5.5
   Exempt: food and prescription drugs.

Local Sales Taxes (up to an additional %) .... None
Inheritance Tax .... No
Estate Tax...Yes
   12% on estates valued over $2 million.

PERSONAL INCOME TAXES

State Income Tax (%) ....0 - 8
   3 income brackets - Lowest $5,200; Highest $20,900.

Personal Exemption $ (single / joint) ....3,900 / 7,800
Standard Deduction $ (single / joint).........6,100 / 10,150
Federal Income Tax Paid - Deduction Allowed .... None
Social Security Income - Tax Exempt ....Yes
Retired Military Pay - Tax Exempt .... Limits
State & Local Government Pensions - Tax Exempt .. Limits
Federal Civil Service Pensions - Tax Exempt .... Limits
Railroad Retirement - Tax Exempt ....Yes
Private Pension - Tax Exempt .... Limits

Note: Limits include a maximum combined exemption of $6,000 ($10,000 for certain retirement benefits) from all retirement income sources including Social Security and Railroad Retirement.

VEHICLES

Registration Fees .... 1 Year
   Passenger vehicle and trucks under 6,000 lbs, $35.
   Truck camper, $12.
   Motor homes, based on weight:
   0 - 16,000 lbs, $21 - $50.
   16,001 - 26,000 lbs, $72 - $119.
   26,001 - 28,000 lbs, $137 - $166.
   28,001 - 38,000 lbs, $166 - $265.

Annual Vehicle Tax ....Yes
   An annual excise tax is paid to the town like a property tax and is based on the age and vehicle MSRP.

State Emissions Test Required ....Yes
   In Cumberland County only. Diesel powered vehicles under 18,000 lbs are exempt. Web Site: www.maine.gov/ dep/air/mobile/enhancedautoinsp.htm

Vehicle Safety Inspection Required ....Yes
   Annual.

Mandatory Minimum Liability Insurance 50/100/25
Uninsured and Underinsured Motorists coverage required. There is also a mandatory $2,000 medical payments coverage.

COST OF LIVING INDICATORS

Rank: 1 highest; 51 lowest

Cost of Living - average statewide (rank) 13
Fuel - $ per gallon, Dec. 2013 (diesel / gas)......3.97 / 3.47
The following "Tax Collections" are all Per Capita
State Individual Income Tax (rank / $)................12 / 1,069
Local Individual Income Tax (rank / $)........................14 / 0
State General Sales Tax (rank / $) .... 22 / 760
Local General Sales Tax (rank / $) .... 35 / 0
State Property Tax (rank / $) .... 16 / 34
Local Property Tax (rank / $) ....10 / 1,772
State - All Tax Collections (rank / $)....................14 / 2,765
Local - All Tax Collections (rank / $)....................19 / 1,789
State & Local - All Tax Collections (rank / $) ......16 / 4,555

STATE TAX COLLECTIONS

Rank: 1 highest; 50 lowest
Rank and % of total taxes collected from:

Property Tax..18 / 1.01
Sales & Gross Receipts ....26 / 46.30
Motor Vehicle & Driver License................................ 23 / 2.91
Individual Income Tax...22 / 38.17
Corporate Income Tax..10 / 6.14
Other Taxes ....23 / 5.46
The following tax collections are Per Capita
Total Tax Collections - Ind. & Biz (rank / $) ....15 / 2,842
Total Tax Collections - Ind. only (rank / $) ....13 / 2,546

STATE FACTS & NUMBERS

Rank: 1 highest; 51 lowest

State Revenue - Per Capita (rank / $) ....19 / 7,983
State & Local Rev. - Per Capita (rank / $)..........26 / 10,522
Personal Income - Per Capita (rank / $) ....30 / 40,087
Median Household Income (rank / $) ....36 / 46,709
Median House Value (rank / $)..........................23 / 173,900
Total Area - Square Miles (rank / count) ....39 / 35,380
Land Area - Square Miles (rank / count) ....39 / 30,843
Water Area - Square Miles (rank / count) ....12 / 4,537
Number of Counties.. 16
Name for Residents.. Mainers
Capital City.. Augusta
Nickname ....Pine Tree State
State Motto...I Direct

State Bird .... Black-Capped Chickadee
State Flower...............................White Pine Cone and Tassel
State Tree...Eastern White Pine
State Song..State Song of Maine

POPULATION

Rank: 1 highest; 51 lowest

State Population (rank / count) ....41 / 1,329,192
Population Per Square Mile (rank / count) .... 40 / 38
Male Population (rank / %).....................................34 / 48.94
Female Population (rank / %)................................18 / 51.06
Sex Ratio & Population Median Age..................95.8 / 42.7
(Sex Ratio = the # of males per 100 females)
Population % by age (under 18 / 18-44) ....20.7 / 32.5
Population % by age (45-64 / 65+) ....30.9 / 15.9

RESOURCES

Maine State Government
Phone: 207-287-5608
Web Site: www.maine.gov

Maine Revenue Services
Phone: 207-626-8475
Web Site: www.maine.gov/revenue

Maine Bureau of Motor Vehicles
Phone: 207-624-9000
Web Site: www.maine.gov/sos/bmv

Maine Office of Tourism
Phone: 888-624-6345
Web Site: www.visitmaine.com

Voting Information
Phone: 207-624-7736
Web Site: www.maine.gov/sos/cec/elec/

Maryland

STATE AND LOCAL TAXES

State Sales Tax (%) 6
  Exempt: food and prescription drugs.

Local Sales Taxes (up to an additional %) .... None

Inheritance Tax ....Yes
  *Ranges from 0% to 10% depending on the relationship
  of the recipient to the decedent.*

Estate Tax ....Yes
  16% on estates valued over $1 million.

PERSONAL INCOME TAXES

State Income Tax (%) ....2 - 5.75
  *8 income brackets - Lowest $1,000; Highest $250,000.
  ($1,000 to $300,000 for joint filers.) Any city and/or
  county income taxes are additional.*

Personal Exemption $ (single / joint) ....3,200 / 6,400
  *Additional $1,000 if 65 or older. Exemptions begin to
  phase out with adjusted gross income above $100,000
  and is eliminated with AGI above 150,000.*

Standard Deduction $ (single / joint)............2,000 / 4,000
  *Deduction is 15% of income with a minimum of $1,500
  and a maximum of $2,000 for single filers and $3,000
  minimum or $4,000 maximum for joint returns.*

Federal Income Tax Paid - Deduction Allowed .... None

Social Security Income - Tax Exempt ....Yes

Retired Military Pay - Tax Exempt ....Limits

State & Local Government Pensions - Tax Exempt .. Limits

Federal Civil Service Pensions - Tax Exempt ....Limits

Railroad Retirement - Tax Exempt ....Yes

Private Pension - Tax Exempt ....Limits

> *Note: If you are 65 or older you may qualify for a pension
> exclusion (maximum $27,100) under certain conditions.
> Out-of-state government pensions do not qualify for the
> exemption.*

VEHICLES

Registration Fees .... 2 Years
  *Passenger and multi purpose vehicles including RVs up
  to 3,700 lbs, $135.*

  *Passenger and multi purpose vehicles including RVs over
  3,700 lbs, $187.*

*Trucks, 3/4 ton or 7,000 lbs or less, $161.50.
Trucks, 10,000 lbs GVW (1/2 or 3/4 ton), $214.*

*Trailers 3,000 lbs or less, $51.
Trailers 3,001 - 5,000 lbs, $102.
Trailers 5,001 - 10,000 lbs, $160.
Trailers 10,001 - 20,000 lbs, 248.*

Annual Vehicle Tax .... No
  No property tax on vehicles.

State Emissions Test Required ....Yes
  *Every 2 years. Tests vary with year and weight of vehicle.
  The "Diesel Vehicle Emissions Program" requires testing
  for vehicles over 10,000 lbs. Web Site: www.mde.state.
  md.us/programs/Air/MobileSources/VehicleEmissionsI
  nspectionProgram/Pages/index.aspx*

Vehicle Safety Inspection Required ....Yes
  Annual. Required before a vehicle can be registered.

Mandatory Minimum Liability Insurance 30/60/15
  *Personal Injury Protection, Uninsured and Underinsured
  Motorists coverage is also required.*

COST OF LIVING INDICATORS

  Rank: 1 highest; 51 lowest

Cost of Living - average statewide (rank) 12

Fuel - $ per gallon, Dec. 2013 (diesel / gas)......3.83 / 3.38

The following "Tax Collections" are all Per Capita

State Individual Income Tax (rank / $)..................10 / 1,129

Local Individual Income Tax (rank / $)....................02 / 672

State General Sales Tax (rank / $) ....30 / 662

Local General Sales Tax (rank / $)................................35 / 0

State Property Tax (rank / $) ....10 / 135

Local Property Tax (rank / $) ....23 / 1,297

State - All Tax Collections (rank / $).....................15 / 2,723

Local - All Tax Collections (rank / $).....................10 / 2,211

State & Local - All Tax Collections (rank / $) ......11 / 4,934

STATE TAX COLLECTIONS

  Rank: 1 highest; 50 lowest
  Rank and % of total taxes collected from:

Property Tax...10 / 4.43

Sales & Gross Receipts ....36 / 42.04

Motor Vehicle & Driver License................................25 / 2.75

Individual Income Tax..15 / 41.70

Corporate Income Tax..24 / 5.16

Other Taxes ....31 / 3.91

The following tax collections are Per Capita

Total Tax Collections - Ind. & Biz (rank / $) ....13 / 2,900

Total Tax Collections - Ind. only (rank / $) ....09 / 2,670

STATE FACTS & NUMBERS

Rank: 1 highest; 51 lowest

State Revenue - Per Capita (rank / $) ....29 / 7,093

State & Local Rev. - Per Capita (rank / $) ....22 / 10,679

Personal Income - Per Capita (rank / $) ....06 / 53,816

Median Household Income (rank / $) ....01 / 71,122

Median House Value (rank / $)..........................06 / 289,300

Total Area - Square Miles (rank / count) ....42 / 12,406

Land Area - Square Miles (rank / count) ....42 / 9,707

Water Area - Square Miles (rank / count) ....18 / 2,699

Number of Counties 23

Name for Residents................................. Marylanders

Capital City...Annapolis

Nickname ....Old Line State / Free State

State Motto...........................Manly Deeds, Womanly Words

State Bird .... Baltimore Oriole

State Flower....................................... Black-Eyed Susan

State Tree.. White Oak

State Song...........................Maryland, My Maryland

POPULATION

Rank: 1 highest; 51 lowest

State Population (rank / count) ....19 / 5,884,563

Population Per Square Mile (rank / count) ....06 / 474

Male Population (rank / %)......................................49 / 48.35

Female Population (rank / %)................................03 / 51.65

Sex Ratio & Population Median Age...................93.6 / 38.0
(Sex Ratio = the # of males per 100 females)

Population % by age (under 18 / 18-44) ....23.4 / 36.6

Population % by age (45-64 / 65+) ....27.7 / 12.3

RESOURCES

Maryland State Government

Phone: 877-634-6361

Web Site: www.maryland.gov

Comptroller of Maryland

Phone: 410-260-7980 or 800-638-2937

Web Site: www.marylandtaxes.com

Maryland Motor Vehicle Administration

Phone: 410-768-7000

Web Site: www.mva.maryland.gov

Maryland Office of Tourism

Phone: 866-639-3526

Web Site: www.visitmaryland.org

Voting Information

Phone: 410-269-2840 or 800-222-8683

Web Site: www.elections.state.md.us/

Massachusetts

STATE AND LOCAL TAXES

State Sales Tax (%) 6.25
   Exempt: food and prescription drugs.

Local Sales Taxes (up to an additional %) .... None

Inheritance Tax .... No

Estate Tax ....Yes
   16% on estates valued over $1 million.

PERSONAL INCOME TAXES

State Income Tax (%) 5.25
   Flat rate, no income brackets.

Personal Exemption $ (single / joint) ....4,400 / 8,800

Standard Deduction $ (single / joint)........................... None

Federal Income Tax Paid - Deduction Allowed .... None

Social Security Income - Tax Exempt ....Yes

Retired Military Pay - Tax Exempt ....Yes

State & Local Government Pensions - Tax Exempt .. Limits
   Full exemption for Massachusetts state pensions and
   some out-of-state pensions.

Federal Civil Service Pensions - Tax Exempt ....Yes

Railroad Retirement - Tax Exempt ....Yes

Private Pension - Tax Exempt .... No

VEHICLES

Registration Fees .... 1 & 2 Years
   Passenger vehicles, $50. For two years.
   Motor homes, $50. For one year.

Annual Vehicle Tax ....Yes
   An annual Motor Vehicle Excise Tax is levied by the city
   or town. The rate is $25 per $1,000 of valuation. Age and
   list price (in year of manufacture) is used to figure the
   valuation. For detailed information see: www.sec.state.
   ma.us/cis/cisexc/excidx.htm.

State Emissions Test Required ....Yes
   Annual. Vehicle safety inspection and emissions test are
   done at the same time.
   Web Site: www.massvehiclecheck.state.ma.us

Vehicle Safety Inspection Required ....Yes
   Annual.

Mandatory Minimum Liability Insurance 20/40/5
   Personal Injury Protection, Uninsured and Underinsured
   Motorists coverage is also required.

COST OF LIVING INDICATORS

   Rank: 1 highest; 51 lowest

Cost of Living - average statewide (rank) 09

Fuel - $ per gallon, Dec. 2013 (diesel / gas)......3.91 / 3.43

The following "Tax Collections" are all Per Capita

State Individual Income Tax (rank / $)...............03 / 1,745

Local Individual Income Tax (rank / $)........................ 14 / 0

State General Sales Tax (rank / $) .... 25 / 740

Local General Sales Tax (rank / $) .... 35 / 0

State Property Tax (rank / $) .... 32 / 1

Local Property Tax (rank / $) ....07 / 1,998

State - All Tax Collections (rank / $) ....10 / 3,323

Local - All Tax Collections (rank / $)....................12 / 2,069

State & Local - All Tax Collections (rank / $) ......08 / 5,393

STATE TAX COLLECTIONS

   Rank: 1 highest; 50 lowest
   Rank and % of total taxes collected from:

Property Tax...33 / 0.02

Sales & Gross Receipts ....44 / 32.09

Motor Vehicle & Driver License...............................39 / 2.08

Individual Income Tax...............................04 / 52.33

Corporate Income Tax..............................05 / 8.78

Other Taxes ....27 / 4.70

The following tax collections are Per Capita

Total Tax Collections - Ind. & Biz (rank / $) ....10 / 3,431

Total Tax Collections - Ind. only (rank / $) ....07 / 3,013

STATE FACTS & NUMBERS

   Rank: 1 highest; 51 lowest

State Revenue - Per Capita (rank / $) ....13 / 8,521

State & Local Rev. - Per Capita (rank / $) ....07 / 12,344

Personal Income - Per Capita (rank / $) ....03 / 55,976

Median Household Income (rank / $) ....07 / 65,339

Median House Value (rank / $)........................04 / 328,300

Total Area - Square Miles (rank / count) ....44 / 10,554

Land Area - Square Miles (rank / count) ....45 / 7,800

Water Area - Square Miles (rank / count) ....16 / 2,754

Number of Counties 14

Name for Residents...................................Massachusettsans

Capital City.. Boston

Nickname .... Bay State / Old Colony State

State Motto..........By the Sword We Seek Peace, But Peace
   Only Under Liberty

State Bird .... Black-Capped Chickadee

State Flower..Mayflower

State Tree.. American Elm
State Song.. All Hail To Massachusetts

POPULATION

Rank: 1 highest; 51 lowest

State Population (rank / count) .... 14 / 6,646,144
Population Per Square Mile (rank / count) ....05 / 630
Male Population (rank / %)................................48 / 48.36
Female Population (rank / %)...............................04 / 51.64
Sex Ratio & Population Median Age..................93.7 / 39.1
   (Sex Ratio = the # of males per 100 females)

Population % by age (under 18 / 18-44) ....21.7 / 36.8
Population % by age (45-64 / 65+) ....27.7 / 13.8

RESOURCES

Massachusetts State Government
Phone: 617-727-7030 or 800-392-6090
Web Site: www.mass.gov

Massachusetts Department of Revenue
Phone: 617-887-6367
Web Site: www.mass.gov/dor

Massachusetts Registry of Motor Vehicles
Phone: 857-368-8000 or 800-858-3926
Web Site: www.massrmv.com

Massachusetts Office of Tourism
Phone: 800-227-6277
Web Site: www.massvacation.com

Voting Information
Phone: 617-727-7030 or 800-392-6090
Web Site: www.sec.state.ma.us/ele/eleidx.htm

Michigan

STATE AND LOCAL TAXES

State Sales Tax (%)...6
   Exempt: food and prescription drugs.

Local Sales Taxes (up to an additional %) .... None
Inheritance Tax .... No
Estate Tax... No

PERSONAL INCOME TAXES

State Income Tax (%)..4.25
   Flat rate, no income brackets. Any city and/or county
   income taxes are additional.

Personal Exemption $ (single / joint) ....3,763 / 7,526
Standard Deduction $ (single / joint)........................... None
Federal Income Tax Paid - Deduction Allowed .... None
Social Security Income - Tax Exempt.................................Yes
Retired Military Pay - Tax Exempt ....Yes
State & Local Government Pensions - Tax Exempt .. Limits
   Full exemption for Michigan state pensions and some
   out-of-state pensions.

Federal Civil Service Pensions - Tax Exempt ....Yes
Railroad Retirement - Tax Exempt ....Yes
Private Pension - Tax Exempt ....Limits
   Exempt up to $47,309, some restrictions.

VEHICLES

Registration Fees .... 1 Year
   Fees for 1984 or newer model years are based on the
   manufacturer's suggested retail price. Model years 1983
   and older are based on the vehicle's weight.

   You can call the Record Information Unit at 1-888-767-
   6424 for an estimate on total fees.

Annual Vehicle Tax ....Yes
   Fees are included in vehicle registration. No property tax
   on vehicles.

State Emissions Test Required .... No
Vehicle Safety Inspection Required .... No
Mandatory Minimum Liability Insurance 20/40/10
   Personal Injury Protection is also required.

COST OF LIVING INDICATORS

Rank: 1 highest; 51 lowest

Cost of Living - average statewide (rank) 34
Fuel - $ per gallon, Dec. 2013 (diesel / gas)......3.93 / 3.25

The following "Tax Collections" are all Per Capita

State Individual Income Tax (rank / $)...................33 / 647
Local Individual Income Tax (rank / $)......................10 / 41
State General Sales Tax (rank / $)..............................10 / 959
Local General Sales Tax (rank / $).................................35 / 0
State Property Tax (rank / $)....................................08 / 192
Local Property Tax (rank / $)..................................25 / 1,181
State - All Tax Collections (rank / $)....................21 / 2,381
Local - All Tax Collections (rank / $)...................34 / 1,272
State & Local - All Tax Collections (rank / $)......30 / 3,653

STATE TAX COLLECTIONS

Rank: 1 highest; 50 lowest
Rank and % of total taxes collected from:

Property Tax...07 / 7.50
Sales & Gross Receipts...11 / 54.73
Motor Vehicle & Driver License...............................11 / 4.06
Individual Income Tax...34 / 28.49
Corporate Income Tax...44 / 2.54
Other Taxes..43 / 2.68
The following tax collections are Per Capita
Total Tax Collections - Ind. & Biz (rank / $).........27 / 2,425
Total Tax Collections - Ind. only (rank / $)...........22 / 2,299

STATE FACTS & NUMBERS

Rank: 1 highest; 51 lowest

State Revenue - Per Capita (rank / $)....................34 / 6,519
State & Local Rev. - Per Capita (rank / $).............36 / 9,451
Personal Income - Per Capita (rank / $)...........37 / 38,291
Median Household Income (rank / $).............34 / 46,859
Median House Value (rank / $).........................47 / 119,200
Total Area - Square Miles (rank / count)...........11 / 96,714
Land Area - Square Miles (rank / count)..........22 / 56,539
Water Area - Square Miles (rank / count)........02 / 40,175
Number of Counties...83
Name for Residents...Michiganders
Capital City.. Lansing
Nickname ....Great Lakes State
State Motto.........If You Are Seeking A Pleasant Peninsula,
   Look About You
State Bird .... Robin
State Flower.. Apple Blossom
State Tree...White Pine
State Song.. Michigan, My Michigan

POPULATION

Rank: 1 highest; 51 lowest

State Population (rank / count) ....09 / 9,883,360
Population Per Square Mile (rank / count) ....23 / 102
Male Population (rank / %)................................30 / 49.05
Female Population (rank / %)................................22 / 50.95
Sex Ratio & Population Median Age...................96.3 / 38.9
   (Sex Ratio = the # of males per 100 females)
Population % by age (under 18 / 18-44) ....23.7 / 34.6
Population % by age (45-64 / 65+) ....27.9 / 13.8

RESOURCES

Michigan State Government
Phone: 877-932-6424
Web Site: www.michigan.gov

Michigan Department of Treasury
Phone: 517-373-3200
Web Site: www.michigan.gov/taxes

Michigan Department of State (Driver License & Vehicle
   Registration)
Phone: 888-767-6424
Web Site: www.michigan.gov/sos

Michigan Office of Tourism
Phone: 888-784-7328
Web Site: www.michigan.org

Voting Information
Phone: 888-767-6424
Web Site: www.mi.gov/sos

Minnesota

STATE AND LOCAL TAXES

State Sales Tax (%) 6.875
Exempt: food and prescription drugs.

Local Sales Taxes (up to an additional %) 1

Inheritance Tax .... No

Estate Tax .... Yes
16% on estates valued over $1 million.

PERSONAL INCOME TAXES

State Income Tax (%) .... 5.35 - 7.85
3 income brackets - Lowest $24,270; Highest $79,730.
($35,480 to $140,961 for joint filers.)

Personal Exemption $ (single / joint) .... 3,900 / 7,800

Standard Deduction $ (single / joint) .... 5,950 / 11,900

Federal Income Tax Paid - Deduction Allowed .... None

Social Security Income - Tax Exempt .... Limits
Taxed same as on your federal return. No tax if Social
Security is your only income.

Retired Military Pay - Tax Exempt .... No

State & Local Government Pensions - Tax Exempt .... No

Federal Civil Service Pensions - Tax Exempt .... No

Railroad Retirement - Tax Exempt .... Yes

Private Pension - Tax Exempt .... No

VEHICLES

Registration Fees .... 1 Year
Basic fee, $7 plus. Varies with type of vehicle and
miscellaneous additional charges.

Annual Vehicle Tax .... Yes
An annual "Registration Tax" is determined by the age
and base value of the vehicle. Minimum tax for vehicles
10 years old or older is $35. Contact Driver and Vehicle
Services for assistance in determining the total tax
amount or call 651-297-2126.

State Emissions Test Required .... No

Vehicle Safety Inspection Required .... No

Mandatory Minimum Liability Insurance 30/60/10
Personal Injury Protection, Uninsured Motorist, and
Underinsured Motorists coverage is also required.

COST OF LIVING INDICATORS

Rank: 1 highest; 51 lowest

Cost of Living - average statewide (rank) 19

Fuel - $ per gallon, Dec. 2013 (diesel / gas) ......3.88 / 3.03

The following "Tax Collections" are all Per Capita

State Individual Income Tax (rank / $) ....05 / 1,391

Local Individual Income Tax (rank / $) .... 14 / 0

State General Sales Tax (rank / $) .... 17 / 866

Local General Sales Tax (rank / $) .... 33 / 20

State Property Tax (rank / $) .... 09 / 144

Local Property Tax (rank / $) .... 17 / 1,377

State - All Tax Collections (rank / $) .... 07 / 3,523

Local - All Tax Collections (rank / $) .... 30 / 1,463

State & Local - All Tax Collections (rank / $) ......10 / 4,986

STATE TAX COLLECTIONS

Rank: 1 highest; 50 lowest
Rank and % of total taxes collected from:

Property Tax ....11 / 3.93

Sales & Gross Receipts ....28 / 44.45

Motor Vehicle & Driver License .... 17 / 3.29

Individual Income Tax ....19 / 38.85

Corporate Income Tax ....23 / 5.18

Other Taxes ....29 / 4.29

The following tax collections are Per Capita

Total Tax Collections - Ind. & Biz (rank / $) ....07 / 3,822

Total Tax Collections - Ind. only (rank / $) ....04 / 3,491

STATE FACTS & NUMBERS

Rank: 1 highest; 51 lowest

State Revenue - Per Capita (rank / $) ....14 / 8,493

State & Local Rev. - Per Capita (rank / $) ....13 / 11,828

Personal Income - Per Capita (rank / $) ....12 / 46,925

Median Household Income (rank / $) ....10 / 58,906

Median House Value (rank / $) ....19 / 185,800

Total Area - Square Miles (rank / count) ....12 / 86,936

Land Area - Square Miles (rank / count) ....14 / 79,627

Water Area - Square Miles (rank / count) ....09 / 7,309

Number of Counties 87

Name for Residents .... Minnesotans

Capital City .... St. Paul

Nickname .... North Star State

State Motto .... The Star Of The North

State Bird .... Common Loon

State Flower .... Pink and White Lady's-Slipper

State Tree .... Red Pine

State Song .... Hail! Minnesota

POPULATION

Rank: 1 highest; 51 lowest

State Population (rank / count) .... 21 / 5,379,139

Population Per Square Mile (rank / count) .... 32 / 62

Male Population (rank / %)..................................15 / 49.63
Female Population (rank / %)..............................37 / 50.37
Sex Ratio & Population Median Age....................98.5 / 37.4
 (Sex Ratio = the # of males per 100 females)

Population % by age (under 18 / 18-44)............24.2 / 35.8
Population % by age (45-64 / 65+) ....27.1 / 12.9

RESOURCES

Minnesota State Government
Phone: 651-201-3400 or 800-657-3717
Web Site: www.state.mn.us

Minnesota Department of Revenue
Phone: 651-556-3000
Web Site: www.revenue.state.mn.us

Minnesota Driver and Vehicle Services
Phone: 651-215-1328
Web Site: http://dps.mn.gov/divisions/dvs

Minnesota Office of Tourism
Phone: 651-296-5029 or 888-868-7476
Web Site: www.exploreminnesota.com

Voting Information
Phone: 877-600-8683
Web Site: www.sos.state.mn.us/index.aspx?page=134

Mississippi

STATE AND LOCAL TAXES

State Sales Tax (%) 7
 Exempt: prescription drugs.

Local Sales Taxes (up to an additional %) 0.25
Inheritance Tax ....No
Estate Tax...No

PERSONAL INCOME TAXES

State Income Tax (%) ....3 - 5
 3 income brackets - Lowest $5,000; Highest $10,000.

Personal Exemption $ (single / joint) ....6,000 / 12,000
 Additional $1,500 if age 65 or over.

Standard Deduction $ (single / joint)............2,300 / 4,600
Federal Income Tax Paid - Deduction Allowed ....None
Social Security Income - Tax Exempt................................Yes
Retired Military Pay - Tax Exempt ....Yes
State & Local Government Pensions - Tax Exempt ....Yes
Federal Civil Service Pensions - Tax Exempt ....Yes
Railroad Retirement - Tax Exempt ....Yes
Private Pension - Tax Exempt ....Limits
 Exempt for qualified plans.

VEHICLES

Registration Fees .... 1 Year
 *Basic fee, $12.75. A Privilege Tax and Ad Valorem Tax is
 due in addition to the basic fee. These taxes are based on
 the type and value of vehicle, and where you live.*

Annual Vehicle Tax ....Yes
 *Motor Vehicle Ad Valorem Tax. Vehicles with a GVWR
 of 10,000 lbs or less must pay this tax at the time of
 registration. The tax is based on the assessed value of
 the vehicle multiplied by the millage rate set by local
 county government.*

 *Assessed value has been established as 30% of MSRP
 plus a reduction of a certain percentage for depreciation
 over 10 years. There is a minimum assessed value of
 $100. Contact the local county tax collector for their
 millage rate and depreciation factor.*

State Emissions Test Required .... No
Vehicle Safety Inspection Required ....Yes
 Annual.

Mandatory Minimum Liability Insurance 25/50/25

COST OF LIVING INDICATORS

Rank: 1 highest; 51 lowest

Cost of Living - average statewide (rank) 51
Fuel - $ per gallon, Dec. 2013 (diesel / gas)......3.67 / 3.11
The following "Tax Collections" are all Per Capita
State Individual Income Tax (rank / $)....................40 / 468
Local Individual Income Tax (rank / $)........................ 14 / 0
State General Sales Tax (rank / $) ....07 / 995
Local General Sales Tax (rank / $)............................. 35 / 0
State Property Tax (rank / $) .... 21 / 8
Local Property Tax (rank / $)............................... 41 / 845
State - All Tax Collections (rank / $)...................32 / 2,194
Local - All Tax Collections (rank / $)........................47 / 911
State & Local - All Tax Collections (rank / $) ......47 / 3,105

STATE TAX COLLECTIONS

Rank: 1 highest; 50 lowest
Rank and % of total taxes collected from:

Property Tax... 22 / 0.34
Sales & Gross Receipts ....08 / 63.23
Motor Vehicle & Driver License............................ 33 / 2.51
Individual Income Tax...40 / 21.59
Corporate Income Tax.. 14 / 5.69
Other Taxes .... 17 / 6.63
The following tax collections are Per Capita
Total Tax Collections - Ind. & Biz (rank / $) ....31 / 2,329
Total Tax Collections - Ind. only (rank / $) ....29 / 2,043

STATE FACTS & NUMBERS

Rank: 1 highest; 51 lowest

State Revenue - Per Capita (rank / $)...................21 / 7,853
State & Local Rev. - Per Capita (rank / $)..........24 / 10,524
Personal Income - Per Capita (rank / $) ....51 / 33,657
Median Household Income (rank / $) ....51 / 37,095
Median House Value (rank / $)........................50 / 100,000
Total Area - Square Miles (rank / count) ....32 / 48,432
Land Area - Square Miles (rank / count)..........31 / 46,923
Water Area - Square Miles (rank / count) ....25 / 1,509
Number of Counties.. 82
Name for Residents...................................Mississippians
Capital City.. Jackson
Nickname ....Magnolia State
State Motto................................... By Valor And Arms
State Bird .... Mockingbird
State Flower... Magnolia
State Tree... Magnolia
State Song.. Go Mis-sis-sip-pi

POPULATION

Rank: 1 highest; 51 lowest

State Population (rank / count) ....31 / 2,984,926
Population Per Square Mile (rank / count) .... 33 / 62
Male Population (rank / %)...............................44 / 48.57
Female Population (rank / %)................................08 / 51.43
Sex Ratio & Population Median Age..................94.4 / 36.0
     (Sex Ratio = the # of males per 100 females)
Population % by age (under 18 / 18-44) ....25.5 / 36.0
Population % by age (45-64 / 65+) ....25.8 / 12.7

RESOURCES

Mississippi State Government
Phone: 877-290-9487
Web Site: www.ms.gov

Mississippi Department of Revenue (Tax information
and vehicle tags & title)
Phone: 601-923-7000
Web Site: www.dor.ms.gov

Mississippi Department of Public Safety (Driver License)
Phone: 601-987-1212
Web Site: www.dps.state.ms.us

Mississippi Office of Tourism
Phone: 601-359-3297 or 866-733-6477
Web Site: www.visitmississippi.org

Voting Information
Phone: 601-576-2550 or 800-829-6786
Web Site: www.sos.ms.gov/elections.aspx

Missouri

STATE AND LOCAL TAXES

State Sales Tax (%)...4.225
Prescription drugs exempt. Food is taxed at 1.225%.

Local Sales Taxes (up to an additional %) 6.625
Inheritance Tax...No
Estate Tax..No

PERSONAL INCOME TAXES

State Income Tax (%) .... 1.5 - 6
*10 income brackets - Lowest $1,000; Highest $9,000. Any
city and/or county income taxes are additional.*

Personal Exemption $ (single / joint) ....2,100 / 4,200
Additional $1,100 if age 65 or over.

Standard Deduction $ (single / joint).........6,100 / 12,200
Federal Income Tax Paid - Deduction Allowed ....Limits
*Up to $5,000 for individuals and $10,000 for joint
returns.*

Social Security Income - Tax Exempt..................................Yes
Retired Military Pay - Tax Exempt ....Limits
State & Local Government Pensions - Tax Exempt ..Limits
Federal Civil Service Pensions - Tax Exempt ....Limits
Railroad Retirement - Tax Exempt ....Yes
Private Pension - Tax Exempt ....Limits

*Note: Limits include exemptions based on age, income,
and other variables.*

VEHICLES

Registration Fees .... 1 Year
*Registration fees for passenger vehicles are determined
by your vehicle's taxable horsepower.
Under 12 horsepower, $21.75.
12 - 71 horsepower, $24.75 - $48.75.
72 or more horsepower, $54.75.*

Recreational Vehicles, $35.75.

Annual Vehicle Tax ....Yes
Annual property tax on vehicles.

State Emissions Test Required ....Yes
*Every two years. Only in St. Louis, St. Charles, Franklin,
and Jefferson counties, and the City of St. Louis.
Web Site: www.dnr.mo.gov/gatewayvip.*

Vehicle Safety Inspection Required ....Yes
Every two years. Vehicles 5 years old or less are exempt.

Mandatory Minimum Liability Insurance 25/50/10
Uninsured Motorist coverage is also required.

COST OF LIVING INDICATORS

Rank: 1 highest; 51 lowest

Cost of Living - average statewide (rank) 35
Fuel - $ per gallon, Dec. 2013 (diesel / gas)......3.62 / 2.94
The following "Tax Collections" are all Per Capita
State Individual Income Tax (rank / $)...................30 / 753
Local Individual Income Tax (rank / $).....................09 / 50
State General Sales Tax (rank / $)..........................42 / 494
Local General Sales Tax (rank / $)..........................13 / 329
State Property Tax (rank / $) ....26 / 4
Local Property Tax (rank / $) ....34 / 972
State - All Tax Collections (rank / $)...................46 / 1,679
Local - All Tax Collections (rank / $)....................27 / 1,583
State & Local - All Tax Collections (rank / $) ......42 / 3,262

STATE TAX COLLECTIONS

*Rank: 1 highest; 50 lowest
Rank and % of total taxes collected from:*

Property Tax...23 / 0.27
Sales & Gross Receipts ....29 / 44.11
Motor Vehicle & Driver License...............................30 / 2.64
Individual Income Tax...09 / 47.51
Corporate Income Tax...43 / 2.79
Other Taxes ....44 / 2.67
The following tax collections are Per Capita
Total Tax Collections - Ind. & Biz (rank / $) ....46 / 1,794
Total Tax Collections - Ind. only (rank / $) ....41 / 1,697

STATE FACTS & NUMBERS

Rank: 1 highest; 51 lowest

State Revenue - Per Capita (rank / $)..................38 / 6,411
State & Local Rev. - Per Capita (rank / $).............35 / 9,481
Personal Income - Per Capita (rank / $) ....34 / 39,133
Median Household Income (rank / $) ....38 / 45,321
Median House Value (rank / $)........................35 / 137,100
Total Area - Square Miles (rank / count) ....21 / 69,707
Land Area - Square Miles (rank / count) ....18 / 68,742
Water Area - Square Miles (rank / count) ....32 / 965
Number of Counties...114
Name for Residents.. Missourians
Capital City..Jefferson City
Nickname .... Show Me State
State Motto...........The Welfare Of The People Shall Be The
Supreme Law

State Bird ....Bluebird
State Flower...White Hawthorn
State Tree...Flowering Dogwood
State Song..Missouri Waltz

POPULATION

Rank: 1 highest; 51 lowest

State Population (rank / count) .... 18 / 6,021,988
Population Per Square Mile (rank / count) .... 29 / 86
Male Population (rank / %).....................................32 / 48.98
Female Population (rank / %).................................20 / 51.02
Sex Ratio & Population Median Age.................96.0 / 37.9
　　(Sex Ratio = the # of males per 100 females)
Population % by age (under 18 / 18-44) ....23.8 / 35.3
Population % by age (45-64 / 65+) ....26.9 / 14.0

RESOURCES

Missouri State Government
Phone: 573-751-2000
Web Site: www.mo.gov

Missouri Department of Revenue
Phone: 573-751-3505
Web Site: www.dor.mo.gov

Missouri Motor Vehicle & Driver Licensing (Missouri
Department of Revenue)
Phone: 573-526-2407 (Driver License) or
　　573-526-3669 (Tags & Registration)
Web Site: www.dor.mo.gov

Missouri Office of Tourism
Phone: 573-751-4133 or 800-519-2100
Web Site: www.visitmo.com

Voting Information
Phone: 573-751-2301 or 800-669-8683
Web Site: www.sos.mo.gov/elections/

Montana

STATE AND LOCAL TAXES

State Sales Tax (%)...None
Local Sales Taxes (up to an additional %) ....None
Inheritance Tax ....No
Estate Tax...No

PERSONAL INCOME TAXES

State Income Tax (%) ....1 - 6.9
　　7 income brackets - Lowest $2,700; Highest $16,400.

Personal Exemption $ (single / joint) ....2,240 / 4,480
　　Additional $2,040 if age 65 or over.

Standard Deduction $ (single / joint)............1,860 / 3,720
　　*Deduction is 20% of adjusted gross income with a
　　minimum of $1,860 and maximum of $4,200 for single
　　filers. Double the amounts for joint returns.*

Federal Income Tax Paid - Deduction Allowed ....Limits
　　*Up to $5,000 for individuals and $10,000 for joint
　　returns.*

Social Security Income - Tax Exempt ....Limits
Retired Military Pay - Tax Exempt ....Limits
State & Local Government Pensions - Tax Exempt ..Limits
Federal Civil Service Pensions - Tax Exempt ....Limits
Railroad Retirement - Tax Exempt ....Yes
Private Pension - Tax Exempt ....Limits

　　*Note: Limits include a maximum combined exemption
　　of $3,600 from all retirement income sources if income
　　limitations are met. To determine taxes on Social Security
　　benefits you will need to complete their worksheet.*

VEHICLES

Registration Fees ....1 Year
　　*Passenger car, pickup truck 1-ton and under, van and
　　SUV rate is based on the age of the vehicle:*
　　0 - 4 years old, $217.
　　5 - 10 years old, $87.
　　11 years or more, $28.
　　*You can choose 1 or 2 year renewal periods. For vehicles
　　11 years old or older you can also choose to permanently
　　register the vehicle for a registration rate of $87.50.*

　　Motor home:
　　Less than 2 years old, $282.50.
　　2 - 4 years old, $224.25.
　　5 - 7 years old, $132.50.

8 years or more, $97.50.

For motor homes 11 years old or older you can choose the permanent registration option for $237.50.

Travel Trailer:

All travel trailers must be permanently registered. The one time fee varies by length of trailer. Under 16 feet, $72. 16-feet and over, $152.

Annual Vehicle Tax ....Yes
An annual "County Option Tax" imposed by most counties is due with the registration fee.

State Emissions Test Required .... No
Vehicle Safety Inspection Required .... No
Mandatory Minimum Liability Insurance 25/50/10

COST OF LIVING INDICATORS

Rank: 1 highest; 51 lowest

Cost of Living - average statewide (rank) 23
Fuel - $ per gallon, Dec. 2013 (diesel / gas)......3.82 / 3.04
The following "Tax Collections" are all Per Capita
State Individual Income Tax (rank / $)....................23 / 808
Local Individual Income Tax (rank / $).........................14 / 0
State General Sales Tax (rank / $) ....46 / 0
Local General Sales Tax (rank / $)..................................35 / 0
State Property Tax (rank / $) ....07 / 242
Local Property Tax (rank / $) ....28 / 1,090
State - All Tax Collections (rank / $)....................29 / 2,292
Local - All Tax Collections (rank / $)....................42 / 1,125
State & Local - All Tax Collections (rank / $) ......37 / 3,417

STATE TAX COLLECTIONS

Rank: 1 highest; 50 lowest
Rank and % of total taxes collected from:

Property Tax...06 / 10.46
Sales & Gross Receipts ....47 / 22.15
Motor Vehicle & Driver License................................03 / 6.17
Individual Income Tax...24 / 36.60
Corporate Income Tax.. 20 / 5.38
Other Taxes ....05 / 19.23
The following tax collections are Per Capita
Total Tax Collections - Ind. & Biz (rank / $) ....25 / 2,447
Total Tax Collections - Ind. only (rank / $) ....26 / 2,152

STATE FACTS & NUMBERS

Rank: 1 highest; 51 lowest

State Revenue - Per Capita (rank / $) ....20 / 7,910
State & Local Rev. - Per Capita (rank / $)..........29 / 10,183
Personal Income - Per Capita (rank / $) ....36 / 38,555

Median Household Income (rank / $) ....40 / 45,076
Median House Value (rank / $)..........................20 / 183,600
Total Area - Square Miles (rank / count) ....04 / 147,040
Land Area - Square Miles (rank / count)........04 / 145,546
Water Area - Square Miles (rank / count) ....26 / 1,494
Number of Counties...56
Name for Residents... Montanans
Capital City...Helena
Nickname .... Big Sky Country
State Motto...Gold and Silver
State Bird ....Western Meadowlark
State Flower..Bitterroot
State Tree...Ponderosa Pine
State Song..Montana

POPULATION

Rank: 1 highest; 51 lowest

State Population (rank / count) ....44 / 1,005,141
Population Per Square Mile (rank / count) .... 49 / 07
Male Population (rank / %)................................06 / 50.20
Female Population (rank / %)................................46 / 49.80
Sex Ratio & Population Median Age............... 100.8 / 39.8
(Sex Ratio = the # of males per 100 females)

Population % by age (under 18 / 18-44) ....22.6 / 33.4
Population % by age (45-64 / 65+) ....29.2 / 14.8

RESOURCES

Montana State Government
Phone: 406-444-2511
Web Site: www.mt.gov

Montana Department of Revenue
Phone: 866-859-2254
Web Site: www.mt.gov/revenue

Montana Motor Vehicle Division
Phone: 406-444-3933 or 406-444-3661 (Tags & Registration)
Web Site: www.doj.mt.gov/driving/

Montana Office of Tourism
Phone: 800-847-4868
Web Site: www.visitmt.com

Voting Information
Phone: 888-884-8683
Web Site: www.sos.mt.gov/Elections/

Nebraska

STATE AND LOCAL TAXES

State Sales Tax (%) 5.5
Exempt: food and prescription drugs.

Local Sales Taxes (up to an additional %) 2

Inheritance Tax .... Yes
Ranges from 1% to 18% depending on the relationship of the recipient to the decedent.

Estate Tax .... No

PERSONAL INCOME TAXES

State Income Tax (%) .... 2.46 - 6.84
4 income brackets - Lowest $2,400; Highest $27,000. Additional tax is imposed on adjusted gross income over $250,000.

Personal Exemption $ (single / joint) .... 126 / 252
Amount is a tax credit.

Standard Deduction $ (single / joint) .... 6,100 / 12,200

Federal Income Tax Paid - Deduction Allowed .... None

Social Security Income - Tax Exempt .... Limits
Taxable to the extent of federal taxation.

Retired Military Pay - Tax Exempt .... No

State & Local Government Pensions - Tax Exempt .... No

Federal Civil Service Pensions - Tax Exempt .... No

Railroad Retirement - Tax Exempt .... Yes

Private Pension - Tax Exempt .... No

VEHICLES

Registration Fees .... 1 Year
Registration fee for passenger vehicles, $15 plus $8.80 in miscellaneous fees. Additional local fees and taxes may be collected.

An annual Motor Vehicle Fee, collected with the registration fee, is based upon the value, weight and use of the vehicle and is adjusted as the vehicle ages. The fee ranges from about $5 to $30.

An annual Motor Vehicle Tax is also assessed on a vehicle at the time of registration. This tax is paid annually until the vehicle reaches 14 years of age or more. It is based upon the MSRP of the vehicle. For a new vehicle the fee can range from $25 for a MSRP up to $3,999 and $1,900 for a MSRP of $100,000 or more. Recreational vehicles range from $160 to $860.

Detailed tables for the Motor Vehicle Fee and Motor Vehicle Tax are available at their web site.

Annual Vehicle Tax .... Yes
All fees are included in the registration process.

State Emissions Test Required .... No

Vehicle Safety Inspection Required .... No

Mandatory Minimum Liability Insurance 25/50/25
Uninsured and Underinsured Motorists coverage is also required.

COST OF LIVING INDICATORS

Rank: 1 highest; 51 lowest

Cost of Living - average statewide (rank) 46

Fuel - $ per gallon, Dec. 2013 (diesel / gas) ...... 3.80 / 3.10

The following "Tax Collections" are all Per Capita

State Individual Income Tax (rank / $) .... 16 / 928

Local Individual Income Tax (rank / $) .... 14 / 0

State General Sales Tax (rank / $) .... 23 / 747

Local General Sales Tax (rank / $) .... 24 / 165

State Property Tax (rank / $) .... 33 / 0

Local Property Tax (rank / $) .... 14 / 1,549

State - All Tax Collections (rank / $) .... 31 / 2,238

Local - All Tax Collections (rank / $) .... 13 / 1,966

State & Local - All Tax Collections (rank / $) ...... 20 / 4,204

STATE TAX COLLECTIONS

Rank: 1 highest; 50 lowest
Rank and % of total taxes collected from:

Property Tax .... 34 / 0.0018

Sales & Gross Receipts .... 24 / 47.85

Motor Vehicle & Driver License .... 22 / 2.95

Individual Income Tax .... 14 / 42.18

Corporate Income Tax .... 21 / 5.37

Other Taxes .... 49 / 1.64

The following tax collections are Per Capita

Total Tax Collections - Ind. & Biz (rank / $) .... 30 / 2,349

Total Tax Collections - Ind. only (rank / $) .... 25 / 2,193

STATE FACTS & NUMBERS

Rank: 1 highest; 51 lowest

State Revenue - Per Capita (rank / $) .... 41 / 6,210

State & Local Rev. - Per Capita (rank / $) .... 15 / 11,669

Personal Income - Per Capita (rank / $) .... 20 / 45,012

Median Household Income (rank / $) .... 26 / 50,723

Median House Value (rank / $) .... 42 / 127,800

Total Area - Square Miles (rank / count) .... 16 / 77,348

Land Area - Square Miles (rank / count) .... 15 / 76,824

Water Area - Square Miles (rank / count) .... 41 / 524

Number of Counties 93

Name for Residents .... Nebraskans

Capital City.. Lincoln
Nickname ....Cornhusker State
State Motto.................................. Equality Before The Law
State Bird ....Western Meadowlark
State Flower... Goldenrod
State Tree...Cottonwood
State Song.. Beautiful Nebraska

POPULATION

Rank: 1 highest; 51 lowest

State Population (rank / count) .... 37 / 1,855,525
Population Per Square Mile (rank / count) .... 44 / 24
Male Population (rank / %)......................................16 / 49.62
Female Population (rank / %)................................36 / 50.38
Sex Ratio & Population Median Age..................98.5 / 36.2
(Sex Ratio = the # of males per 100 females)

Population % by age (under 18 / 18-44)...........25.1 / 35.5
Population % by age (45-64 / 65+) ....25.8 / 13.6

RESOURCES

Nebraska State Government
Phone: 402-471-2311
Web Site: www.nebraska.gov

Nebraska Department of Revenue
Phone: 402-471-5729
Web Site: www.revenue.state.ne.us

Nebraska Department of Motor Vehicles
Phone: 402-471-3861 (Driver License) or
        402-471-3918 (Tags & Registration)
Web Site: www.dmv.ne.gov

Nebraska Office of Tourism
Phone: 888-444-1867
Web Site: www.visitnebraska.com

Voting Information
Phone: 402-471-2555
Web Site: www.sos.ne.gov/dyindex.html#boxingName

Nevada

STATE AND LOCAL TAXES

State Sales Tax (%)...6.5
  Exempt: food and prescription drugs.

Local Sales Taxes (up to an additional %) 1.25
Inheritance Tax .... No
Estate Tax.. No

PERSONAL INCOME TAXES

State Income Tax (%) .... None
Personal Exemption $ (single / joint) .... n/a
Standard Deduction $ (single / joint)............................. n/a
Federal Income Tax Paid - Deduction Allowed .... n/a
Social Security Income - Tax Exempt............................. n/a
Retired Military Pay - Tax Exempt .... n/a
State & Local Government Pensions - Tax Exempt .... n/a
Federal Civil Service Pensions - Tax Exempt .... n/a
Railroad Retirement - Tax Exempt .... n/a
Private Pension - Tax Exempt .... n/a

VEHICLES

Registration Fees .... 1 Year
  Nevada charges a basic Registration Fee, Governmental Services Tax, and other miscellaneous fees.

  Basic registration fee is $33 for passenger cars, trucks and motorcycles under 6,000 lbs. There are graduated scales based on weight for larger vehicles.

  The "Governmental Services Tax" is based on a percentage of the vehicles value. The counties of Clark and Churchill also have a "Supplemental Government Services Tax".

  You can estimate your registration cost online at https:// dmvapp.nv.gov/dmv/vr_estimate/vrestimation input.aspx

Annual Vehicle Tax ....Yes
  All fees are included in the registration process.

State Emissions Test Required ....Yes
  Annual. Only in the urban areas of Clark and Washoe counties. Diesel powered vehicles over 14,000 lbs GVWR are exempt. Web Site: www.dmvnv.com/emission.htm.

Vehicle Safety Inspection Required .... No
Mandatory Minimum Liability Insurance 15/30/10

COST OF LIVING INDICATORS

Rank: 1 highest; 51 lowest

Cost of Living - average statewide (rank) 28
Fuel - $ per gallon, Dec. 2013 (diesel / gas) ......3.84 / 3.30
The following "Tax Collections" are all Per Capita
State Individual Income Tax (rank / $) ....44 / 0
Local Individual Income Tax (rank / $) ....14 / 0
State General Sales Tax (rank / $) ....05 / 1,063
Local General Sales Tax (rank / $) ....28 / 111
State Property Tax (rank / $) ....12 / 116
Local Property Tax (rank / $) ....33 / 975
State - All Tax Collections (rank / $) ....28 / 2,295
Local - All Tax Collections (rank / $) ....32 / 1,407
State & Local - All Tax Collections (rank / $) ......29 / 3,702

STATE TAX COLLECTIONS

Rank: 1 highest; 50 lowest
Rank and % of total taxes collected from:

Property Tax.. 13 / 3.46
Sales & Gross Receipts ....04 / 77.22
Motor Vehicle & Driver License................................28 / 2.70
Individual Income Tax...44 / 0.00
Corporate Income Tax..47 / 0.00
Other Taxes ....8 / 16.61
The following tax collections are Per Capita
Total Tax Collections - Ind. & Biz (rank / $) ....24 / 2,456
Total Tax Collections - Ind. only (rank / $) ....21 / 2,310

STATE FACTS & NUMBERS

Rank: 1 highest; 51 lowest

State Revenue - Per Capita (rank / $) ....39 / 6,378
State & Local Rev. - Per Capita (rank / $) ....38 / 9,393
Personal Income - Per Capita (rank / $) ....38 / 38,221
Median Household Income (rank / $) ....28 / 49,760
Median House Value (rank / $) ....26 / 161,300
Total Area - Square Miles (rank / count) ....07 / 110,572
Land Area - Square Miles (rank / count) ....07 / 109,781
Water Area - Square Miles (rank / count) ....36 / 791
Number of Counties 16
Name for Residents... Nevadans
Capital City.. Carson City
Nickname .... The Silver State
State Motto..All For Our Country
State Bird ....Mountain Bluebird
State Flower...Sagebrush
State Tree...............Single Leaf Piñon and Bristlecone Pine
State Song... Home Means Nevada

POPULATION

Rank: 1 highest; 51 lowest

State Population (rank / count) ....35 / 2,758,931
Population Per Square Mile (rank / count) .... 43 / 25
Male Population (rank / %)....................................04 / 50.49
Female Population (rank / %)................................48 / 49.51
Sex Ratio & Population Median Age............... 102.0 / 36.3
(Sex Ratio = the # of males per 100 females)
Population % by age (under 18 / 18-44) ....24.6 / 37.7
Population % by age (45-64 / 65+) ....25.6 / 12.1

RESOURCES

Nevada State Government
Phone: 800-992-0900
Web Site: www.nv.gov

Nevada Department of Taxation
Phone: 866-962-3707
Web Site: www.tax.state.nv.us

Nevada Department of Motor Vehicles
Phone: 877-368-7828
Web Site: www.dmvnv.com

Nevada Office of Tourism
Phone: 775-687-4322 or 800-638-2328
Web Site: www.travelnevada.com

Voting Information
Phone: 775-684-5705
Web Site: www.nvsos.gov/index.aspx?page=3

New Hampshire

STATE AND LOCAL TAXES

State Sales Tax (%) .... None
Local Sales Taxes (up to an additional %) .... None
Inheritance Tax .... No
Estate Tax.. No

PERSONAL INCOME TAXES

State Income Tax (%) .... None
Dividends and interest income of more than $2,400 ($4,800 joint filers) subject to a 5% tax. A $1,200 exemption is available if you are age 65 or over.

Personal Exemption $ (single / joint) .... n/a
Standard Deduction $ (single / joint)................................ n/a
Federal Income Tax Paid - Deduction Allowed .... n/a
Social Security Income - Tax Exempt .... n/a
Retired Military Pay - Tax Exempt .... n/a
State & Local Government Pensions - Tax Exempt .... n/a
Federal Civil Service Pensions - Tax Exempt .... n/a
Railroad Retirement - Tax Exempt .... n/a
Private Pension - Tax Exempt .... n/a

VEHICLES

Registration Fees .... 1 Year
State registration fees are calculated based on vehicle weight.
0 - 3,000 lbs, $31.20.
3,001 - 5,000 lbs, $43.20.
5,001 - 8,000 lbs, $55.20.
8,001 - 73,280 lbs, $0.96 per hundred pounds gross weight.

In addition to the state rates, local fees are calculated as follows: Current year vehicles are taxed at $18 per $1,000 vehicle value (MSRP when new) for the first year. The rate is then reduced by $3 per $1,000 value per year until the vehicle is six years old. At that time, the rate remains at $3 per $1,000 value.

Annual Vehicle Tax ....Yes
All fees are included in the registration process.

State Emissions Test Required ....Yes
Statewide, part of annual vehicle safety inspection. Required for all 1996 and newer light-duty (8,500 GVWR and less) gasoline-fueled and 1997 and newer diesel powered passenger vehicles.
Web Site: www.nhinspect.com

Vehicle Safety Inspection Required ....Yes
Annual. All vehicles.

Mandatory Minimum Liability Insurance 25/50/25
Amounts shown are the recommended minimum. No mandatory minimum liability requirements, except for high risk drivers. Uninsured Motorist coverage is required as well as a mandatory $2,000 medical payments coverage.

COST OF LIVING INDICATORS
Rank: 1 highest; 51 lowest

Cost of Living - average statewide (rank) 11
Fuel - $ per gallon, Dec. 2013 (diesel / gas) ......3.83 / 3.35
The following "Tax Collections" are all Per Capita
State Individual Income Tax (rank / $) .... 42 / 63
Local Individual Income Tax (rank / $)....................... 14 / 0
State General Sales Tax (rank / $) .... 46 / 0
Local General Sales Tax (rank / $) .... 35 / 0
State Property Tax (rank / $) .... 04 / 299
Local Property Tax (rank / $) ....05 / 2,213
State - All Tax Collections (rank / $) ....43 / 1,773
Local - All Tax Collections (rank / $)...................07 / 2,249
State & Local - All Tax Collections (rank / $) ......25 / 4,022

STATE TAX COLLECTIONS
Rank: 1 highest; 50 lowest
Rank and % of total taxes collected from:

Property Tax...02 / 17.25
Sales & Gross Receipts ....39 / 39.66
Motor Vehicle & Driver License................................06 / 4.84
Individual Income Tax...42 / 3.70
Corporate Income Tax...01 / 23.63
Other Taxes ....14 / 10.92
The following tax collections are Per Capita
Total Tax Collections - Ind. & Biz (rank / $) ....50 / 1,671
Total Tax Collections - Ind. only (rank / $) ....49 / 1,157

STATE FACTS & NUMBERS
Rank: 1 highest; 51 lowest

State Revenue - Per Capita (rank / $) ....36 / 6,468
State & Local Rev. - Per Capita (rank / $).............44 / 9,251
Personal Income - Per Capita (rank / $) ....10 / 49,129
Median Household Income (rank / $) ....08 / 63,280
Median House Value (rank / $)........................13 / 239,100
Total Area - Square Miles (rank / count) ....46 / 9,349
Land Area - Square Miles (rank / count)..............44 / 8,953
Water Area - Square Miles (rank / count) ....47 / 397

Number of Counties 10
Name for Residents.................................. New Hampshirites
Capital City..Concord
Nickname ....Granite State
State Motto..Live Free Or Die
State Bird .... Purple Finch
State Flower..Purple Lilac
State Tree.. White Birch
State Song..Old New Hampshire

POPULATION

Rank: 1 highest; 51 lowest

State Population (rank / count) .... 42 / 1,320,718
Population Per Square Mile (rank / count) .... 20 / 141
Male Population (rank / %)......................................23 / 49.33
Female Population (rank / %)................................29 / 50.67
Sex Ratio & Population Median Age...................97.3 / 41.1
(Sex Ratio = the # of males per 100 females)

Population % by age (under 18 / 18-44) ....21.8 / 33.9
Population % by age (45-64 / 65+) ....30.7 / 13.6

RESOURCES

New Hampshire State Government
Phone: 603-271-1110
Web Site: www.nh.gov

New Hampshire Department of Revenue Administration
Phone: 603-230-5000
Web Site: www.revenue.nh.gov

New Hampshire Division of Motor Vehicles
Phone: 603-227-4000
Web Site: www.nh.gov/safety/divisions/dmv

New Hampshire Office of Tourism
Phone: 603-271-2665 or 800-386-4664
Web Site: www.visitnh.gov

Voting Information
Phone: 603-271-3242
Web Site: http://sos.nh.gov/Elections.aspx

New Jersey

STATE AND LOCAL TAXES

State Sales Tax (%) 7
Exempt: food and prescription drugs.

Local Sales Taxes (up to an additional %) ....See note
*Some counties are not subject to the statewide sales tax
rate and collect a local rate of 3.5%.*

Inheritance Tax ....Yes
*Ranges from 0% to 16% depending on the relationship
of the recipient to the decedent.*

Estate Tax..Yes
16% on estates valued over $675,000.

PERSONAL INCOME TAXES

State Income Tax (%) .... 1.4 - 8.97
*6 income brackets - Lowest $20,000; Highest $500,000.
Any city and/or county income taxes are additional.*

Personal Exemption $ (single / joint) ....1,000 / 2,000
Additional $1,000 if age 65 or over.

Standard Deduction $ (single / joint)........................... None
Federal Income Tax Paid - Deduction Allowed .... None
Social Security Income - Tax Exempt...................................Yes
Retired Military Pay - Tax Exempt ....Yes
State & Local Government Pensions - Tax Exempt .. Limits
Federal Civil Service Pensions - Tax Exempt ....Limits
Railroad Retirement - Tax Exempt ....Yes
Private Pension - Tax Exempt ....Limits

*Note: Limits include a maximum combined exemption
of $15,000 (if 62 or older), income limits apply, from all
retirement income sources.*

VEHICLES

Registration Fees .... 1 Year
*Registration fees are based on the vehicle weight and
model year. Following are the vehicle age groups, your
actual rate will vary by weight.
1970 or older, $35.50 - $65.50.
1971 - 1979, $38.50 - $72.50.
1980 - 2010, $46.50 - $71.50.
2011 - 2013, $59 - 84.*

*Motor homes and station wagons, fee based upon the
vehicle's passenger weight class and model year. Use the
highest dollar amount shown above for the year range.*

*Non-commercial trucks (pick-up truck, van and SUVs),
fee based on the vehicle's gross weight.*

New Jersey requires payment for a four-year registration period on purchases of new vehicles. They offer a rate calculator at: www.state.nj.us/mvc/regfee/index.html.

Annual Vehicle Tax .... No
No property tax on vehicles.

State Emissions Test Required ....Yes
Every 2 years. New vehicles (5 model years) are exempt. Diesel-powered vehicles with a GVWR over 8,500 lbs are also exempt.
Web Site: www.state.nj.us/mvc/Inspections/index.htm

Vehicle Safety Inspection Required .... No
Mandatory Minimum Liability Insurance 15/30/5
Amounts shown are for a "Standard Policy". Other options are available. Personal Injury Protection, Uninsured and Underinsured Motorists coverage is also required. Samples of a Basic Policy and a Standard Policy are available at www.state.nj.us/dobi/division_ consumers/insurance/basicpolicy.shtml.

COST OF LIVING INDICATORS

Rank: 1 highest; 51 lowest

Cost of Living - average statewide (rank) 06
Fuel - $ per gallon, Dec. 2013 (diesel / gas)......3.72 / 3.25
The following "Tax Collections" are all Per Capita
State Individual Income Tax (rank / $)................08 / 1,198
Local Individual Income Tax (rank / $)........................14 / 0
State General Sales Tax (rank / $) ....13 / 919
Local General Sales Tax (rank / $)................................35 / 0
State Property Tax (rank / $) ....33 / 0
Local Property Tax (rank / $) ....01 / 2,878
State - All Tax Collections (rank / $).....................12 / 3,066
Local - All Tax Collections (rank / $).....................03 / 2,929
State & Local - All Tax Collections (rank / $) ......07 / 5,996

STATE TAX COLLECTIONS

Rank: 1 highest; 50 lowest
Rank and % of total taxes collected from:

Property Tax...32 / 0.02
Sales & Gross Receipts ....32 / 43.74
Motor Vehicle & Driver License..............................35 / 2.40
Individual Income Tax...16 / 40.53
Corporate Income Tax...08 / 7.02
Other Taxes ....18 / 6.28
The following tax collections are Per Capita
Total Tax Collections - Ind. & Biz (rank / $) ....11 / 3,097
Total Tax Collections - Ind. only (rank / $) ....08 / 2,757

STATE FACTS & NUMBERS

Rank: 1 highest; 51 lowest

State Revenue - Per Capita (rank / $)....................18 / 7987
State & Local Rev. - Per Capita (rank / $)..........12 / 11,870
Personal Income - Per Capita (rank / $) ....04 / 54,987
Median Household Income (rank / $) ....02 / 69,667
Median House Value (rank / $)..........................05 / 325,800
Total Area - Square Miles (rank / count) ....47 / 8,723
Land Area - Square Miles (rank / count) ....46 / 7,354
Water Area - Square Miles (rank / count) ....27 / 1,368
Number of Counties 21
Name for Residents..New Jerseyites
Capital City.. Trenton
Nickname ....Garden State
State Motto...Liberty And Prosperity
State Bird ....Eastern Goldfinch
State Flower...Purple Violet
State Tree..Northern Red Oak
State Song.. None

POPULATION

Rank: 1 highest; 51 lowest

State Population (rank / count) .... 11 / 8,864,590
Population Per Square Mile (rank / count) ....02 / 1,016
Male Population (rank / %)......................................41 / 48.68
Female Population (rank / %)...................................11 / 51.32
Sex Ratio & Population Median Age..................94.8 / 39.0
(Sex Ratio = the # of males per 100 females)
Population % by age (under 18 / 18-44) ....23.5 / 35.4
Population % by age (45-64 / 65+) ....27.6 / 13.5

RESOURCES

New Jersey State Government
Phone: 609-292-2121
Web Site: www.nj.gov

New Jersey Division of the Treasury
Phone: 609-826-4400
Web Site: www.state.nj.us/treasury/taxation

New Jersey Motor Vehicle Commission
Phone: 888-486-3339 (in-state) or
          609-292-6500 (out-of-state)
Web Site: www.state.nj.us/mvc

New Jersey Office of Tourism
Phone: 800-847-4865
Web Site: www.visitnj.org

Voting Information
Phone: 609-292-3760
Web Site: www.njelections.org/

New Mexico

STATE AND LOCAL TAXES

State Sales Tax (%) 5.125
Exempt: food and prescription drugs.

Local Sales Taxes (up to an additional %) 6.625
Inheritance Tax .... No
Estate Tax .... No

PERSONAL INCOME TAXES

State Income Tax (%) ....1.7 - 4.9
4 income brackets - Lowest $5,500; Highest $16,000.
($8,000 to $24,000 for joint filers.)

Personal Exemption $ (single / joint) ....3,900 / 7,800
Additional deduction up to $10,900 if age 65 or over.

Standard Deduction $ (single / joint) ....6,100 / 12,200
Federal Income Tax Paid - Deduction Allowed .... None
Social Security Income - Tax Exempt .... Limits
Retired Military Pay - Tax Exempt .... Limits
State & Local Government Pensions - Tax Exempt .. Limits
Federal Civil Service Pensions - Tax Exempt .... Limits
Railroad Retirement - Tax Exempt .... Limits
Private Pension - Tax Exempt .... Limits

Note: Limits include a maximum combined exemption
of $2,500 (if 62 or older), income limits apply, from all
retirement income sources.

VEHICLES

Registration Fees .... 1 Year
Basic fees, $27 - $62. Rate is determined by weight and
model year of vehicle.

Basic fees for travel trailers under 2,100 lbs, $9.50 -
$14.50. For trailers over 2,100 lbs the following options
are available. One year registration $7 for first 550
lbs plus $1 for every 100 lbs of half the empty weight.
Permanent registration $33 plus $1 for every 100 lbs.

Trucks with a declared gross vehicle weight under 26,000
lbs, $38 - $207. Rate based on weight and model year of
vehicle.

Annual Vehicle Tax .... No
No property tax on vehicles.

State Emissions Test Required ....Yes
Every 2 years. Albuquerque and Bernalillo Counties only.
Vehicles with a GVWR of 10,001 lbs or more are exempt.

Diesel vehicles are required to pass a visible emissions
test with each change of ownership.
Web Site: www.cabq.gov/aircare

Vehicle Safety Inspection Required .... No
Mandatory Minimum Liability Insurance 20/50/10

COST OF LIVING INDICATORS

Rank: 1 highest; 51 lowest

Cost of Living - average statewide (rank) 39
Fuel - $ per gallon, Dec. 2013 (diesel / gas)......3.78 / 3.05
The following "Tax Collections" are all Per Capita
State Individual Income Tax (rank / $)................38 / 526
Local Individual Income Tax (rank / $)......................14 / 0
State General Sales Tax (rank / $) ....14 / 907
Local General Sales Tax (rank / $) ....07 / 434
State Property Tax (rank / $) .... 17 / 32
Local Property Tax (rank / $) ....47 / 623
State - All Tax Collections (rank / $).....................25 / 2,342
Local - All Tax Collections (rank / $)......................41 / 1,134
State & Local - All Tax Collections (rank / $) ......35 / 3,476

STATE TAX COLLECTIONS

Rank: 1 highest; 50 lowest
Rank and % of total taxes collected from:

Property Tax..16 / 1.18
Sales & Gross Receipts ....15 / 52.10
Motor Vehicle & Driver License.................................45 / 1.89
Individual Income Tax..38 / 22.61
Corporate Income Tax..17 / 5.52
Other Taxes ....07 / 16.69
The following tax collections are Per Capita
Total Tax Collections - Ind. & Biz (rank / $) ....26 / 2,440
Total Tax Collections - Ind. only (rank / $) ....34 / 1,898

STATE FACTS & NUMBERS

Rank: 1 highest; 51 lowest

State Revenue - Per Capita (rank / $) ....08 / 9,480
State & Local Rev. - Per Capita (rank / $) ....16 / 11,639
Personal Income - Per Capita (rank / $) ....44 / 35,682
Median Household Income (rank / $) ....46 / 42,558
Median House Value (rank / $)........................28 / 159,300
Total Area - Square Miles (rank / count) ....05 / 121,590
Land Area - Square Miles (rank / count) ....05 / 121,298
Water Area - Square Miles (rank / count) ....49 / 292
Number of Counties 33
Name for Residents... New Mexicans
Capital City.. Santa Fe

Nickname ....Land Of Enchantment
State Motto...It Grows As It Goes
State Bird... Roadrunner
State Flower...Yucca Flower
State Tree...Piñon
State Song.. O, Fair New Mexico

POPULATION

Rank: 1 highest; 51 lowest

State Population (rank / count) .... 36 / 2,085,538
Population Per Square Mile (rank / count) .... 46 / 17
Male Population (rank / %)..................................22 / 49.41
Female Population (rank / %)................................30 / 50.59
Sex Ratio & Population Median Age..................97.7 / 36.7
    (Sex Ratio = the # of males per 100 females)
Population % by age (under 18 / 18-44) ....25.2 / 34.9
Population % by age (45-64 / 65+) ....26.7 / 13.2

RESOURCES

New Mexico State Government
Phone: 800-825-6639
Web Site: www.newmexico.gov

New Mexico Taxation and Revenue Department
Phone: 505-827-0700
Web Site: www.tax.newmexico.gov

New Mexico Motor Vehicle Division
Phone: 888-683-4636
Web Site: www.mvd.newmexico.gov

New Mexico Office of Tourism
Phone: 505-827-7336
Web Site: www.newmexico.org

Voting Information
Phone: 505-827-3614 or 800-477-3632
Web Site: www.sos.state.nm.us/Voter_Information

New York

STATE AND LOCAL TAXES

State Sales Tax (%) 4
    Exempt: food and prescription drugs.

Local Sales Taxes (up to an additional %) 5
Inheritance Tax .... No
Estate Tax..Yes
    16% on estates valued over $1 million.

PERSONAL INCOME TAXES

State Income Tax (%) ....4 - 8.82
    8 income brackets - Lowest $8,200; Highest $1,029,250.
    Any city and/or county income taxes are additional.

Personal Exemption $ (single / joint) .... None
Standard Deduction $ (single / joint)......... 7,500 / 15,000
Federal Income Tax Paid - Deduction Allowed .... None
Social Security Income - Tax Exempt................................Yes
Retired Military Pay - Tax Exempt ....Yes
State & Local Government Pensions - Tax Exempt..Limits
    Full exemption for New York state pensions. For out-of-
    state pensions see Private Pensions.

Federal Civil Service Pensions - Tax Exempt ....Yes
Railroad Retirement - Tax Exempt ....Yes
Private Pension - Tax Exempt ....Limits
    Up to $20,000 exempt for taxpayers 59 1/2 or older.

VEHICLES

Registration Fees .... 2 Years
    Registration fees for most vehicles are based on weight.
    0 - 2,950 lbs, $26 - $47.
    2,951 - 3,950 lbs, $48.50 - $66.50.
    3,951 - 5,050 lbs, $69 - $93.
    5,051 - 6,950 lbs, $95.50 - $139.
    6,951 lbs or more, $140.

    A Vehicle Use Tax ($10 - $80 for 2 years) is also charge in
    New York City and some counties.

Annual Vehicle Tax .... No
    No property tax on vehicles.

State Emissions Test Required ....Yes
    Annual. For model years 1996 and newer.
    Web Site: www.dec.ny.gov/chemical/8391.html

Vehicle Safety Inspection Required ....Yes
    Annual. Performed with the emissions test.

Mandatory Minimum Liability Insurance 25/50/10
Additional requirements include: $50,000 per person and

$100,000 per accident for death, Uninsured Motorists and basis no-fault insurance.

COST OF LIVING INDICATORS

Rank: 1 highest; 51 lowest

Cost of Living - average statewide (rank) 03
Fuel - $ per gallon, Dec. 2013 (diesel / gas) ......4.16 / 3.63
The following "Tax Collections" are all Per Capita
State Individual Income Tax (rank / $) ....01 / 1,850
Local Individual Income Tax (rank / $) ....03 / 425
State General Sales Tax (rank / $) ....36 / 592
Local General Sales Tax (rank / $) ....03 / 635
State Property Tax (rank / $) ....33 / 0
Local Property Tax (rank / $) ....04 / 2,321
State - All Tax Collections (rank / $) ....09 / 3,472
Local - All Tax Collections (rank / $) ....02 / 3,924
State & Local - All Tax Collections (rank / $) ......03 / 7,396

STATE TAX COLLECTIONS

Rank: 1 highest; 50 lowest
Rank and % of total taxes collected from:

Property Tax ....37 / 0.00
Sales & Gross Receipts ....45 / 31.96
Motor Vehicle & Driver License ....37 / 2.17
Individual Income Tax ....03 / 54.19
Corporate Income Tax ....09 / 6.38
Other Taxes ....24 / 5.29
The following tax collections are Per Capita
Total Tax Collections - Ind. & Biz (rank / $) ....09 / 3,656
Total Tax Collections - Ind. only (rank / $) ....05 / 3,284

STATE FACTS & NUMBERS

Rank: 1 highest; 51 lowest

State Revenue - Per Capita (rank / $) ....05 / 10,503
State & Local Rev. - Per Capita (rank / $) ....04 / 16,544
Personal Income - Per Capita (rank / $) ....07 / 53,241
Median Household Income (rank / $) ....16 / 56,448
Median House Value (rank / $) ....07 / 286,700
Total Area - Square Miles (rank / count) ....27 / 54,555
Land Area - Square Miles (rank / count) ....30 / 47,126
Water Area - Square Miles (rank / count) ....07 / 7,429
Number of Counties 62
Name for Residents ....New Yorkers
Capital City .... Albany
Nickname .... The Empire State
State Motto ....Ever Upward
State Bird ....Eastern Bluebird
State Flower ....Rose

State Tree ....Sugar Maple
State Song ....I Love New York

POPULATION

Rank: 1 highest; 51 lowest

State Population (rank / count) ....03 / 19,570,261
Population Per Square Mile (rank / count) ....08 / 359
Male Population (rank / %) ....47 / 48.39
Female Population (rank / %) ....05 / 51.61
Sex Ratio & Population Median Age ....93.8 / 38.0
   (Sex Ratio = the # of males per 100 females)
Population % by age (under 18 / 18-44) ....22.3 / 37.4
Population % by age (45-64 / 65+) ....26.7 / 13.6

RESOURCES

New York State Government
Phone: 518-474-8390
Web Site: www.ny.gov

New York Department of Taxation and Finance
Phone: 518-457-5181
Web Site: www.tax.ny.gov

New York Department of Motor Vehicles
Phone: 518-473-5595
Web Site: www.dmv.ny.gov

New York Office of Tourism
Phone: 800-225-5697
Web Site: www.iloveny.com

Voting Information
Phone: 518-473-5086 or 800-367-8683
Web Site: www.elections.ny.gov

North Carolina

STATE AND LOCAL TAXES

State Sales Tax (%) 4.75
Exempt: prescription drugs. Food is subject to local taxes.

Local Sales Taxes (up to an additional %) 3
Inheritance Tax .... No
Estate Tax.. No

PERSONAL INCOME TAXES

State Income Tax (%) ....6 - 7.75
3 income brackets - Lowest $12,750; Highest $60,000. ($21,250 to $100,000 for joint filers.)

Personal Exemption $ (single / joint) ....2,500 / 5,000
Deductions are maximum amount. Adjustments are made based on income level.

Standard Deduction $ (single / joint)............3,000 / 6,000
Federal Income Tax Paid - Deduction Allowed .... None
Social Security Income - Tax Exempt..................................Yes
Retired Military Pay - Tax Exempt ....Limits
100% exemption with 5 years of creditable service.

State & Local Government Pensions - Tax Exempt..Limits
Federal Civil Service Pensions - Tax Exempt ....Limits
Railroad Retirement - Tax Exempt ....Limits
Private Pension - Tax Exempt ....Limits
Up to $2,000 on qualifying private pensions.

Note: Limits include at least $4,000 in exemptions (full exemption on some pensions depending on dates and length of service) from federal, state and local pensions.

VEHICLES

Registration Fees .... 1 Year
Passenger vehicles $28.

Private trucks 4,000 - 6,000 lbs, $28 - $51.60.

House trailer and/or camping trailer, $11.

Annual Vehicle Tax ....Yes
Annual property tax on vehicles. Varies by county.

State Emissions Test Required ....Yes
Annual In 48 counties. Motor homes and diesel powered vehicles are exempt. Web Site: www.daq.state.nc.us/ motor/inspect/htdocs/en

Vehicle Safety Inspection Required ....Yes
Annual.

Mandatory Minimum Liability Insurance 30/60/25
Uninsured and Underinsured Motorists coverage is also required.

COST OF LIVING INDICATORS

Rank: 1 highest; 51 lowest

Cost of Living - average statewide (rank) 26
Fuel - $ per gallon, Dec. 2013 (diesel / gas)......3.82 / 3.28
The following "Tax Collections" are all Per Capita
State Individual Income Tax (rank / $)................13 / 1,012
Local Individual Income Tax (rank / $)........................14 / 0
State General Sales Tax (rank / $) ....34 / 634
Local General Sales Tax (rank / $) ....20 / 215
State Property Tax (rank / $) ....33 / 0
Local Property Tax (rank / $) ....39 / 886
State - All Tax Collections (rank / $) ....27 / 2,297
Local - All Tax Collections (rank / $).....................40 / 1,160
State & Local - All Tax Collections (rank / $) ......36 / 3,457

STATE TAX COLLECTIONS

Rank: 1 highest; 50 lowest
Rank and % of total taxes collected from:

Property Tax..37 / 0.00
Sales & Gross Receipts ....37 / 42.00
Motor Vehicle & Driver License...........................20 / 3.05
Individual Income Tax..10 / 45.72
Corporate Income Tax..22 / 5.37
Other Taxes ....33 / 3.86
The following tax collections are Per Capita
Total Tax Collections - Ind. & Biz (rank / $) ....32 / 2,329
Total Tax Collections - Ind. only (rank / $) ....28 / 2,120

STATE FACTS & NUMBERS

Rank: 1 highest; 51 lowest

State Revenue - Per Capita (rank / $) ....35 / 6,480
State & Local Rev. - Per Capita (rank / $).............34 / 9,567
Personal Income - Per Capita (rank / $) ....40 / 37,910
Median Household Income (rank / $) ....39 / 45,150
Median House Value (rank / $)........................31 / 152,800
Total Area - Square Miles (rank / count) ....28 / 53,819
Land Area - Square Miles (rank / count) ....29 / 48,618
Water Area - Square Miles (rank / count) ....10 / 5,201
Number of Counties...100
Name for Residents.................................... North Carolinians
Capital City...Raleigh
Nickname ....Tar Heel State
State Motto................................ To Be Rather Than To Seem

State Bird ....Cardinal
State Flower..Flowering Dogwood
State Tree...Longleaf Pine
State Song.................................The Old North Song

POPULATION

Rank: 1 highest; 51 lowest

State Population (rank / count) .... 10 / 9,752,073
Population Per Square Mile (rank / count) ....15 / 181
Male Population (rank / %)..40 / 48.72
Female Population (rank / %)................................12 / 51.28
Sex Ratio & Population Median Age....................95.0 / 37.4
    (Sex Ratio = the # of males per 100 females)
Population % by age (under 18 / 18-44) ....23.9 / 36.8
Population % by age (45-64 / 65+) ....26.3 / 13.0

RESOURCES

North Carolina State Government
Phone: 919-733-1110 or 800-662-7030
Web Site: www.nc.gov

North Carolina Department of Revenue
Phone: 877-252-3052
Web Site: www.dor.state.nc.us

North Carolina Division of Motor Vehicles
Phone: 919-715-7000
Web Site: www.ncdot.gov/dmv

North Carolina Office of Tourism
Phone: 800-847-4862
Web Site: www.visitnc.com

Voting Information
Phone: 919-733-7173
Web Site: www..ncsbe.gov

North Dakota

STATE AND LOCAL TAXES

State Sales Tax (%)...5
    Exempt: food and prescription drugs.

Local Sales Taxes (up to an additional %) 3
Inheritance Tax .... No
Estate Tax.. No

PERSONAL INCOME TAXES

State Income Tax (%) ....1.51 - 3.99
    5 income brackets - Lowest $36,250; Highest $398,350.
    ($60,650 to $398,350 for joint filers.)

Personal Exemption $ (single / joint) ....3,900 / 7,800
Standard Deduction $ (single / joint).........6,100 / 12,200
Federal Income Tax Paid - Deduction Allowed .... None
Social Security Income - Tax Exempt...........................Limits
    Taxable to the extent of federal taxation.

Retired Military Pay - Tax Exempt ....Limits
State & Local Government Pensions - Tax Exempt ..Limits
Federal Civil Service Pensions - Tax Exempt ....Limits
Railroad Retirement - Tax Exempt ....Yes
Private Pension - Tax Exempt .... No

> *Note: Limits include a maximum combined exemption of $5,000 from all retirement income sources including Social Security benefits.*

VEHICLES

Registration Fees .... 1 Year
    Registration fees are based on the weight of vehicle and the year it is first registered (model year has no bearing). Rates below are for "Year First Registered 2009 and newer", rates decline as first registration year gets older.

    Passenger vehicles:
    0 - 4,999 lbs, $73 - $111.
    5,000 - 7,999 lbs, $142 - $208.
    8,000 lbs and over, $241 - $274.

    Pickup trucks:
    0 - 10,000 lbs, $73 - $111.
    10,001 - 16,000 lbs, $142 - $208.
    16,001 lbs and over, $241 - $274.

    You can estimate your vehicle registration fees online at: https://apps.nd.gov/dot/mv/mvrenewal/feeCalc.htm.

Annual Vehicle Tax .... No
  No property tax on vehicles.

State Emissions Test Required .... No
Vehicle Safety Inspection Required .... No
Mandatory Minimum Liability Insurance 25/50/25
  Personal Injury Protection, Uninsured and Underinsured
  Motorists coverage is also required.

COST OF LIVING INDICATORS
  Rank: 1 highest; 51 lowest

Cost of Living - average statewide (rank) 17
Fuel - $ per gallon, Dec. 2013 (diesel / gas) ......4.04 / 3.16
The following "Tax Collections" are all Per Capita
State Individual Income Tax (rank / $) .... 35 / 619
Local Individual Income Tax (rank / $) .... 14 / 0
State General Sales Tax (rank / $) ....04 / 1,110
Local General Sales Tax (rank / $) .... 23 / 181
State Property Tax (rank / $) .... 28 / 3
Local Property Tax (rank / $) ....29 / 1,040
State - All Tax Collections (rank / $) ....02 / 5,463
Local - All Tax Collections (rank / $) ....35 / 1,268
State & Local - All Tax Collections (rank / $) ......04 / 6,731

STATE TAX COLLECTIONS
  Rank: 1 highest; 50 lowest
  Rank and % of total taxes collected from:

Property Tax .... 31 / 0.04
Sales & Gross Receipts ....46 / 28.37
Motor Vehicle & Driver License .... 43 / 1.97
Individual Income Tax .... 41 / 7.70
Corporate Income Tax .... 37 / 3.84
Other Taxes ....02 / 58.08
The following tax collections are Per Capita
Total Tax Collections - Ind. & Biz (rank / $) ....02 / 8,033
Total Tax Collections - Ind. only (rank / $) ....06 / 3,059

STATE FACTS & NUMBERS
  Rank: 1 highest; 51 lowest

State Revenue - Per Capita (rank / $) ....04 / 11,157
State & Local Rev. - Per Capita (rank / $) ....05 / 13,786
Personal Income - Per Capita (rank / $) ....05 / 54,871
Median Household Income (rank / $) ....20 / 53,585
Median House Value (rank / $) ....39 / 130,500
Total Area - Square Miles (rank / count) .... 19 / 70,698
Land Area - Square Miles (rank / count) .... 17 / 69,001
Water Area - Square Miles (rank / count) ....24 / 1,698
Number of Counties 53

Name for Residents... North Dakotans
Capital City..Bismarck
Nickname .... Peace Garden State
State Motto ..... Liberty and Union, Now and Forever, One
  and Inseparable
State Bird ....Western Meadowlark
State Flower..Wild Prairie Rose
State Tree .... American Elm
State Song..North Dakota Hymn

POPULATION
  Rank: 1 highest; 51 lowest

State Population (rank / count) ....48 / 699,628
Population Per Square Mile (rank / count) .... 48 / 10
Male Population (rank / %).................................03 / 50.53
Female Population (rank / %)................................49 / 49.47
Sex Ratio & Population Median Age............... 102.1 / 37.0
  (Sex Ratio = the # of males per 100 females)
Population % by age (under 18 / 18-44) ....22.3 / 36.7
Population % by age (45-64 / 65+) ....26.5 / 14.5

RESOURCES

North Dakota State Government
Phone: 701-328-2000
Web Site: www.nd.gov

North Dakota Office of State Tax Commissioner
Phone: 701-328-7088
Web Site: www.nd.gov/tax

North Dakota Motor Vehicle Division
Phone: 701-328-2500 or 855-637-6237
Web Site: www.dot.nd.gov/public/licensing.htm

North Dakota Office of Tourism
Phone: 701-328-2525 or 800-435-5663
Web Site: www.ndtourism.com

Voting Information
Phone: 701-328-4146 or 800-352-0867 ext. 328-4146
Web Site: www.nd.gov/sos/electvote/

Ohio

STATE AND LOCAL TAXES

State Sales Tax (%)..5.75
Exempt: food and prescription drugs.

Local Sales Taxes (up to an additional %) 2.25
Inheritance Tax .... No
Estate Tax.. No

PERSONAL INCOME TAXES

State Income Tax (%) ....0.587 - 5.925
   9 income brackets - Lowest $5,200; Highest $208,500.
   Any city and/or county income taxes are additional.

Personal Exemption $ (single / joint) ....1,650 / 3,300
Standard Deduction $ (single / joint)........................... None
Federal Income Tax Paid - Deduction Allowed .... None
Social Security Income - Tax Exempt ....Yes
Retired Military Pay - Tax Exempt ....Yes
   Some exceptions based on age.

State & Local Government Pensions - Tax Exempt .... No
Federal Civil Service Pensions - Tax Exempt .... No
Railroad Retirement - Tax Exempt ....Yes
Private Pension - Tax Exempt .... No

   Note: A credit up to $200 is available if retirement income
   is at least $8,000. Seniors age 65 or over receive a $50 tax
   credit.

VEHICLES

Registration Fees .... 1 Year
   Passenger vehicles, $34.50.
   Motor home, $49.50.
   Trucks up to 3/4 ton, $49.50.
   Trucks 3/4 -1 ton, $84.50.

   A local "Permissive Tax" may be added, maximum of
   $20.

Annual Vehicle Tax .... No
   No property tax on vehicles.

State Emissions Test Required ....Yes
   Every two years. Seven counties in the Cleveland and
   Akron area. Motor homes and vehicles over 10,000 lbs
   are exempt.
   Web Site: www.epa.state.oh.us/dapc/mobile.aspx

Vehicle Safety Inspection Required .... No
Mandatory Minimum Liability Insurance 25/50/25

COST OF LIVING INDICATORS

   Rank: 1 highest; 51 lowest

Cost of Living - average statewide (rank) 41
Fuel - $ per gallon, Dec. 2013 (diesel / gas)......3.86 / 3.23
The following "Tax Collections" are all Per Capita
State Individual Income Tax (rank / $)...................29 / 764
Local Individual Income Tax (rank / $)...................04 / 370
State General Sales Tax (rank / $) ....29 / 673
Local General Sales Tax (rank / $) ....25 / 150
State Property Tax (rank / $) ....33 / 0
Local Property Tax (rank / $) ....27 / 1,140
State - All Tax Collections (rank / $) ....33 / 2,167
Local - All Tax Collections (rank / $).....................21 / 1,742
State & Local - All Tax Collections (rank / $) ......27 / 3,909

STATE TAX COLLECTIONS

   Rank: 1 highest; 50 lowest
   Rank and % of total taxes collected from:

Property Tax...37 / 0.00
Sales & Gross Receipts ....18 / 50.61
Motor Vehicle & Driver License..............................18 / 3.07
Individual Income Tax..26 / 34.83
Corporate Income Tax.....................................46 / 0.45
Other Taxes ....13 / 11.04
The following tax collections are Per Capita
Total Tax Collections - Ind. & Biz (rank / $) ....34 / 2,246
Total Tax Collections - Ind. only (rank / $) ....33 / 1,993

STATE FACTS & NUMBERS

   Rank: 1 highest; 51 lowest

State Revenue - Per Capita (rank / $) ....15 / 8,391
State & Local Rev. - Per Capita (rank / $)..........18 / 11,405
Personal Income - Per Capita (rank / $) ....32 / 40,057
Median Household Income (rank / $) ....35 / 46,829
Median House Value (rank / $)........................38 / 130,600
Total Area - Square Miles (rank / count) ....34 / 44,826
Land Area - Square Miles (rank / count)..........35 / 40,861
Water Area - Square Miles (rank / count) ....14 / 3,965
Number of Counties 88
Name for Residents.................................... Ohioans
Capital City...Columbus
Nickname ....Buckeye State
State Motto..................... With God, All Things Are Possible
State Bird ....Cardinal
State Flower..Scarlet Carnation
State Tree .... Buckeye
State Song.. Beautiful Ohio

POPULATION

Rank: 1 highest; 51 lowest

State Population (rank / count) ....07 / 11,544,225
Population Per Square Mile (rank / count) ....11 / 258
Male Population (rank / %)..36 / 48.82
Female Population (rank / %)..16 / 51.18
Sex Ratio & Population Median Age....................95.4 / 38.8
(Sex Ratio = the # of males per 100 females)

Population % by age (under 18 / 18-44) ....23.7 / 34.6
Population % by age (45-64 / 65+) ....27.7 / 14.0

RESOURCES

Ohio State Government
Phone: 614-466-2000
Web Site: www.ohio.gov

Ohio Department of Taxation
Phone: 800-282-1780
Web Site: www.tax.ohio.gov

Ohio Bureau of Motor Vehicles
Phone: 614-752-7500
Web Site: www.bmv.ohio.gov

Ohio Office of Tourism
Phone: 800-282-5393
Web Site: www.discoverohio.com

Voting Information
Phone: 614-466-2655 or 877-767-6446
Web Site: www.sos.state.oh.us/sos/elections.aspx

Oklahoma

STATE AND LOCAL TAXES

State Sales Tax (%)..4.5
Exempt: prescription drugs.

Local Sales Taxes (up to an additional %) 6.35
Inheritance Tax ....No
Estate Tax..No

PERSONAL INCOME TAXES

State Income Tax (%) ....0.5 - 5.25
8 income brackets - Lowest $1,000; Highest $8,700.
($2,000 to $15,000 for joint filers.)

Personal Exemption $ (single / joint) ....1,000 / 2,000
Additional $1,000 if age 65 or over.

Standard Deduction $ (single / joint)..........5,950 / 11,900
Federal Income Tax Paid - Deduction Allowed ....None
Social Security Income - Tax Exempt................................Yes
Retired Military Pay - Tax Exempt ....Limits
State & Local Government Pensions - Tax Exempt ..Limits
Federal Civil Service Pensions - Tax Exempt ....Limits
Railroad Retirement - Tax Exempt ....Yes
Private Pension - Tax Exempt ....Limits

Note: Limits include a maximum combined exemption of $10,000 (income restrictions on private pensions) from all retirement income sources other than Social Security and Railroad Retirement.

VEHICLES

Registration Fees .... 1 Year
Fees are based on how long you've had the vehicle registered in the state.
1st - 4th year, $91.
5th - 8th year, $81.
9th - 12th year, $61.
13th - 16th year, $41.
17th year and over, $21.

Note: An excise tax is due upon every transfer of ownership. The tax is collected at the time of issuance of the new Oklahoma title. For most vehicles the tax is based on the purchase price. The tax for new vehicles is 3.25% of the purchase price (or taxable value, if different). Used vehicles are taxed $20 on the first $1,500 of value plus 3.25% of the remainder.

Annual Vehicle Tax .... No
   No property tax on vehicles.

State Emissions Test Required .... No
Vehicle Safety Inspection Required .... No
Mandatory Minimum Liability Insurance 25/50/25

COST OF LIVING INDICATORS
   Rank: 1 highest; 51 lowest

Cost of Living - average statewide (rank) 47
Fuel - $ per gallon, Dec. 2013 (diesel / gas) ...... 3.61 / 2.97
The following "Tax Collections" are all Per Capita
State Individual Income Tax (rank / $) .... 34 / 625
Local Individual Income Tax (rank / $) .... 14 / 0
State General Sales Tax (rank / $) .... 39 / 571
Local General Sales Tax (rank / $) .... 06 / 457
State Property Tax (rank / $) .... 33 / 0
Local Property Tax (rank / $) .... 48 / 583
State - All Tax Collections (rank / $) .... 37 / 2,038
Local - All Tax Collections (rank / $) .... 43 / 1,110
State & Local - All Tax Collections (rank / $) ...... 45 / 3,148

STATE TAX COLLECTIONS
   Rank: 1 highest; 50 lowest
   Rank and % of total taxes collected from:

Property Tax .... 37 / 0.00
Sales & Gross Receipts .... 35 / 42.20
Motor Vehicle & Driver License .... 01 / 7.71
Individual Income Tax .... 30 / 31.43
Corporate Income Tax .... 25 / 5.05
Other Taxes .... 09 / 13.61
The following tax collections are Per Capita
Total Tax Collections - Ind. & Biz (rank / $) .... 33 / 2,314
Total Tax Collections - Ind. only (rank / $) .... 36 / 1,882

STATE FACTS & NUMBERS
   Rank: 1 highest; 51 lowest

State Revenue - Per Capita (rank / $) .... 31 / 6,877
State & Local Rev. - Per Capita (rank / $) .... 43 / 9,274
Personal Income - Per Capita (rank / $) .... 29 / 40,620
Median Household Income (rank / $) .... 42 / 44,312
Median House Value (rank / $) .... 48 / 112,900
Total Area - Square Miles (rank / count) .... 20 / 69,899
Land Area - Square Miles (rank / count) .... 19 / 68,595
Water Area - Square Miles (rank / count) .... 30 / 1,304
Number of Counties 77
Name for Residents .... Oklahomans
Capital City .... Oklahoma City

Nickname .... Sooner State
State Motto .... Labor Conquers All Things
State Bird .... Scissor-Tailed Flycatcher
State Flower .... Oklahoma Rose
State Tree .... Redbud
State Song .... Oklahoma!

POPULATION
   Rank: 1 highest; 51 lowest

State Population (rank / count) .... 28 / 3,814,820
Population Per Square Mile (rank / count) .... 37 / 55
Male Population (rank / %) .... 20 / 49.50
Female Population (rank / %) .... 32 / 50.50
Sex Ratio & Population Median Age .... 98.0 / 36.2
   (Sex Ratio = the # of males per 100 females)
Population % by age (under 18 / 18-44) .... 24.8 / 36.0
Population % by age (45-64 / 65+) .... 25.8 / 13.4

RESOURCES

Oklahoma State Government
Phone: 405-521-2011
Web Site: www.ok.gov

Oklahoma Tax Commission
Phone: 405-521-3160
Web Site: www.oktax.state.ok.us

Oklahoma Department of Public Safety (Driver License)
Phone: 405-425-2300
Web Site: www.dps.state.ok.us/dls

Oklahoma Motor Vehicle Division
Phone: 405-521-3221
Web Site: www.tax.ok.gov/motveh.html

Oklahoma Office of Tourism
Phone: 800-652-6552
Web Site: www.travelok.com

Voting Information
Phone: 405-521-2391
Web Site: www.ok.gov/elections/

Oregon

STATE AND LOCAL TAXES

State Sales Tax (%) .... None
Local Sales Taxes (up to an additional %) .... None
Inheritance Tax .... No
Estate Tax .... Yes
  16% on estates valued over $1 million.

PERSONAL INCOME TAXES

State Income Tax (%) .... 5 - 9.9
  4 income brackets - Lowest $3,250; Highest $125,000.
  Any city and/or county income taxes are additional.

Personal Exemption $ (single / joint) .... 188 / 376
  Amount is a tax credit.

Standard Deduction $ (single / joint) .... 2,025 / 4,050
  Additional $1,200 if age 65 or over.

Federal Income Tax Paid - Deduction Allowed .... Limits
  Up to $6,100 for all filers.

Social Security Income - Tax Exempt .... Yes
Retired Military Pay - Tax Exempt .... Limits
  Deduction amount based on dates of service.

State & Local Government Pensions - Tax Exempt .. Limits
Federal Civil Service Pensions - Tax Exempt .... Limits
Railroad Retirement - Tax Exempt .... Yes
Private Pension - Tax Exempt .... Limits

  Note: Depending on your age and income, you may
  qualify for an income credit on your Oregon return.

VEHICLES

Registration Fees .... 2 Years
  Passenger vehicles (under 10,000 lbs), $86.

  Camper and travel trailer, $81. Add $6.75 for each
  additional foot over 10 feet. (No vehicle over 45 feet can
  be registered.)

  Motor homes 6 - 14 feet, $54.
  Motor homes 15 feet, $163.50. Add $7.50 for each
  additional foot. (No vehicle over 45 feet can be
  registered.)

Annual Vehicle Tax .... No
  No property tax on vehicles.

State Emissions Test Required .... Yes
  Every 2 years. Within and near the Medford or Portland-
  Metro areas only. Diesel powered vehicles 8,501 lbs or
  more are exempt. Web Site: www.deq.state.or.us/aq/vip

Vehicle Safety Inspection Required .... No
Mandatory Minimum Liability Insurance 25/50/20
  Personal Injury Protection, Uninsured and Underinsured
  Motorists coverage is also required.

COST OF LIVING INDICATORS

  Rank: 1 highest; 51 lowest

Cost of Living - average statewide (rank) 14
Fuel - $ per gallon, Dec. 2013 (diesel / gas) ...... 3.86 / 3.29
The following "Tax Collections" are all Per Capita
State Individual Income Tax (rank / $) .... 04 / 1,409
Local Individual Income Tax (rank / $) .... 14 / 0
State General Sales Tax (rank / $) .... 46 / 0
Local General Sales Tax (rank / $) .... 35 / 0
State Property Tax (rank / $) .... 23 / 6
Local Property Tax (rank / $) .... 24 / 1,291
State - All Tax Collections (rank / $) .... 35 / 2,082
Local - All Tax Collections (rank / $) .... 28 / 1,537
State & Local - All Tax Collections (rank / $) ...... 31 / 3,619

STATE TAX COLLECTIONS

  Rank: 1 highest; 50 lowest
  Rank and % of total taxes collected from:

Property Tax .... 25 / 0.18
Sales & Gross Receipts .... 48 / 16.08
Motor Vehicle & Driver License .... 04 / 5.82
Individual Income Tax .... 01 / 66.97
Corporate Income Tax .... 27 / 4.98
Other Taxes .... 20 / 5.97
The following tax collections are Per Capita
Total Tax Collections - Ind. & Biz (rank / $) .... 35 / 2,231
Total Tax Collections - Ind. only (rank / $) .... 32 / 2,013

STATE FACTS & NUMBERS

  Rank: 1 highest; 51 lowest

State Revenue - Per Capita (rank / $) .... 11 / 8,924
State & Local Rev. - Per Capita (rank / $) .... 11 / 12,065
Personal Income - Per Capita (rank / $) .... 33 / 39,166
Median Household Income (rank / $) .... 29 / 49,161
Median House Value (rank / $) .... 16 / 233,900
Total Area - Square Miles (rank / count) .... 09 / 98,379
Land Area - Square Miles (rank / count) .... 10 / 95,988
Water Area - Square Miles (rank / count) .... 20 / 2,391
Number of Counties 36
Name for Residents .... Oregonians
Capital City .... Salem
Nickname .... Beaver State
State Motto .... She Flies With Her Own Wings

State Bird ....Western Meadowlark
State Flower...Oregon Grape
State Tree...Douglas Fir
State Song... Oregon, My Oregon

POPULATION

Rank: 1 highest; 51 lowest

State Population (rank / count) .... 27 / 3,899,353
Population Per Square Mile (rank / count) .... 39 / 40
Male Population (rank / %)......................................21 / 49.49
Female Population (rank / %)................................31 / 50.51
Sex Ratio & Population Median Age...................98.0 / 38.4
   (Sex Ratio = the # of males per 100 females)
Population % by age (under 18 / 18-44) ....22.6 / 36.1
Population % by age (45-64 / 65+) ....27.4 / 13.9

RESOURCES

Oregon State Government
Phone: 503-378-4582
Web Site: www.oregon.gov

Oregon Department of Revenue
Phone: 503-378-4988
Web Site: www.oregon.gov/dor

Oregon Driver and Motor Vehicles
Phone: 503-945-5000
Web Site: www.oregon.gov/odot/dmv

Oregon Office of Tourism
Phone: 800-547-7842
Web Site: www.traveloregon.com

Voting Information
Phone: 503-986-1518 or 866-673-8683
Web Site: www.oregonvotes.org

Pennsylvania

STATE AND LOCAL TAXES

State Sales Tax (%)..6
   Exempt: food and prescription drugs.

Local Sales Taxes (up to an additional %) 2
Inheritance Tax ....Yes
   Ranges from 0% to 15% depending on the relationship
   of the recipient to the decedent.

Estate Tax.. No

PERSONAL INCOME TAXES

State Income Tax (%) 3.07
   Flat rate, no income brackets. Any city and/or county
   income taxes are additional.

Personal Exemption $ (single / joint) .... None
Standard Deduction $ (single / joint)........................... None
Federal Income Tax Paid - Deduction Allowed .... None
Social Security Income - Tax Exempt.................................Yes
Retired Military Pay - Tax Exempt ....Yes
State & Local Government Pensions - Tax Exempt ....Yes
Federal Civil Service Pensions - Tax Exempt ....Yes
Railroad Retirement - Tax Exempt ....Yes
Private Pension - Tax Exempt ....Yes

VEHICLES

Registration Fees .... 1 Year
   Passenger vehicle, $36.

   Truck registration fees vary by gross weight of vehicle.
   5,000 lbs or less, $58.50.
   5,001 - 7,000 lbs, $81.
   7,001 - 9,000 lbs, $153.
   9,001 - 11,000 lbs, $198.
   11,001 - 33,000 lbs, $243 - 567.
   33,001 - 60,000 lbs, $621 - 999.00.

   Motor home 8,000 lbs or less, $45.
   Motor home 8,001 - 11,000 lbs, $63.
   Motor home 11,000 lbs or more, $81.

Annual Vehicle Tax .... No
   No property tax on vehicles.

State Emissions Test Required ....Yes
   Annual. In four regions covering 25 counties.
   Web Site: www.drivecleanpa.state.pa.us

Vehicle Safety Inspection Required ....Yes
   Annual.

Mandatory Minimum Liability Insurance 15/30/5
Personal Injury Protection is also required.

COST OF LIVING INDICATORS

Rank: 1 highest; 51 lowest

Cost of Living - average statewide (rank) 20
Fuel - $ per gallon, Dec. 2013 (diesel / gas) ...... 3.92 / 3.40
The following "Tax Collections" are all Per Capita
State Individual Income Tax (rank / $) .... 27 / 770
Local Individual Income Tax (rank / $) .... 05 / 321
State General Sales Tax (rank / $) .... 28 / 701
Local General Sales Tax (rank / $) .... 32 / 50
State Property Tax (rank / $) .... 27 / 4
Local Property Tax (rank / $) .... 22 / 1,298
State - All Tax Collections (rank / $) .... 19 / 2,535
Local - All Tax Collections (rank / $) .... 14 / 1,835
State & Local - All Tax Collections (rank / $) ...... 19 / 4,370

STATE TAX COLLECTIONS

Rank: 1 highest; 50 lowest
Rank and % of total taxes collected from:

Property Tax .... 27 / 0.12
Sales & Gross Receipts .... 16 / 52.05
Motor Vehicle & Driver License .... 26 / 2.73
Individual Income Tax .... 31 / 30.66
Corporate Income Tax .... 16 / 5.58
Other Taxes .... 16 / 8.86
The following tax collections are Per Capita
Total Tax Collections - Ind. & Biz (rank / $) .... 19 / 2,582
Total Tax Collections - Ind. only (rank / $) .... 23 / 2,272

STATE FACTS & NUMBERS

Rank: 1 highest; 51 lowest

State Revenue - Per Capita (rank / $) .... 28 / 7,121
State & Local Rev. - Per Capita (rank / $) .... 25 / 10,523
Personal Income - Per Capita (rank / $) .... 19 / 45,083
Median Household Income (rank / $) .... 22 / 51,230
Median House Value (rank / $) .... 25 / 164,700
Total Area - Square Miles (rank / count) .... 33 / 46,054
Land Area - Square Miles (rank / count) .... 32 / 44,743
Water Area - Square Miles (rank / count) .... 28 / 1,312
Number of Counties 66
Name for Residents .... Pennsylvanians
Capital City .... Harrisburg
Nickname .... Keystone State
State Motto .... Virtue, Liberty, and Independence
State Bird .... Ruffed Grouse

State Flower .... Mountain Laurel
State Tree .... Eastern Hemlock
State Song .... Pennsylvania

POPULATION

Rank: 1 highest; 51 lowest

State Population (rank / count) .... 06 / 12,763,536
Population Per Square Mile (rank / count) .... 10 / 277
Male Population (rank / %) .... 39 / 48.73
Female Population (rank / %) .... 13 / 51.27
Sex Ratio & Population Median Age .... 95.1 / 40.1
(Sex Ratio = the # of males per 100 females)
Population % by age (under 18 / 18-44) .... 22.0 / 34.5
Population % by age (45-64 / 65+) .... 28.0 / 15.5

RESOURCES

Pennsylvania State Government
Phone: 800-932-0784
Web Site: www.pa.gov

Pennsylvania Department of Revenue
Phone: 717-787-8201
Web Site: www.revenue.state.pa.us

Pennsylvania Driver and Vehicle Services
Phone: 800-932-4600 (in-state) or
        717-412-5300 (out-of-state)
Web Site: www.dmv.state.pa.us

Pennsylvania Office of Tourism
Phone: 800-847-4872
Web Site: www.visitpa.com

Voting Information
Phone: 877-868-3772
Web Site: www.votespa.com/

Rhode Island

STATE AND LOCAL TAXES

State Sales Tax (%) 7
Exempt: food and prescription drugs.

Local Sales Taxes (up to an additional %) .... None
Inheritance Tax .... No
Estate Tax .... Yes
16% on estates valued over $910, 725. Exemption amount is adjusted for inflation on an annual basis.

PERSONAL INCOME TAXES

State Income Tax (%) ....3.75 - 5.99
3 income brackets - Lowest $58,600; Highest $133,250.

Personal Exemption $ (single / joint) ....3,750 / 7,500
Deduction is phased out with adjusted gross income starting at $192,000 and eliminated with AGI of $207,950.

Standard Deduction $ (single / joint) ....8,000 / 16,000
Deduction is phased out with adjusted gross income starting at $192,000 and eliminated with AGI of $207,950.

Federal Income Tax Paid - Deduction Allowed .... None
Social Security Income - Tax Exempt .... Limits
Taxed to the extent it is federally taxed.

Retired Military Pay - Tax Exempt .... No
State & Local Government Pensions - Tax Exempt .... No
Federal Civil Service Pensions - Tax Exempt .... No
Railroad Retirement - Tax Exempt ....Yes
Private Pension - Tax Exempt .... No

VEHICLES

Registration Fees .... 1 Year
Passenger vehicles under 4,000 lbs, $44.75.
Trucks under 4,000 lbs, $48.75.
Vehicles 4,000 lbs or more:
4,001 - 10,000 lbs, $57.00 - $106.25.
10,001 - 22,000 lbs, $141.00 - $266.50.
22,001 - 42,000 lbs, $287.00 - $671.50
42,001 - 74,000 lbs, $734.50 - $1,161.50.

Annual Vehicle Tax ....Yes
Annual property tax on vehicles, varies by municipality.

State Emissions Test Required ....Yes
Every two years. Statewide.
Web Site: www.riinspection.org

Vehicle Safety Inspection Required ....Yes
Every 2 years. Annual for all vehicles over 8,500 lbs.

Mandatory Minimum Liability Insurance 25/50/25

COST OF LIVING INDICATORS

Rank: 1 highest; 51 lowest

Cost of Living - average statewide (rank) 08
Fuel - $ per gallon, Dec. 2013 (diesel / gas)......3.94 / 3.47
The following "Tax Collections" are all Per Capita
State Individual Income Tax (rank / $)...................14 / 968
Local Individual Income Tax (rank / $)......................14 / 0
State General Sales Tax (rank / $)..........................21 / 785
Local General Sales Tax (rank / $)..............................35 / 0
State Property Tax (rank / $) ....30 / 2
Local Property Tax (rank / $)..............................06 / 2,163
State - All Tax Collections (rank / $).................18 / 2,623
Local - All Tax Collections (rank / $).....................09 / 2,214
State & Local - All Tax Collections (rank / $) ......13 / 4,837

STATE TAX COLLECTIONS

Rank: 1 highest; 50 lowest
Rank and % of total taxes collected from:

Property Tax...30 / 0.07
Sales & Gross Receipts ....13 / 52.57
Motor Vehicle & Driver License.........................41 / 2.05
Individual Income Tax....................................23 / 37.94
Corporate Income Tax.....................................33 / 4.35
Other Taxes ....41 / 3.00
The following tax collections are Per Capita
Total Tax Collections - Ind. & Biz (rank / $) ....18 / 2,671
Total Tax Collections - Ind. only (rank / $) ....14 / 2,501

STATE FACTS & NUMBERS

Rank: 1 highest; 51 lowest

State Revenue - Per Capita (rank / $) ....10 / 8,939
State & Local Rev. - Per Capita (rank / $)..........09 / 12,132
Personal Income - Per Capita (rank / $) ....15 / 45,877
Median Household Income (rank / $) ....19 / 54,554
Median House Value (rank / $)..........................10 / 245,300
Total Area - Square Miles (rank / count) ....50 / 1,545
Land Area - Square Miles (rank / count).............50 / 1,034
Water Area - Square Miles (rank / count) ....43 / 511
Number of Counties 5
Name for Residents.................................... Rhode Islanders
Capital City...Providence
Nickname .... The Ocean State
State Motto..Hope

State Bird .... Rhode Island Red
State Flower...Violet
State Tree...Red Maple
State Song...........................Rhode Island, It's For Me

POPULATION

Rank: 1 highest; 51 lowest

State Population (rank / count) .... 43 / 1,050,292
Population Per Square Mile (rank / count) .... 03 / 680
Male Population (rank / %)....................................50 / 48.30
Female Population (rank / %)................................02 / 51.70
Sex Ratio & Population Median Age..................93.4 / 39.4
  (Sex Ratio = the # of males per 100 females)

Population % by age (under 18 / 18-44) ....21.3 / 36.5
Population % by age (45-64 / 65+) ....27.8 / 14.4

RESOURCES

Rhode Island State Government
Phone: 401-222-2000
Web Site: www.ri.gov

Rhode Island Division of Taxation
Phone: 401-574-8829
Web Site: www.tax.ri.gov

Rhode Island Division of Motor Vehicles
Phone: 401-462-4368
Web Site: www.dmv.ri.gov

Rhode Island Office of Tourism
Phone: 800-556-2484
Web Site: www.visitrhodeisland.com

Voting Information
Phone: 401-222-2345
Web Site: www.elections.state.ri.us/

South Carolina

STATE AND LOCAL TAXES

State Sales Tax (%) 6
  Exempt: food and prescription drugs.

Local Sales Taxes (up to an additional %) 3
Inheritance Tax .... No
Estate Tax... No

PERSONAL INCOME TAXES

State Income Tax (%) ....0 - 7
  6 income brackets - Lowest $2,850; Highest $14,250.

Personal Exemption $ (single / joint) ....3,900 / 7,800
Standard Deduction $ (single / joint).........6,100 / 12,200
Federal Income Tax Paid - Deduction Allowed .... None
Social Security Income - Tax Exempt ....Yes
Retired Military Pay - Tax Exempt ....Limits
State & Local Government Pensions - Tax Exempt ..Limits
Federal Civil Service Pensions - Tax Exempt ....Limits
Railroad Retirement - Tax Exempt ....Yes
Private Pension - Tax Exempt ....Limits

> *Note: Limits include a maximum combined exemption of $3,000 ($15,000 if 65 or older) from all retirement income sources.*

VEHICLES

Registration Fees .... 2 Years
  Passenger cars and RV's, $24.
  Utility or camper trailer, $10.
  Trucks, rate based on weight:
  0 - 6,000 lbs, $30 - $60.
  6,001 - 10,000 lbs, $70 - $100.

Annual Vehicle Tax ....Yes
  Annual property tax on vehicles.

State Emissions Test Required .... No
Vehicle Safety Inspection Required .... No
Mandatory Minimum Liability Insurance 25/50/25
  Uninsured Motorist coverage is also required.

COST OF LIVING INDICATORS

Rank: 1 highest; 51 lowest

Cost of Living - average statewide (rank) 33
Fuel - $ per gallon, Dec. 2013 (diesel / gas)......3.67 / 3.12
The following "Tax Collections" are all Per Capita
State Individual Income Tax (rank / $)...................36 / 616

Local Individual Income Tax (rank / $)........................14 / 0
State General Sales Tax (rank / $)...........................37 / 591
Local General Sales Tax (rank / $)............................30 / 75
State Property Tax (rank / $) ....31 / 2
Local Property Tax (rank / $) ....31 / 1,015
State - All Tax Collections (rank / $)...................49 / 1,627
Local - All Tax Collections (rank / $)...................33 / 1,282
State & Local - All Tax Collections (rank / $) ......50 / 2,910

STATE TAX COLLECTIONS

Rank: 1 highest; 50 lowest
Rank and % of total taxes collected from:

Property Tax..29 / 0.11
Sales & Gross Receipts ....14 / 52.24
Motor Vehicle & Driver License.............................36 / 2.23
Individual Income Tax......................................21 / 38.54
Corporate Income Tax......................................42 / 3.15
Other Taxes ....35 / 3.74
The following tax collections are Per Capita
Total Tax Collections - Ind. & Biz (rank / $) ....48 / 1,701
Total Tax Collections - Ind. only (rank / $) ....44 / 1,584

STATE FACTS & NUMBERS

Rank: 1 highest; 51 lowest

State Revenue - Per Capita (rank / $) ....32 / 6,718
State & Local Rev. - Per Capita (rank / $)..............33 / 9,691
Personal Income - Per Capita (rank / $) ....49 / 35,056
Median Household Income (rank / $) ....43 / 43,107
Median House Value (rank / $)........................36 / 136,300
Total Area - Square Miles (rank / count) ....40 / 32,020
Land Area - Square Miles (rank / count) ....40 / 30,061
Water Area - Square Miles (rank / count) ....21 / 1,960
Number of Counties 46
Name for Residents........................South Carolinians
Capital City..Columbia
Nickname ....Palmetto State
State Motto....................Prepared In Mind And Resources
State Bird ....Great Carolina Wren
State Flower.............................Yellow Jessamine
State Tree.............................Cabbage Palmetto
State Song.....................................Carolina

POPULATION

Rank: 1 highest; 51 lowest

State Population (rank / count) ....24 / 4,723,723
Population Per Square Mile (rank / count) ....19 / 148
Male Population (rank / %)................................43 / 48.65

Female Population (rank / %)................................09 / 51.35
Sex Ratio & Population Median Age..................94.7 / 37.9
   (Sex Ratio = the # of males per 100 females)
Population % by age (under 18 / 18-44) ....23.4 / 36.1
Population % by age (45-64 / 65+) ....26.9 / 13.6

RESOURCES

South Carolina State Government
Phone: 803-896-0000
Web Site: www.sc.gov

South Carolina Department of Revenue
Phone: 803-898-5709
Web Site: www.sctax.org

South Carolina Department of Motor Vehicles
Phone: 803-896-5000
Web Site: www.scdmvonline.com

South Carolina Office of Tourism
Phone: 803-734-1700
Web Site: www.discoversouthcarolina.com

Voting Information
Phone: 803-734-9060
Web Site: www.scvotes.org/

South Dakota

STATE AND LOCAL TAXES

State Sales Tax (%) 4
Prescription drugs exempt.

Local Sales Taxes (up to an additional %) 2
Inheritance Tax .... No
Estate Tax... No

PERSONAL INCOME TAXES

State Income Tax (%) .... None
Personal Exemption $ (single / joint) .... n/a
Standard Deduction $ (single / joint)............................... n/a
Federal Income Tax Paid - Deduction Allowed .... n/a
Social Security Income - Tax Exempt .... n/a
Retired Military Pay - Tax Exempt .... n/a
State & Local Government Pensions - Tax Exempt .... n/a
Federal Civil Service Pensions - Tax Exempt .... n/a
Railroad Retirement - Tax Exempt .... n/a
Private Pension - Tax Exempt .... n/a

VEHICLES

Registration Fees .... 1 Year
Registration fees are based on weight and age of vehicle.
Cars, pickups, and vans. 0 to 9 years old:
1 - 2,000 lbs, $30.
2,001 - 4,000 lbs, $60.
4,001 - 6,000 lbs, $90.
6,001 lbs or more, $120.

Cars, pickups, and vans. 10 or more years old:
1 - 2,000 lbs, $21.
2,001 - 4,000 lbs, $42.
4,001 - 6,000 lbs, $63.
6,001 lbs or more, $84.

Motor home, 0 - 9 years old:
1 - 6,000 lbs, $75.
Each additional 2,000 lbs, $25.

Motor home, 10 or more years old:
1 - 6,000 lbs, $52.50.
Each additional 2,000 lbs, $17.50.

Annual Vehicle Tax .... No
No property tax on vehicles.

State Emissions Test Required .... No

Vehicle Safety Inspection Required .... No
Mandatory Minimum Liability Insurance 25/50/25
Uninsured and Underinsured Motorists coverage is also required.

COST OF LIVING INDICATORS

Rank: 1 highest; 51 lowest

Cost of Living - average statewide (rank) 22
Fuel - $ per gallon, Dec. 2013 (diesel / gas)......3.85 / 3.15
The following "Tax Collections" are all Per Capita
State Individual Income Tax (rank / $).........................44 / 0
Local Individual Income Tax (rank / $).........................14 / 0
State General Sales Tax (rank / $) ....08 / 970
Local General Sales Tax (rank / $)...........................11 / 347
State Property Tax (rank / $) ....33 / 0
Local Property Tax (rank / $) ....26 / 1,177
State - All Tax Collections (rank / $)....................48 / 1,655
Local - All Tax Collections (rank / $)....................26 / 1,583
State & Local - All Tax Collections (rank / $) ......43 / 3,239

STATE TAX COLLECTIONS

Rank: 1 highest; 50 lowest
Rank and % of total taxes collected from:

Property Tax..37 / 0.00
Sales & Gross Receipts ....03 / 78.68
Motor Vehicle & Driver License...............................09 / 4.50
Individual Income Tax...44 / 0.00
Corporate Income Tax..36 / 3.93
Other Taxes ....10 / 12.88
The following tax collections are Per Capita

Total Tax Collections - Ind. & Biz (rank / $) ....45 / 1,826
Total Tax Collections - Ind. only (rank / $) ....45 / 1,519

STATE FACTS & NUMBERS

Rank: 1 highest; 51 lowest

State Revenue - Per Capita (rank / $).................27 / 7,220
State & Local Rev. - Per Capita (rank / $)..........30 / 10,156
Personal Income - Per Capita (rank / $) ....18 / 45,381
Median Household Income (rank / $) ....30 / 48,362
Median House Value (rank / $).........................37 / 131,600
Total Area - Square Miles (rank / count) ....17 / 77,116
Land Area - Square Miles (rank / count) ....16 / 75,811
Water Area - Square Miles (rank / count) ....29 / 1,305
Number of Counties 64
Name for Residents................................... South Dakotans
Capital City...Pierre
Nickname ....Mt. Rushmore State

State Motto..................................Under God The People Rule
State Bird ....Ring-Necked Pheasant
State Flower.................................American Pasqueflower
State Tree...Black Hills Spruce
State Song.......................................Hail, South Dakota

POPULATION

Rank: 1 highest; 51 lowest

State Population (rank / count) ....46 / 833,354
Population Per Square Mile (rank / count) .... 47 / 11
Male Population (rank / %)......................................10 / 50.04
Female Population (rank / %)................................42 / 49.96
Sex Ratio & Population Median Age................ 100.1 / 36.9
(Sex Ratio = the # of males per 100 females)

Population % by age (under 18 / 18-44) ....24.9 / 34.4
Population % by age (45-64 / 65+) ....26.4 / 14.3

RESOURCES

South Dakota State Government
Phone: 605-773-3011
Web Site: www.sd.gov

South Dakota Department of Revenue and Regulation
Phone: 605-773-3311
Web Site: http://dor.sd.gov

South Dakota Driver Licensing Program
Phone: 605-773-6883
Web Site: www.dps.sd.gov/licensing

South Dakota Motor Vehicles Division
Phone: 605-773-3541
Web Site: www.state.sd.us/drr2/motorvehicle

South Dakota Office of Tourism
Phone: 800-732-5682
Web Site: www.travelsd.com

Voting Information
Phone: 605-773-3537
Web Site: http://sdsos.gov/Elections/Default.aspx

Tennessee

STATE AND LOCAL TAXES

State Sales Tax (%) 7
Prescription drugs exempt. Food is taxed at 5.25%.

Local Sales Taxes (up to an additional %) 2.75
Inheritance Tax .... No
Estate Tax..Yes
Referred to as an Inheritance Tax in state statues but is taxed like an Estate Tax. 9.5% on estates valued over $2 million. Tax will be phased out by 2016.

PERSONAL INCOME TAXES

State Income Tax (%) .... None
State income tax of 6% applies only to dividend and interest income. The first $1,250 ($2,500 for joint filers) is exempt. Persons 65 and older may exclude $26,200 single, $37,000 married filing jointly.

Personal Exemption $ (single / joint) .... n/a
Standard Deduction $ (single / joint)............................... n/a
Federal Income Tax Paid - Deduction Allowed .... n/a
Social Security Income - Tax Exempt............................... n/a
Retired Military Pay - Tax Exempt .... n/a
State & Local Government Pensions - Tax Exempt .... n/a
Federal Civil Service Pensions - Tax Exempt .... n/a
Railroad Retirement - Tax Exempt .... n/a
Private Pension - Tax Exempt .... n/a

VEHICLES

Registration Fees .... 1 Year
Vehicle registrations are processed at a local county clerk's office.
Passenger vehicles, $24.
A "Privilege Tax" is also charged in some cities and counties. Fee ranges from $10 - $97.

Annual Vehicle Tax .... No
No property tax on vehicles.

State Emissions Test Required ....Yes
Annual for all gas or diesel-fueled vehicles up to 10,500 lbs in Davidson, Hamilton, Rutherford, Sumner, Williamson, and Wilson counties. Web Site: www.state. tn.us/environment/air/air_emissions-testing.shtml

Vehicle Safety Inspection Required .... No
Mandatory Minimum Liability Insurance 25/50/15

COST OF LIVING INDICATORS

Rank: 1 highest; 51 lowest

Cost of Living - average statewide (rank) 49
Fuel - $ per gallon, Dec. 2013 (diesel / gas)......3.75 / 3.13
The following "Tax Collections" are all Per Capita
State Individual Income Tax (rank / $)...................... 43 / 29
Local Individual Income Tax (rank / $)........................ 14 / 0
State General Sales Tax (rank / $) .... 11 / 958
Local General Sales Tax (rank / $) .... 16 / 303
State Property Tax (rank / $) ....33 / 0
Local Property Tax (rank / $) .... 42 / 790
State - All Tax Collections (rank / $)....................44 / 1,736
Local - All Tax Collections (rank / $).....................39 / 1,219
State & Local - All Tax Collections (rank / $) ......48 / 2,955

STATE TAX COLLECTIONS

Rank: 1 highest; 50 lowest

Rank and % of total taxes collected from:

Property Tax...37 / 0.00
Sales & Gross Receipts ....06 / 74.79
Motor Vehicle & Driver License..............................32 / 2.58
Individual Income Tax..43 / 1.52
Corporate Income Tax...02 / 10.23
Other Taxes ....15 / 10.88
The following tax collections are Per Capita
Total Tax Collections - Ind. & Biz (rank / $) ....44 / 1,856
Total Tax Collections - Ind. only (rank / $) ....48 / 1,487

STATE FACTS & NUMBERS

Rank: 1 highest; 51 lowest

State Revenue - Per Capita (rank / $) ....48 / 5,367
State & Local Rev. - Per Capita (rank / $).............40 / 9,344
Personal Income - Per Capita (rank / $) .... 35 / 38,752
Median Household Income (rank / $) .... 45 / 42,764
Median House Value (rank / $)........................34 / 138,400
Total Area - Square Miles (rank / count) .... 36 / 42,144
Land Area - Square Miles (rank / count)..........34 / 41,235
Water Area - Square Miles (rank / count) ....35 / 909
Number of Counties 95
Name for Residents......................................Tennesseans
Capital City...Nashville
Nickname ....The Volunteer State
State Motto................................Agriculture and Commerce
State Bird .... Mockingbird
State Flower.. Iris
State Tree.. Tulip Poplar
State Song.................................The Tennessee Waltz

POPULATION

Rank: 1 highest; 51 lowest

State Population (rank / count) .... 17 / 6,456,243
Population Per Square Mile (rank / count) .... 18 / 153
Male Population (rank / %)..............................38 / 48.75
Female Population (rank / %)............................14 / 51.25
Sex Ratio & Population Median Age...................95.1 / 38.0
(Sex Ratio = the # of males per 100 females)
Population % by age (under 18 / 18-44) ....23.6 / 36.0
Population % by age (45-64 / 65+) ....27.0 / 13.4

RESOURCES

Tennessee State Government
Phone: 615-355-8066
Web Site: www.tn.gov

Tennessee Department of Revenue
Phone: 615-253-0600
Web Site: www.tn.gov/revenue

Tennessee Department of Safety (Driver License)
Phone: 615-253-5221 or 866-849-3548
Web Site: www.tn.gov/safety/dlmain.htm

Tennessee Vehicle Services
Phone: 888-871-3171 (in-state) or
        615-741-3101 (out-of-state)
Web Site: www.state.tn.us/revenue/vehicle

Tennessee Office of Tourism
Phone: 800-462-8366
Web Site: www.tnvacation.com

Voting Information
Phone: 615-741-7956 or 877-850-4959
Web Site: www.state.tn.us/sos/election/

Texas

STATE AND LOCAL TAXES

State Sales Tax (%) 6.25
  Exempt: food and prescription drugs.

Local Sales Taxes (up to an additional %) 2
Inheritance Tax .... No
Estate Tax .... No

PERSONAL INCOME TAXES

State Income Tax (%) .... None
Personal Exemption $ (single / joint) .... n/a
Standard Deduction $ (single / joint) .... n/a
Federal Income Tax Paid - Deduction Allowed .... n/a
Social Security Income - Tax Exempt .... n/a
Retired Military Pay - Tax Exempt .... n/a
State & Local Government Pensions - Tax Exempt .... n/a
Federal Civil Service Pensions - Tax Exempt .... n/a
Railroad Retirement - Tax Exempt .... n/a
Private Pension - Tax Exempt .... n/a

VEHICLES

Registration Fees .... 1 Year
  Passenger vehicles and light trucks (6,000 lbs or less),
  $50.75.

  Travel trailers 6,000 lbs or less, $45.

  All vehicles 6,001 lbs to 10,000 lbs, $54.

  Heavy vehicles including Motor homes
  10,001 lbs - 18,000 lbs, $110.
  18,001 lbs - 40,000 lbs, $205 - $340.
  40,001 lbs - 70,000 lbs, $535 - $740.

  There is a Local Fee of $5 to $20 in addition to registration
  fee. The fee varies by county.

Annual Vehicle Tax .... No
  No property tax on vehicles.

State Emissions Test Required ....Yes
  Annual for vehicles in Brazoria, Fort Bend, Galveston,
  Harris, Montgomery, Collin, Dallas, Denton, Ellis,
  Johnson, Kaufman, Parker, Rockwell, Tarrant, Travis,
  Williamson and El Paso counties. Diesel powered vehicles
  are exempt. Web Site: www.txdps.state.tx.us/rsd/vi.

Vehicle Safety Inspection Required ....Yes
  Annual.

Mandatory Minimum Liability Insurance 30/60/25

COST OF LIVING INDICATORS

  Rank: 1 highest; 51 lowest

Cost of Living - average statewide (rank) 42
Fuel - $ per gallon, Dec. 2013 (diesel / gas) ......3.68 / 3.09
The following "Tax Collections" are all Per Capita
State Individual Income Tax (rank / $) ....44 / 0
Local Individual Income Tax (rank / $) ....14 / 0
State General Sales Tax (rank / $) .... 19 / 836
Local General Sales Tax (rank / $) ....21 / 209
State Property Tax (rank / $) .... 33 / 0
Local Property Tax (rank / $) ....15 / 1,519
State - All Tax Collections (rank / $) ....47 / 1,656
Local - All Tax Collections (rank / $) ....15 / 1,828
State & Local - All Tax Collections (rank / $) ......34 / 3,484

STATE TAX COLLECTIONS

  Rank: 1 highest; 50 lowest
  Rank and % of total taxes collected from:

Property Tax ....37 / 0.00
Sales & Gross Receipts ....05 / 77.03
Motor Vehicle & Driver License .... 12 / 4.04
Individual Income Tax ....44 / 0.00
Corporate Income Tax ....47 / 0.00
Other Taxes ....06 / 18.93
The following tax collections are Per Capita
Total Tax Collections - Ind. & Biz (rank / $) ....43 / 1,865
Total Tax Collections - Ind. only (rank / $) ....46 / 1,512

STATE FACTS & NUMBERS

  Rank: 1 highest; 51 lowest

State Revenue - Per Capita (rank / $) ....51 / 5,114
State & Local Rev. - Per Capita (rank / $) ....49 / 8,614
Personal Income - Per Capita (rank / $) ....26 / 42,638
Median Household Income (rank / $) ....25 / 50,740
Median House Value (rank / $) ....41 / 128,400
Total Area - Square Miles (rank / count) ....02 / 268,596
Land Area - Square Miles (rank / count) ....02 / 261,232
Water Area - Square Miles (rank / count) ....08 / 7,365
Number of Counties 254
Name for Residents ....Texans
Capital City .... Austin
Nickname .... The Lone Star State
State Motto ....Friendship
State Bird .... Mockingbird
State Flower ....Bluebonnet
State Tree ....Pecan
State Song ....Texas, Our Texas

POPULATION

Rank: 1 highest; 51 lowest

State Population (rank / count) ....02 / 26,059,203
Population Per Square Mile (rank / count) .... 24 / 97
Male Population (rank / %)....................................18 / 49.60
Female Population (rank / %)...............................34 / 50.40
Sex Ratio & Population Median Age..................98.4 / 33.6
     (Sex Ratio = the # of males per 100 females)

Population % by age (under 18 / 18-44) ....27.3 / 38.4
Population % by age (45-64 / 65+) ....24.0 / 10.3

RESOURCES

Texas State Government
Phone: 877-541-7905
Web Site: www.texas.gov

Texas Comptroller of Public Accounts
Phone: 888-334-4112
Web Site: www.window.state.tx.us

Texas Department of Public Safety (Driver License)
Phone: 512-424-2600
Web Site: www.txdps.state.tx.us/DriverLicense/

Texas Department of Motor Vehicles
Phone: 888-368-4689
Web Site: www.txdmv.gov

Texas Office of Tourism
Phone: 800-452-9292
Web Site: www.traveltex.com

Voting Information
Phone: 800-252-8683
Web Site: www.sos.state.tx.us/elections/index.shtml

Utah

STATE AND LOCAL TAXES

State Sales Tax (%) 4.7
     Exempt: prescription drugs. Food is taxed at 1.75%.

Local Sales Taxes (up to an additional %) 6.25
Inheritance Tax .... No
Estate Tax... No

PERSONAL INCOME TAXES

State Income Tax (%) 5
     Flat tax, no income brackets.

Personal Exemption $ (single / joint) ....2,925 / 5,850
     *Exemption is 75% of federal exemption amount, adjusted
     each year.*

Standard Deduction $ (single / joint)............................ None
Federal Income Tax Paid - Deduction Allowed .... None
Social Security Income - Tax Exempt........................... Limits
Retired Military Pay - Tax Exempt .... Limits
State & Local Government Pensions - Tax Exempt .. Limits
Federal Civil Service Pensions - Tax Exempt .... Limits
Railroad Retirement - Tax Exempt .... Limits
Private Pension - Tax Exempt .... Limits

     *Note: A tax credit up to $450 may be available, amount
     phases-out with higher income levels. Age and date
     restrictions also apply.*

VEHICLES

Registration Fees .... 1 Year
     *Vehicle registration fee varies depending on vehicle
     type, fuel type, county, and other factors. To find out the
     amount for your vehicle call the DMV at 801-297-7780
     or 1-800-368-8824.*

Annual Vehicle Tax ....Yes
     *The vehicle property assessment fee is a uniform fee
     based on the age of the vehicle. These fees are paid at
     time of vehicle registration. Below are rates for the most
     common types of vehicles.*

     Passenger Vehicles:
     Less than 3 years old, $150.
     3 - 11 years old, $50 - $110.
     12 or more years old, $10.

Travel Trailers:
Less than 3 years old, $175.
3 - 11 years old, $65 - $135.
12 or more years old, $20.

Tent Trailers and Truck Campers:
Less than 3 years old, $70.
3 - 11 years old, $25 - $50.
12 or more years old, $10.

Motor homes are subject to a uniform fee of 1% of the fair market value as established by the Tax Commission.

State Emissions Test Required ....Yes
Every two years for vehicles less than six years old, annual for vehicles over six years old. In Davis, Salt Lake, Utah, and Weber counties only. Web Site: http://dmv. utah.gov/vehicles-services-menu/vehicle-inspections

Vehicle Safety Inspection Required ....Yes
Annual for vehicles 10 years and older. Varies for newer models.

Mandatory Minimum Liability Insurance 25/65/15
Personal Injury Protection is also required.

COST OF LIVING INDICATORS

Rank: 1 highest; 51 lowest

Cost of Living - average statewide (rank) 45
Fuel - $ per gallon, Dec. 2013 (diesel / gas) ......3.81 / 3.10
The following "Tax Collections" are all Per Capita
State Individual Income Tax (rank / $) .... 24 / 805
Local Individual Income Tax (rank / $) .... 14 / 0
State General Sales Tax (rank / $) .... 33 / 646
Local General Sales Tax (rank / $) .... 22 / 209
State Property Tax (rank / $) .... 33 / 0
Local Property Tax (rank / $) .... 38 / 893
State - All Tax Collections (rank / $) ....39 / 1,918
Local - All Tax Collections (rank / $) ....37 / 1,254
State & Local - All Tax Collections (rank / $) ......44 / 3,172

STATE TAX COLLECTIONS

Rank: 1 highest; 50 lowest
Rank and % of total taxes collected from:

Property Tax.. 37 / 0.00
Sales & Gross Receipts ....25 / 46.85
Motor Vehicle & Driver License............................. 21 / 2.98
Individual Income Tax...12 / 42.45
Corporate Income Tax.. 32 / 4.45
Other Taxes .... 38 / 3.26

The following tax collections are Per Capita
Total Tax Collections - Ind. & Biz (rank / $) ....38 / 2,035
Total Tax Collections - Ind. only (rank / $) ....37 / 1,878

STATE FACTS & NUMBERS

Rank: 1 highest; 51 lowest

State Revenue - Per Capita (rank / $) ....44 / 5,949
State & Local Rev. - Per Capita (rank / $) ....47 / 8,821
Personal Income - Per Capita (rank / $) ....47 / 35,430
Median Household Income (rank / $) .... 14 / 57,049
Median House Value (rank / $)..........................18 / 209,000
Total Area - Square Miles (rank / count) .... 13 / 84,987
Land Area - Square Miles (rank / count) .... 12 / 82,170
Water Area - Square Miles (rank / count) ....17 / 2,727
Number of Counties 29
Name for Residents.. Utahans
Capital City..Salt Lake City
Nickname ....Beehive State
State Motto .... Industry
State Bird .... California Seagull
State Flower...Sego Lily
State Tree.. Blue Spruce
State Song....................................Utah, We Love Thee

POPULATION

Rank: 1 highest; 51 lowest

State Population (rank / count) ....34 / 2,855,287
Population Per Square Mile (rank / count) .... 42 / 34
Male Population (rank / %)................................05 / 50.23
Female Population (rank / %)................................47 / 49.77
Sex Ratio & Population Median Age............... 100.9 / 29.2
(Sex Ratio = the # of males per 100 females)
Population % by age (under 18 / 18-44) ....31.5 / 39.7
Population % by age (45-64 / 65+) ....19.8 / 9.0

RESOURCES

Utah State Government
Phone: 801-538-3000
Web Site: www.utah.gov

Utah State Tax Commission
Phone: 801-297-2200
Web Site: www.tax.utah.gov

Utah Driver License Division
Phone: 801-965-4437 or 888-353-4224
Web Site: www.publicsafety.utah.gov/dld

Utah Division of Motor Vehicles
Phone: 801-297-7780 or 800-368-8824
Web Site: www.dmv.utah.gov

Utah Office of Tourism
Phone: 800-200-1160
Web Site: www.visitutah.com

Voting Information
Phone: 801-538-1041
Web Site: http://elections.utah.gov/

Vermont

STATE AND LOCAL TAXES

State Sales Tax (%) 6
 Exempt: food and prescription drugs.

Local Sales Taxes (up to an additional %) 1
Inheritance Tax .... No
Estate Tax...Yes
 16% on estates valued over $2.75 million.

PERSONAL INCOME TAXES

State Income Tax (%) ....3.55 - 8.95
 5 income brackets - Lowest $35,350; Highest $388,350.
 ($59,050 to $388,350 for joint filers.)

Personal Exemption $ (single / joint) ....3,900 / 7,800
Standard Deduction $ (single / joint).........6,100 / 12,200
Federal Income Tax Paid - Deduction Allowed .... None
Social Security Income - Tax Exempt................................. No
Retired Military Pay - Tax Exempt .... No
State & Local Government Pensions - Tax Exempt........ No
Federal Civil Service Pensions - Tax Exempt .... No
Railroad Retirement - Tax Exempt ....Yes
Private Pension - Tax Exempt .... No

VEHICLES

Registration Fees .... 1 Year
 Cars, Trucks (up to 6,099 lbs), and Motor homes:
 Gas powered, $70.
 Diesel powered, $27.

Annual Vehicle Tax .... No
 No property tax on vehicles.

State Emissions Test Required ....Yes
 Annual with safety inspection. Vehicles over 8,500 lbs
 GVWR are exempt. Web Site: http://dmv.vermont.gov/
 safety/detailedinformation

Vehicle Safety Inspection Required ....Yes
 Annual.

Mandatory Minimum Liability Insurance 25/50/10
 Uninsured and Underinsured Motorists coverage is also
 required.

COST OF LIVING INDICATORS

 Rank: 1 highest; 51 lowest

Cost of Living - average statewide (rank) 10
Fuel - $ per gallon, Dec. 2013 (diesel / gas)......4.03 / 3.50

The following "Tax Collections" are all Per Capita

State Individual Income Tax (rank / $) .... 20 / 888
Local Individual Income Tax (rank / $) .... 14 / 0
State General Sales Tax (rank / $) .... 40 / 520
Local General Sales Tax (rank / $) .... 34 / 15
State Property Tax (rank / $) .... 01 / 1,526
Local Property Tax (rank / $) .... 46 / 671
State - All Tax Collections (rank / $) .... 03 / 4,294
Local - All Tax Collections (rank / $) .... 50 / 722
State & Local - All Tax Collections (rank / $) ...... 09 / 5,016

STATE TAX COLLECTIONS

Rank: 1 highest; 50 lowest

Rank and % of total taxes collected from:

Property Tax .... 01 / 34.41
Sales & Gross Receipts .... 41 / 35.12
Motor Vehicle & Driver License .... 31 / 2.62
Individual Income Tax .... 39 / 21.70
Corporate Income Tax .... 40 / 3.50
Other Taxes .... 45 / 2.65

The following tax collections are Per Capita

Total Tax Collections - Ind. & Biz (rank / $) .... 04 / 4,405
Total Tax Collections - Ind. only (rank / $) .... 01 / 4,155

STATE FACTS & NUMBERS

Rank: 1 highest; 51 lowest

State Revenue - Per Capita (rank / $) .... 06 / 10,393
State & Local Rev. - Per Capita (rank / $) .... 10 / 12,109
Personal Income - Per Capita (rank / $) .... 22 / 44,545
Median Household Income (rank / $) .... 21 / 52,977
Median House Value (rank / $) .... 17 / 215,700
Total Area - Square Miles (rank / count) .... 45 / 9,616
Land Area - Square Miles (rank / count) .... 43 / 9,217
Water Area - Square Miles (rank / count) .... 46 / 400
Number of Counties 14
Name for Residents .... Vermonters
Capital City .... Montpelier
Nickname .... Green Mountain State
State Motto .... Freedom and Unity
State Bird .... Hermit Thrush
State Flower .... Red Clover
State Tree .... Sugar Maple
State Song .... These Green Mountains

POPULATION

Rank: 1 highest; 51 lowest

State Population (rank / count) .... 50 / 626,011

Population Per Square Mile (rank / count) .... 31 / 65
Male Population (rank / %) .... 25 / 49.25
Female Population (rank / %) .... 27 / 50.75
Sex Ratio & Population Median Age .... 97.1 / 41.5
(Sex Ratio = the # of males per 100 females)

Population % by age (under 18 / 18-44) .... 20.7 / 34.0
Population % by age (45-64 / 65+) .... 30.8 / 14.5

RESOURCES

Vermont State Government
Phone: 802-652-4636 (out-of-state) or
    866-652-4636 (in-state)
Web Site: www.vermont.gov

Vermont Department of Taxes
Phone: 802-828-2505
Web Site: www.state.vt.us/tax

Vermont Department of Motor Vehicles
Phone: 802-828-2000 or 888-998-3766
Web Site: www.dmv.vermont.gov

Vermont Office of Tourism
Phone: 800-837-6668
Web Site: www.vermontvacation.com

Voting Information
Phone: 802-828-2464 or 800-439-8683 (In-State)
Web Site: www.vermont-elections.org/

Virginia

STATE AND LOCAL TAXES

State Sales Tax (%) 4.3
   Exempt: prescription drugs. Food is taxed at 2.5%.

Local Sales Taxes (up to an additional %) 2.2
Inheritance Tax .... No
Estate Tax... No

PERSONAL INCOME TAXES

State Income Tax (%) .... 2 - 5.75
   4 income brackets - Lowest $3,000; Highest $17,000.

Personal Exemption $ (single / joint) .... 930 / 1,860
Standard Deduction $ (single / joint)............ 3,000 / 6,000
Federal Income Tax Paid - Deduction Allowed .... None
Social Security Income - Tax Exempt .... Yes
Retired Military Pay - Tax Exempt .... Limits
   Follows federal tax rules.

State & Local Government Pensions - Tax Exempt .. Limits
Federal Civil Service Pensions - Tax Exempt .... Limits
Railroad Retirement - Tax Exempt .... Yes
Private Pension - Tax Exempt .... Limits

Note: Limits include a maximum combined exemption of $6,000 if age 64 by midnight, January 1, 2006 ($12,000 if age 65 by 1/1/2006) from all retirement income sources. Some income limitations.

VEHICLES

Registration Fees .... 1 Year
   Passenger cars and motor homes $40.75 - $45.75, depending on weight.

   Pickup truck $40.75 - $51.75, depending on weight.

   Travel trailer, $29.50.

Annual Vehicle Tax .... Yes
   Annual property tax on vehicles.

State Emissions Test Required .... Yes
   Every two years. Operated primarily in the counties of Arlington, Fairfax, Loudoun, Prince William, Stafford and the cities of Alexandria, Fairfax, Falls Church, Manassas, and Manassas Park. Web Site: www.deq.state.va.us/Programs/AirCheckVirginia.aspx

Vehicle Safety Inspection Required .... Yes
   Annual.

Mandatory Minimum Liability Insurance 25/50/20
   Uninsured and Underinsured Motorists coverage is also required.

COST OF LIVING INDICATORS

   Rank: 1 highest; 51 lowest

Cost of Living - average statewide (rank) 29
Fuel - $ per gallon, Dec. 2013 (diesel / gas)...... 3.76 / 3.19
The following "Tax Collections" are all Per Capita
State Individual Income Tax (rank / $)................ 09 / 1,164
Local Individual Income Tax (rank / $)..................... 14 / 0
State General Sales Tax (rank / $) .... 44 / 423
Local General Sales Tax (rank / $) .... 27 / 124
State Property Tax (rank / $) .... 24 / 5
Local Property Tax (rank / $) .... 18 / 1,352
State - All Tax Collections (rank / $) .... 34 / 2,127
Local - All Tax Collections (rank / $)................... 17 / 1,801
State & Local - All Tax Collections (rank / $) ...... 26 / 3,928

STATE TAX COLLECTIONS

   Rank: 1 highest; 50 lowest
   Rank and % of total taxes collected from:

Property Tax... 24 / 0.19
Sales & Gross Receipts .... 43 / 32.27
Motor Vehicle & Driver License........................... 27 / 2.71
Individual Income Tax...................................... 02 / 56.32
Corporate Income Tax.. 30 / 4.62
Other Taxes .... 32 / 3.88
The following tax collections are Per Capita
Total Tax Collections - Ind. & Biz (rank / $) .... 36 / 2,216
Total Tax Collections - Ind. only (rank / $) .... 31 / 2,027

STATE FACTS & NUMBERS

   Rank: 1 highest; 51 lowest

State Revenue - Per Capita (rank / $) .... 42 / 6,204
State & Local Rev. - Per Capita (rank / $)............. 41 / 9,328
Personal Income - Per Capita (rank / $) .... 11 / 48,377
Median Household Income (rank / $) .... 09 / 61,741
Median House Value (rank / $)........................ 11 / 243,100
Total Area - Square Miles (rank / count) .... 35 / 42,775
Land Area - Square Miles (rank / count) .... 36 / 39,490
Water Area - Square Miles (rank / count) .... 15 / 3,285
Number of Counties 95
Name for Residents... Virginians
Capital City.. Richmond
Nickname .... Old Dominion

State Motto...Thus Always To Tyrants
State Bird ....Cardinal
State Flower...American Dogwood
State Tree..American Dogwood
State Song..............................Carry Me Back To Old Virginia

POPULATION

Rank: 1 highest; 51 lowest

State Population (rank / count) .... 12 / 8,185,867
Population Per Square Mile (rank / count) .... 14 / 191
Male Population (rank / %)...............................29 / 49.07
Female Population (rank / %).................................23 / 50.93
Sex Ratio & Population Median Age...................96.3 / 37.5
(Sex Ratio = the # of males per 100 females)

Population % by age (under 18 / 18-44) ....23.2 / 37.5
Population % by age (45-64 / 65+) ....27.1 / 12.2

RESOURCES

Virginia State Government
Phone: 804-786-0000 or 800-422-2319
Web Site: www.virginia.gov

Virginia Department of Taxation
Phone: 804-367-8031
Web Site: www.tax.virginia.gov

Virginia Department of Motor Vehicles
Phone: 804-497-7100
Web Site: www.dmv.virginia.gov

Virginia Office of Tourism
Phone: 800-847-4882
Web Site: www.virginia.org

Voting Information
Phone: 804-864-8901 or 800-552-9745
Web Site: www.sbe.virginia.gov/

Washington

STATE AND LOCAL TAXES

State Sales Tax (%)..6.5
Exempt: food and prescription drugs.

Local Sales Taxes (up to an additional %) 3.1
Inheritance Tax .... No
Estate Tax...Yes
20% on estates valued over $2 million. Exemption amount is adjusted for inflation on an annual basis.

PERSONAL INCOME TAXES

State Income Tax (%) .... None
Personal Exemption $ (single / joint) .... n/a
Standard Deduction $ (single / joint)............................... n/a
Federal Income Tax Paid - Deduction Allowed .... n/a
Social Security Income - Tax Exempt................................ n/a
Retired Military Pay - Tax Exempt .... n/a
State & Local Government Pensions - Tax Exempt .... n/a
Federal Civil Service Pensions - Tax Exempt .... n/a
Railroad Retirement - Tax Exempt .... n/a
Private Pension - Tax Exempt .... n/a

VEHICLES

Registration Fees .... 1 Year
Vehicle fees are based on several factors including the vehicle weight and where you live.

Vehicles from 0 to 8,000 lbs, $43.75 - $63.75.

Motor home, $111.75.

Travel trailer, $36.75.

Trucks:
0 - 8,000 lbs, $41 - $61.
8,001 - 12,000 lbs, $63 - $80.

If you live in the areas of King, Pierce, or Snohomish counties you may be required to pay the Regional Transit Authority (RTA) tax. The RTA is an annual excise tax of 0.3% based on the value of your vehicle.

City or county governments can also impose an annual "Local Transportation Benefit District Fee", due with the registration. There are currently 35 areas charging this fee which adds an additional $10 - $20 per vehicle.

Annual Vehicle Tax .... No
No property tax on vehicles.

State Emissions Test Required ....Yes
Every two years in most of Clark, King, Pierce, Snohomish,
and Spokane counties. Diesel passenger vehicles under
6,001 lbs and any diesel model year 2007 and newer are
exempt. Web Site: www.emissiontestwa.com

Vehicle Safety Inspection Required .... No
Mandatory Minimum Liability Insurance 25/50/10

COST OF LIVING INDICATORS
Rank: 1 highest; 51 lowest

Cost of Living - average statewide (rank) 16
Fuel - $ per gallon, Dec. 2013 (diesel / gas)......3.95 / 3.32
The following "Tax Collections" are all Per Capita
State Individual Income Tax (rank / $)..................44 / 0
Local Individual Income Tax (rank / $).....................14 / 0
State General Sales Tax (rank / $) ....02 / 1,534
Local General Sales Tax (rank / $) ....12 / 338
State Property Tax (rank / $) ....05 / 269
Local Property Tax (rank / $) ....32 / 988
State - All Tax Collections (rank / $) ....20 / 2,524
Local - All Tax Collections (rank / $).....................25 / 1,595
State & Local - All Tax Collections (rank / $) ......22 / 4,119

STATE TAX COLLECTIONS
Rank: 1 highest; 50 lowest
Rank and % of total taxes collected from:

Property Tax.......................................05 / 10.76
Sales & Gross Receipts ....02 / 80.41
Motor Vehicle & Driver License................................19 / 3.07
Individual Income Tax...44 / 0.00
Corporate Income Tax..47 / 0.00
Other Taxes ....22 / 5.76
The following tax collections are Per Capita
Total Tax Collections - Ind. & Biz (rank / $) ....22 / 2,555
Total Tax Collections - Ind. only (rank / $) ....17 / 2,423

STATE FACTS & NUMBERS
Rank: 1 highest; 51 lowest

State Revenue - Per Capita (rank / $) ....26 / 7,310
State & Local Rev. - Per Capita (rank / $)........... 19 / 11,286
Personal Income - Per Capita (rank / $) .... 14 / 46,045
Median Household Income (rank / $) .... 13 / 57,573
Median House Value (rank / $)..........................09 / 256,500
Total Area - Square Miles (rank / count) .... 18 / 71,298
Land Area - Square Miles (rank / count)........... 20 / 66,456
Water Area - Square Miles (rank / count)........... 11 / 4,842
Number of Counties 39

Name for Residents..Washingtonians
Capital City..Olympia
Nickname .... The Evergreen State
State Motto...By and By
State Bird ....Willow Goldfinch
State Flower.. Coast Rhododendron
State Tree ....Western Hemlock
State Song.. Washington, My Home

POPULATION
Rank: 1 highest; 51 lowest

State Population (rank / count) .... 13 / 6,897,012
Population Per Square Mile (rank / count) .... 25 / 97
Male Population (rank / %).................................11 / 49.81
Female Population (rank / %)................................41 / 50.19
Sex Ratio & Population Median Age...................99.3 / 37.3
    (Sex Ratio = the # of males per 100 females)
Population % by age (under 18 / 18-44) ....23.5 / 37.1
Population % by age (45-64 / 65+) ....27.1 / 12.3

RESOURCES

Washington State Government
Phone: 360-753-5000 or 800-321-2808
Web Site: www.access.wa.gov

Washington State Department of Revenue
Phone: 800-647-7706
Web Site: www.dor.wa.gov

Washington State Department of Licensing
Phone: 360-902-3900 (Driver License) or 360-902-3770
(Tags & Registration)
Web Site: www.dol.wa.gov

Washington Office of Tourism
Phone: 800-544-1800
Web Site: www.experiencewa.com

Voting Information
Phone: 360-902-4180 or 800-448-4881
Web Site: www.sos.wa.gov/elections

West Virginia

STATE AND LOCAL TAXES

State Sales Tax (%) 6
Exempt: food and prescription drugs.

Local Sales Taxes (up to an additional %) 1
Inheritance Tax ....No
Estate Tax ....No

PERSONAL INCOME TAXES

State Income Tax (%) .... 3 - 6.5
5 income brackets - Lowest $10,000; Highest $60,000.

Personal Exemption $ (single / joint) ....2,000 / 4,000
Standard Deduction $ (single / joint) ....None
Federal Income Tax Paid - Deduction Allowed .... None
Social Security Income - Tax Exempt ....Limits
Taxable to extent federally taxable.

Retired Military Pay - Tax Exempt ....Limits
First $2,000 is exempt. Balance based on formula with years of military service, maximum $20,000.

State & Local Government Pensions - Tax Exempt .. Limits
Up to $2,000 exempt.

Federal Civil Service Pensions - Tax Exempt ....Limits
Up to $2,000 is exempt. Full exemption for some law enforcement occupations.

Railroad Retirement - Tax Exempt ....Yes
Private Pension - Tax Exempt ....Limits

Note: Taxpayers 65 and older may exclude the first $8,000 of any retirement income. Pension exemptions count toward the $8,000.

VEHICLES

Registration Fees .... 1 Year
Basic registration fee for passenger vehicles and pickup trucks weighing 8,000 lbs or less, $30.

Annual Vehicle Tax ....Yes
Annual property tax on vehicles.

State Emissions Test Required .... No
Vehicle Safety Inspection Required ....Yes
Annual.

Mandatory Minimum Liability Insurance 20/40/10
Uninsured Motorist coverage is also required.

COST OF LIVING INDICATORS

Rank: 1 highest; 51 lowest

Cost of Living - average statewide (rank) 27
Fuel - $ per gallon, Dec. 2013 (diesel / gas)......3.96 / 3.36
The following "Tax Collections" are all Per Capita
State Individual Income Tax (rank / $)....................18 / 898
Local Individual Income Tax (rank / $).....................14 / 0
State General Sales Tax (rank / $) ....32 / 652
Local General Sales Tax (rank / $) ....35 / 0
State Property Tax (rank / $) ....29 / 3
Local Property Tax (rank / $) ....43 / 767
State - All Tax Collections (rank / $) ....13 / 2,808
Local - All Tax Collections (rank / $).................46 / 951
State & Local - All Tax Collections (rank / $) ......28 / 3,759

STATE TAX COLLECTIONS

Rank: 1 highest; 50 lowest
Rank and % of total taxes collected from:

Property Tax..28 / 0.11
Sales & Gross Receipts ....21 / 49.10
Motor Vehicle & Driver License................................42 / 2.01
Individual Income Tax.................................29 / 32.78
Corporate Income Tax................................38 / 3.59
Other Taxes ....12 / 12.40
The following tax collections are Per Capita
Total Tax Collections - Ind. & Biz (rank / $) ....14 / 2,887
Total Tax Collections - Ind. only (rank / $) ....16 / 2,425

STATE FACTS & NUMBERS

Rank: 1 highest; 51 lowest

State Revenue - Per Capita (rank / $) ....16 / 8,299
State & Local Rev. - Per Capita (rank / $)..........31 / 10,099
Personal Income - Per Capita (rank / $) ....48 / 35,082
Median Household Income (rank / $) ....49 / 40,196
Median House Value (rank / $)...........................51 / 98,300
Total Area - Square Miles (rank / count) ....41 / 24,230
Land Area - Square Miles (rank / count)..........41 / 24,038
Water Area - Square Miles (rank / count) ....50 / 192
Number of Counties 55
Name for Residents....................................West Virginians
Capital City.. Charleston
Nickname .... Mountain State
State Motto.........................Mountaineers Are Always Free
State Bird ....Cardinal
State Flower..Big Rhododendron
State Tree ....Sugar Maple
State Song................ West Virginia, My Home Sweet Home

POPULATION

Rank: 1 highest; 51 lowest

State Population (rank / count) .... 38 / 1,855,413
Population Per Square Mile (rank / count) .... 30 / 77
Male Population (rank / %)....................................24 / 49.30
Female Population (rank / %)................................28 / 50.70
Sex Ratio & Population Median Age.................97.3 / 41.3
(Sex Ratio = the # of males per 100 females)
Population % by age (under 18 / 18-44) ....20.9 / 33.8
Population % by age (45-64 / 65+) ....29.2 / 16.1

RESOURCES

West Virginia State Government
Phone: 304-558-3456
Web Site: www.wv.gov

West Virginia Department Revenue
Phone: 304-558-3333 (State Tax Dept.)
Web Site: www.wvrevenue.gov

West Virginia Division of Motor Vehicles
Phone: 304-926-3871 or 800-642-9066
Web Site: www.transportation.wv.gov

West Virginia Office of Tourism
Phone: 800-225-5982
Web Site: www.wvtourism.com

Voting Information
Phone: 304-558-6000
Web Site: www.sos.wv.gov/elections/

Wisconsin

STATE AND LOCAL TAXES

State Sales Tax (%) 5
Exempt: food and prescription drugs.

Local Sales Taxes (up to an additional %) 1.5
Inheritance Tax .... No
Estate Tax.. No

PERSONAL INCOME TAXES

State Income Tax (%) ....4.6 - 7.75
5 income brackets - Lowest $10,750; Highest $236,600.
($14,330 to $315,460 for joint filers.)

Personal Exemption $ (single / joint) .... 700 / 1,400
Deduction is $1,250 if 65 or older.

Standard Deduction $ (single / joint).........9,930 / 17,880
Amounts are the maximum, reduced as income rises.
Reaches zero for single filers at $97,069 and for joint
filers at $110,493.

Federal Income Tax Paid - Deduction Allowed .... None
Social Security Income - Tax Exempt...................................Yes
Retired Military Pay - Tax Exempt ....Yes
State & Local Government Pensions - Tax Exempt ..Limits
Federal Civil Service Pensions - Tax Exempt .... Limits
Railroad Retirement - Tax Exempt ....Yes
Private Pension - Tax Exempt ....Limits

Note: Limits include a maximum combined exemption
of $5,000, with age and income limitations, for benefits
from qualified plans.

VEHICLES

Registration Fees .... 1 Year
Automobile, $75.

Truck:
4,500 - 8,000 lbs, $75 - $106.
8,001 - 12,000 lbs, $155 - 209.

RV Trailers and Camping trailer, $15.

Motor home fee varies by weight:
up to 12,000 lbs, $48.50 - $67.50
12,000 - 26,000 lbs, $80.50 - $106.50.
Over 26,000 lbs, $119.50.

Plus a $10 - $20 Wheel tax for the cities of Beloit,
Janesville, Mayville, Milwaukee, and St. Croix County.

Annual Vehicle Tax .... No
   No property tax on vehicles.

State Emissions Test Required ....Yes
   Every two years in these southern counties: Kenosha, Milwaukee, Ozaukee, Racine, Sheboygan, Washington, and Waukesha. Diesel powered vehicles with a model year 2006 and older are exempt.
   Web Site: www.wisconsinvip.org

Vehicle Safety Inspection Required .... No

Mandatory Minimum Liability Insurance 25/50/10
   Uninsured and Underinsured Motorists coverage is also required.

COST OF LIVING INDICATORS
   Rank: 1 highest; 51 lowest

Cost of Living - average statewide (rank) 25
Fuel - $ per gallon, Dec. 2013 (diesel / gas)......3.87 / 3.14
The following "Tax Collections" are all Per Capita
State Individual Income Tax (rank / $)................11 / 1,123
Local Individual Income Tax (rank / $)......................... 14 / 0
State General Sales Tax (rank / $) .... 27 / 718
Local General Sales Tax (rank / $)................................ 31 / 57
State Property Tax (rank / $) .... 18 / 26
Local Property Tax (rank / $) ....11 / 1,690
State - All Tax Collections (rank / $).....................17 / 2,680
Local - All Tax Collections (rank / $)....................18 / 1,791
State & Local - All Tax Collections (rank / $) ....17 / 4,471

STATE TAX COLLECTIONS
   Rank: 1 highest; 50 lowest
   Rank and % of total taxes collected from:

Property Tax...17 / 1.05
Sales & Gross Receipts ....33 / 43.36
Motor Vehicle & Driver License.......................... 16 / 3.36
Individual Income Tax..13 / 42.45
Corporate Income Tax... 13 / 6.03
Other Taxes .... 36 / 3.74
The following tax collections are Per Capita
Total Tax Collections - Ind. & Biz (rank / $) ....20 / 2,575
Total Tax Collections - Ind. only (rank / $) ....20 / 2,324

STATE FACTS & NUMBERS
   Rank: 1 highest; 51 lowest

State Revenue - Per Capita (rank / $) ....23 / 7,825
State & Local Rev. - Per Capita (rank / $)..........21 / 10,948
Personal Income - Per Capita (rank / $) ....27 / 42,121
Median Household Income (rank / $) ....23 / 51,059

Median House Value (rank / $)..........................24 / 167,200
Total Area - Square Miles (rank / count) .... 23 / 65,496
Land Area - Square Miles (rank / count) .... 25 / 54,158
Water Area - Square Miles (rank / count) ....04 / 11,339
Number of Counties 72
Name for Residents...Wisconsinites
Capital City...Madison
Nickname .... Badger State
State Motto.. Forward
State Bird .... Robin
State Flower..Wood Violet
State Tree..Sugar Maple
State Song..On, Wisconsin!

POPULATION
   Rank: 1 highest; 51 lowest

State Population (rank / count) ....20 / 5,726,398
Population Per Square Mile (rank / count) .... 28 / 87
Male Population (rank / %)......................................14 / 49.63
Female Population (rank / %)................................38 / 50.37
Sex Ratio & Population Median Age...................98.5 / 38.5
   (Sex Ratio = the # of males per 100 females)
Population % by age (under 18 / 18-44) ....23.6 / 35.1
Population % by age (45-64 / 65+) ....27.7 / 13.6

RESOURCES

Wisconsin State Government
Phone: 608-266-2211
Web Site: www.wisconsin.gov

Wisconsin Department of Revenue
Phone: 608-266-2486
Web Site: www.revenue.wi.gov

Wisconsin Division of Motor Vehicles
Phone: 414-266-1000
Web Site: www.dot.wisconsin.gov/drivers

Wisconsin Office of Tourism
Phone: 608-266-2161 or 800-432-8747
Web Site: www.travelwisconsin.com

Voting Information
Phone: 608-261-2028 or 866-868-3947
Web Site: http://gab.wi.gov/elections-voting

Wyoming

STATE AND LOCAL TAXES

State Sales Tax (%) 4
  Exempt: food and prescription drugs.

Local Sales Taxes (up to an additional %) 4
Inheritance Tax .... No
Estate Tax.. No

PERSONAL INCOME TAXES

State Income Tax (%) .... None
Personal Exemption $ (single / joint) .... n/a
Standard Deduction $ (single / joint) .... n/a
Federal Income Tax Paid - Deduction Allowed .... n/a
Social Security Income - Tax Exempt .... n/a
Retired Military Pay - Tax Exempt .... n/a
State & Local Government Pensions - Tax Exempt .... n/a
Federal Civil Service Pensions - Tax Exempt .... n/a
Railroad Retirement - Tax Exempt .... n/a
Private Pension - Tax Exempt .... n/a

VEHICLES

Registration Fees .... 1 Year
  Rates available from the local county treasurer's office.
  Fees vary by vehicle type, cost, age, and weight. The
  Wyoming County Treasurer's Association provides a fee
  calculator at: www.wcta.us

Annual Vehicle Tax .... No
  All fees are included in the registration process.

State Emissions Test Required .... No
Vehicle Safety Inspection Required .... No
Mandatory Minimum Liability Insurance 25/50/20

COST OF LIVING INDICATORS

  Rank: 1 highest; 51 lowest

Cost of Living - average statewide (rank) 30
Fuel - $ per gallon, Dec. 2013 (diesel / gas) ......3.89 / 3.20
The following "Tax Collections" are all Per Capita
State Individual Income Tax (rank / $) ....44 / 0
Local Individual Income Tax (rank / $) ....14 / 0
State General Sales Tax (rank / $) ....03 / 1,497
Local General Sales Tax (rank / $) ....14 / 321
State Property Tax (rank / $) ....02 / 493
Local Property Tax (rank / $) ....12 / 1,642
State - All Tax Collections (rank / $) ....04 / 4,271

Local - All Tax Collections (rank / $) ....11 / 2,102
State & Local - All Tax Collections (rank / $) ......05 / 6,373

STATE TAX COLLECTIONS

  Rank: 1 highest; 50 lowest
  Rank and % of total taxes collected from:

Property Tax...03 / 12.42
Sales & Gross Receipts ....30 / 43.91
Motor Vehicle & Driver License ....29 / 2.66
Individual Income Tax................................44 / 0.00
Corporate Income Tax................................47 / 0.00
Other Taxes..03 / 41.01
The following tax collections are Per Capita
Total Tax Collections - Ind. & Biz (rank / $) ....03 / 4,426
Total Tax Collections - Ind. only (rank / $) ....11 / 2,611

STATE FACTS & NUMBERS

  Rank: 1 highest; 51 lowest

State Revenue - Per Capita (rank / $) ....03 / 13,003
State & Local Rev. - Per Capita (rank / $) ....03 / 17,710
Personal Income - Per Capita (rank / $) ....08 / 50,567
Median Household Income (rank / $) ....18 / 54,901
Median House Value (rank / $)....................21 / 183,200
Total Area - Square Miles (rank / count) ....10 / 97,813
Land Area - Square Miles (rank / count) ....09 / 97,093
Water Area - Square Miles (rank / count) ....37 / 720
Number of Counties 23
Name for Residents....................................Wyomingites
Capital City...Cheyenne
Nickname ....Equality State / Cowboy State
State Motto... Equal Rights
State Bird ....Western Meadowlark
State Flower.......................................Indian Paintbrush
State Tree .... Plains Cottonwood
State Song..Wyoming

POPULATION

  Rank: 1 highest; 51 lowest

State Population (rank / count) ....51 / 576,412
Population Per Square Mile (rank / count) .... 50 / 06
Male Population (rank / %).....................................02 / 51.00
Female Population (rank / %)................................50 / 49.00
Sex Ratio & Population Median Age.............. 104.1 / 36.8
  (Sex Ratio = the # of males per 100 females)

Population % by age (under 18 / 18-44) ....24.0 / 35.7
Population % by age (45-64 / 65+) ....27.9 / 12.4

RESOURCES

Wyoming State Government
Phone: 307-777-7220
Web Site: www.wyoming.gov

Wyoming Department of Revenue
Phone: 307-777-5275
Web Site: http://revenue.state.wy.us

Wyoming Motor Vehicle Services
Phone: 307-777-4810 (Driver License) or 307-777-4851
(Tags & Registration)
Web Site: www.dot.state.wy.us

Wyoming Office of Tourism
Phone: 307-777-7777 or 800-225-5996
Web Site: www.wyomingtourism.org

Voting Information
Phone: 307-777-5860
Web Site: http://soswy.state.wy.us/Elections/
    Elections.aspx

CHARTS

INFORMATION TOPICS

STATE AND LOCAL TAXES

Column	Chart 1
A	State Sales Tax (%)
B	Local Sales Taxes (up to an additional %)
C	Food exempt from sales tax (Yes/No)
D	Prescription drugs exempt from sales tax (Yes/No)
E	Inheritance Tax (Yes/No)
F	Estate Tax (Yes/No)

PERSONAL INCOME TAXES

Column	Chart 1
A	State Income Tax - Lowest (%)
B	State Income Tax - Highest (%)
C	State Income Brackets (Qty)
D	Bracket Amount - Lowest ($)
E	Bracket Amount - Highest ($)

Column	Chart 2
F	Personal Exemption - Single ($)
G	Personal Exemption - Joint ($)
H	Standard Deduction - Single ($)
I	Standard Deduction -Joint ($)

Column	Chart 3
J	Federal Income Tax Paid - Deduction Allowed (Amount)
K	Social Security Income - Tax Exempt (Yes/No)
L	Retired Military Pay - Tax Exempt (Yes/No)
M	State & Local Government Pensions - Tax Exempt (Yes/No)

Column	Chart 4
N	Federal Civil Service Pensions - Tax Exempt (Yes/No)
O	Railroad Retirement - Tax Exempt (Yes/No)
P	Private Pension - Tax Exempt (Yes/No)

VEHICLES

Column	Chart 1
A	Annual Vehicle Tax
B	State Emissions Test Required
C	Vehicle Safety Inspection Required
D	Mandatory Minimum Liability Insurance

COST OF LIVING INDICATORS

Column	Chart 1
A	Cost of Living - average statewide (Rank)
B	Fuel - average $ per gallon, Dec. 2013 (Diesel)
C	Fuel - average $ per gallon, Dec. 2013 (Gas)

Column	Chart 2
D	State Individual Income Tax Collections (Rank)
E	State Individual Income Tax Collections ($ Per Capita)
F	Local Individual Income Tax Collections (Rank)
G	Local Individual Income Tax Collections ($ Per Capita)

Column	Chart 3
H	State General Sales Tax Collections (Rank)
I	State General Sales Tax Collections ($ Per Capita)
J	Local General Sales Tax Collections (Rank)
K	Local General Sales Tax Collections ($ Per Capita)

Column	Chart 4
L	State Property Tax Collections (Rank)
M	State Property Tax Collections ($ Per Capita)
N	Local Property Tax Collections (Rank)
O	Local Property Tax Collections ($ Per Capita)

Column	Chart 5
P	State - All Tax Collections (Rank)
Q	State - All Tax Collections ($ Per Capita)
R	Local - All Tax Collections (Rank)
S	Local - All Tax Collections ($ Per Capita)
T	State & Local - All Tax Collections (Rank)
U	State & Local - All Tax Collections ($ Per Capita)

STATE TAX COLLECTIONS

Column	Chart 1
	Total Revenue From (Rank):
A	Property Tax
B	Sales & Gross Receipts
C	Motor Vehicle & Driver License
D	Individual Income Tax
E	Corporate Income Tax
F	Other Taxes

Column	Chart 2
	Total Revenue From (%):
G	Property Tax
H	Sales & Gross Receipts
I	Motor Vehicle & Driver License
J	Individual Income Tax
K	Corporate Income Tax
L	Other Taxes

Column	Chart 3
M	Total Tax Collections - Individual & Biz (Rank)
N	Total Tax Collections - Individual & Biz ($ Per Capita)
O	Total Tax Collections - Individual only (Rank)
P	Total Tax Collections - Individual only ($ Per Capita)

STATE FACTS & NUMBERS

Column	Chart 1
A	State Revenue - Per Capita (Rank)
B	State Revenue - Per Capita ($)
C	State & Local Revenue - Per Capita (Rank)
D	State & Local Revenue - Per Capita ($)

Column	Chart 2
E	Personal Income - Per Capita (Rank)
F	Personal Income - Per Capita ($)
G	Median Household Income (Rank)
H	Median Household Income ($)
I	Median House Value (Rank)
J	Median House Value ($)

Column	Chart 3
K	Total Area - Square Miles (Rank)
L	Total Area - Square Miles (Count)
M	Land Area - Square Miles (Rank)
N	Land Area - Square Miles (Count)
O	Water Area - Square Miles (Rank)
P	Water Area - Square Miles (Count)

Column	Chart 4
Q	Number of Counties
R	Name for Residents
S	Capital City

Column	Chart 5
T	Nickname
U	State Motto

Column	Chart 6
V	State Bird
W	State Flower
X	State Tree

Column	Chart 7
Y	State Song

POPULATION

Column	Chart 1
A	Population (Count)
B	Population (Rank)
C	Population Per Square Mile (Count)
D	Population Per Square Mile (Rank)

Column	Chart 2
E	Male Population (Rank)
F	Male Population (%)
G	Female Population (Rank)
H	Female Population (%)

Column	Chart 3
I	Sex Ratio - # of Males Per 100 Females
J	Population - Median Age
K	Population % By Age - Under 18
L	Population % By Age - 18-44
M	Population % By Age - 45-64
N	Population % By Age - 65+

A - State Sales Tax (%) / B - Local Sales Tax (%) C - Food Exempt / D - Rx Drugs Exempt E - Inheritance Tax / F - Estate Tax						**State & Local Taxes**
Taxes & Exemptions	**A**	**B**	**C**	**D**	**E**	**F**
Alabama	4	8.5	No	Yes	No	No
Alaska	None	7.5	No	No	No	No
Arizona	5.6	7.1	Yes	Yes	No	No
Arkansas	6.5	5.5	No	Yes	No	No
California	7.5	2.5	Yes	Yes	No	No
Colorado	2.9	7	Yes	Yes	No	No
Connecticut	6.35	None	Yes	Yes	No	Yes
Delaware	None	None	No	No	No	Yes
District of Columbia	5.75	None	Yes	Yes	No	Yes
Florida	6	1.5	Yes	Yes	No	No
Georgia	4	4	No	Yes	No	No
Hawaii	4	0.5	No	Yes	No	Yes
Idaho	6	3	No	Yes	No	No
Illinois	6.25	4.25	No	No	No	Yes
Indiana	7.00	None	Yes	Yes	No	No
Iowa	6	2	Yes	Yes	Yes	No
Kansas	5.7	5	No	Yes	No	No
Kentucky	6	None	Yes	Yes	Yes	No
Louisiana	4	6.75	No	Yes	No	No
Maine	5.5	None	Yes	Yes	No	Yes
Maryland	6	None	Yes	Yes	Yes	Yes
Massachusetts	6.25	None	Yes	Yes	No	Yes
Michigan	6	None	Yes	Yes	No	No
Minnesota	6.875	1	Yes	Yes	No	Yes
Mississippi	7	0.25	No	Yes	No	No
Missouri	4.225	6.625	No	Yes	No	No
Montana	None	None	No	No	No	No
Nebraska	5.5	2	Yes	Yes	Yes	No
Nevada	6.5	1.25	Yes	Yes	No	No
New Hampshire	None	None	No	No	No	No
New Jersey	7	Notes	Yes	Yes	Yes	Yes
New Mexico	5.125	6.625	Yes	Yes	No	No
New York	4	5	Yes	Yes	No	Yes
North Carolina	4.75	3	No	Yes	No	No
North Dakota	5	3	Yes	Yes	No	No
Ohio	5.75	2.25	Yes	Yes	No	No
Oklahoma	4.5	6.35	No	Yes	No	No
Oregon	None	None	No	No	No	Yes
Pennsylvania	6	2	Yes	Yes	Yes	No
Rhode Island	7	None	Yes	Yes	No	Yes
South Carolina	6	3	Yes	Yes	No	No
South Dakota	4	2	No	Yes	No	No
Tennessee	7	2.75	No	Yes	No	Yes
Texas	6.25	2	Yes	Yes	No	No
Utah	4.7	6.25	No	Yes	No	No
Vermont	6	1	Yes	Yes	No	Yes
Virginia	4.3	2.2	No	Yes	No	No
Washington	6.5	3.1	Yes	Yes	No	Yes
West Virginia	6	1	Yes	Yes	No	No
Wisconsin	5	1.5	Yes	Yes	No	No
Wyoming	4	4	Yes	Yes	No	No

State Income Tax (%): A - Lowest, B - Highest C - Number of Income Brackets Bracket Amount ($): D - Lowest, E - Highest					**Personal Income Taxes**
Taxes & Brackets	**A**	**B**	**C**	**D**	**E**
Alabama	2	5	3	500	3,000
Alaska	None	None	n/a	n/a	n/a
Arizona	2.59	4.54	5	10,000	150,000
Arkansas	1	7	6	4,099	34,000
California	1	12.3	9	7,455	500,000
Colorado	4.63	4.63	None	n/a	n/a
Connecticut	3	6.7	6	10,000	250,000
Delaware	2.2	6.75	6	5,000	60,000
District of Columbia	4	8.95	4	10,000	350,000
Florida	None	None	n/a	n/a	n/a
Georgia	1	6	6	750	7,000
Hawaii	1.4	11	12	2,400	200,000
Idaho	1.6	7.4	7	1,380	10,350
Illinois	5	5	None	n/a	n/a
Indiana	3.4	3.4	None	n/a	n/a
Iowa	0.36	8.98	9	1,494	67,230
Kansas	3	4.9	2	15,000	30,000
Kentucky	2	6	6	3,000	75,000
Louisiana	2	6	3	12,500	50,000
Maine	0	8	3	5,200	20,900
Maryland	2	5.75	8	1,000	250,000
Massachusetts	5.25	5.25	None	n/a	n/a
Michigan	4.25	4.25	None	n/a	n/a
Minnesota	5.35	7.85	3	24,270	79,730
Mississippi	3	5	3	5,000	10,000
Missouri	1.5	6	10	1,000	9,000
Montana	1	6.9	7	2,700	16,400
Nebraska	2.46	6.84	4	2,400	27,000
Nevada	None	None	n/a	n/a	n/a
New Hampshire	None	None	n/a	n/a	n/a
New Jersey	1.4	8.97	6	20,000	500,000
New Mexico	1.7	4.9	4	5,500	16,000
New York	4	8.82	8	8,200	1,029,250
North Carolina	6	7.75	3	12,750	60,000
North Dakota	1.51	3.99	5	36,250	398,350
Ohio	0.587	5.925	9	5,200	208,500
Oklahoma	0.5	5.25	7	1,000	8,700
Oregon	5	9.9	4	3,250	125,000
Pennsylvania	3.07	3.07	None	n/a	n/a
Rhode Island	3.75	5.99	3	58,600	133,250
South Carolina	0	7	6	2,850	14,250
South Dakota	None	None	n/a	n/a	n/a
Tennessee	None	None	n/a	n/a	n/a
Texas	None	None	n/a	n/a	n/a
Utah	5	5	None	n/a	n/a
Vermont	3.55	8.95	5	35,350	388,350
Virginia	2	5.75	4	3,000	17,000
Washington	None	None	n/a	n/a	n/a
West Virginia	3	6.5	5	10,000	60,000
Wisconsin	4.6	7.75	5	10,750	236,600
Wyoming	None	None	n/a	n/a	n/a

Personal Exemption ($): **F** - Single, **G** - Joint Standard Deduction ($): **H** - Single, **I** - Joint				**Personal Income Taxes**
Deductions	**F**	**G**	**H**	**I**
Alabama	1,500	3,000	2,500	7,500
Alaska	n/a	n/a	n/a	n/a
Arizona	2,100	4,200	4,833	9,665
Arkansas	23	46	2,000	4,000
California	104	208	3,692	7,384
Colorado	3,900	7,800	None	None
Connecticut	13,000	24,000	None	None
Delaware	110	220	3,250	6,500
District of Columbia	1,675	3,350	2,000	4,000
Florida	n/a	n/a	n/a	n/a
Georgia	2,700	5,400	2,300	3,000
Hawaii	1,040	2,080	2,200	4,400
Idaho	3,900	7,800	5,950	11,900
Illinois	2,000	4,000	None	None
Indiana	1,000	2,000	None	None
Iowa	40	80	1,900	4,670
Kansas	2,250	4,500	3,000	6,000
Kentucky	20	40	2,290	4,580
Louisiana	4,500	9,000	n/a	n/a
Maine	3,900	7,800	6,100	10,150
Maryland	3,200	6,400	2,000	4,000
Massachusetts	4,400	8,800	None	None
Michigan	3,763	7,526	None	None
Minnesota	3,900	7,800	5,950	11,900
Mississippi	6,000	12,000	2,300	4,600
Missouri	2,100	4,200	6,100	12,200
Montana	2,240	4,480	1,860	3,720
Nebraska	126	252	6,100	12,200
Nevada	n/a	n/a	n/a	n/a
New Hampshire	n/a	n/a	n/a	n/a
New Jersey	1,000	2,000	None	None
New Mexico	3,900	7,800	6,100	12,200
New York	0	0	7,500	15,000
North Carolina	2,500	5,000	3,000	6,000
North Dakota	3,900	7,800	6,100	12,200
Ohio	1,650	3,300	None	None
Oklahoma	1,000	2,000	5,950	11,900
Oregon	188	376	2,025	4,055
Pennsylvania	None	None	None	None
Rhode Island	3,750	7,500	8,000	16,000
South Carolina	3,900	7,800	6,100	12,200
South Dakota	n/a	n/a	n/a	n/a
Tennessee	n/a	n/a	n/a	n/a
Texas	n/a	n/a	n/a	n/a
Utah	2,925	5,850	None	None
Vermont	3,900	7,800	6,100	12,200
Virginia	930	1,860	3,000	6,000
Washington	n/a	n/a	n/a	n/a
West Virginia	2,000	4,000	None	None
Wisconsin	700	1,400	9,930	17,880
Wyoming	n/a	n/a	n/a	n/a

J - Federal Income Tax Paid / **K** - Social Security Income / **L** - Retired Military Pay **M** - State & Local Government Pensions				**Personal Income Taxes**
Tax Exemptions	**J**	**K**	**L**	**M**
Alabama	Full	Yes	Yes	Yes
Alaska	n/a	n/a	n/a	n/a
Arizona	None	Yes	Limits	Limits
Arkansas	None	Yes	Limits	Limits
California	None	Yes	No	No
Colorado	None	Yes	Limits	Limits
Connecticut	None	Limits	Limits	No
Delaware	None	Yes	Limits	Limits
District of Columbia	None	Yes	Limits	Limits
Florida	n/a	n/a	n/a	n/a
Georgia	None	Yes	Limits	Limits
Hawaii	None	Yes	Yes	Yes
Idaho	None	Yes	Limits	Limits
Illinois	None	Yes	Yes	Yes
Indiana	None	Yes	Limits	No
Iowa	Full	Yes	Limits	Limits
Kansas	None	Limits	Yes	Limits
Kentucky	None	Yes	Limits	Limits
Louisiana	Full	Yes	Yes	Limits
Maine	None	Yes	Limits	Limits
Maryland	None	Yes	Limits	Limits
Massachusetts	None	Yes	Yes	Limits
Michigan	None	Yes	Yes	Limits
Minnesota	None	Limits	No	No
Mississippi	None	Yes	Yes	Yes
Missouri	Limits	Yes	Limits	Limits
Montana	Limits	Limits	Limits	Limits
Nebraska	None	Limits	No	No
Nevada	n/a	n/a	n/a	n/a
New Hampshire	n/a	n/a	n/a	n/a
New Jersey	None	Yes	Yes	Limits
New Mexico	None	Limits	Limits	Limits
New York	None	Yes	Yes	Limits
North Carolina	None	Yes	Limits	Limits
North Dakota	None	Limits	Limits	Limits
Ohio	None	Yes	Yes	No
Oklahoma	None	Yes	Limits	Limits
Oregon	Limits	Yes	Limits	Limits
Pennsylvania	None	Yes	Yes	Yes
Rhode Island	None	Limits	No	No
South Carolina	None	Yes	Limits	Limits
South Dakota	n/a	n/a	n/a	n/a
Tennessee	n/a	n/a	n/a	n/a
Texas	n/a	n/a	n/a	n/a
Utah	None	Limits	Limits	Limits
Vermont	None	No	No	No
Virginia	None	Yes	Limits	Limits
Washington	n/a	n/a	n/a	n/a
West Virginia	None	Limits	Limits	Limits
Wisconsin	None	Yes	Yes	Limits
Wyoming	n/a	n/a	n/a	n/a

N - Federal Civil Service Pensions O - Railroad Retirement P - Private Pensions	Personal Income Taxes		
Tax Exemptions	**N**	**O**	**P**
Alabama	Yes	Yes	Limits
Alaska	n/a	n/a	n/a
Arizona	Limits	Yes	No
Arkansas	Limits	Yes	Limits
California	No	Yes	No
Colorado	Limits	Yes	Limits
Connecticut	No	Yes	No
Delaware	Limits	Yes	Limits
District of Columbia	Limits	Yes	No
Florida	n/a	n/a	n/a
Georgia	Limits	Yes	Limits
Hawaii	Yes	Yes	Yes
Idaho	Limits	Yes	No
Illinois	Yes	Yes	Limits
Indiana	Limits	Yes	No
Iowa	Limits	Yes	Limits
Kansas	Yes	Yes	No
Kentucky	Limits	Yes	Limits
Louisiana	Yes	Yes	Limits
Maine	Limits	Yes	Limits
Maryland	Limits	Yes	Limits
Massachusetts	Yes	Yes	No
Michigan	Yes	Yes	Limits
Minnesota	No	Yes	No
Mississippi	Yes	Yes	Limits
Missouri	Limits	Yes	Limits
Montana	Limits	Yes	Limits
Nebraska	No	Yes	No
Nevada	n/a	n/a	n/a
New Hampshire	n/a	n/a	n/a
New Jersey	Limits	Yes	Limits
New Mexico	Limits	Limits	Limits
New York	Yes	Yes	Limits
North Carolina	Limits	Limits	Limits
North Dakota	Limits	Yes	No
Ohio	No	Yes	No
Oklahoma	Limits	Yes	Limits
Oregon	Limits	Yes	Limits
Pennsylvania	Yes	Yes	Yes
Rhode Island	No	Yes	No
South Carolina	Limits	Yes	Limits
South Dakota	n/a	n/a	n/a
Tennessee	n/a	n/a	n/a
Texas	n/a	n/a	n/a
Utah	Limits	Limits	Limits
Vermont	No	Yes	No
Virginia	Limits	Yes	Limits
Washington	n/a	n/a	n/a
West Virginia	Limits	Yes	Limits
Wisconsin	Limits	Yes	Limits
Wyoming	n/a	n/a	n/a

A - Annual Vehicle Tax / B - State Emissions Test Required / C - Vehicle Safety Inspection Required / D - Minimum Liability Insurance	Vehicles			
Tax Exemptions	**A**	**B**	**C**	**D**
Alabama	Yes	No	No	25/50/25
Alaska	Yes	No	No	50/100/25
Arizona	Yes	Yes	No	15/30/10
Arkansas	Yes	No	No	25/50/25
California	Yes	Yes	No	15/30/5
Colorado	Yes	Yes	No	25/50/15
Connecticut	Yes	Yes	Yes	20/40/10
Delaware	No	Yes	Yes	15/30/10
District of Columbia	No	Yes	Yes	25/50/10
Florida	No	No	No	10/20/10
Georgia	No	Yes	No	25/50/25
Hawaii	Yes	No	Yes	20/40/10
Idaho	Yes	Yes	No	25/50/15
Illinois	No	Yes	No	20/40/15
Indiana	Yes	Yes	No	25/50/10
Iowa	Yes	No	No	20/40/15
Kansas	Yes	No	No	25/50/10
Kentucky	Yes	No	No	25/50/10
Louisiana	No	Yes	Yes	15/30/25
Maine	Yes	Yes	Yes	50/100/25
Maryland	No	Yes	Yes	30/60/15
Massachusetts	Yes	Yes	Yes	20/40/5
Michigan	Yes	No	No	20/40/10
Minnesota	Yes	No	No	30/60/10
Mississippi	Yes	No	Yes	25/50/25
Missouri	Yes	Yes	Yes	25/50/10
Montana	Yes	No	No	25/50/10
Nebraska	Yes	No	No	25/50/25
Nevada	Yes	Yes	No	15/30/10
New Hampshire	Yes	Yes	Yes	25/50/25
New Jersey	No	Yes	No	15/30/5
New Mexico	No	Yes	No	25/50/10
New York	No	Yes	Yes	25/50/10
North Carolina	Yes	Yes	Yes	30/60/25
North Dakota	No	No	No	25/50/25
Ohio	No	Yes	No	25/50/25
Oklahoma	No	No	No	25/50/25
Oregon	No	Yes	No	25/50/20
Pennsylvania	No	Yes	Yes	15/30/5
Rhode Island	Yes	Yes	Yes	25/50/25
South Carolina	Yes	No	No	25/50/25
South Dakota	No	No	No	25/50/25
Tennessee	No	Yes	No	25/50/15
Texas	No	Yes	Yes	30/60/25
Utah	Yes	Yes	Yes	25/65/15
Vermont	No	Yes	Yes	25/50/10
Virginia	Yes	Yes	Yes	25/50/20
Washington	No	Yes	No	25/50/10
West Virginia	Yes	No	Yes	20/40/10
Wisconsin	No	Yes	No	25/50/10
Wyoming	No	No	No	25/50/20

A - Cost of Living - Average Statewide (Rank) **B** - Fuel - average $ per gallon (Diesel) **C** - Fuel - average $ per gallon (Gasoline)	**Cost of Living Indicators**		
Statewide Average & Fuel $	**A**	**B**	**C**
Alabama	36	3.76	3.15
Alaska	4	4.07	3.68
Arizona	18	3.77	3.15
Arkansas	43	3.73	3.05
California	7	4.07	3.58
Colorado	21	3.74	3.13
Connecticut	5	4.17	3.64
Delaware	15	3.81	3.36
District of Columbia	2	3.95	3.51
Florida	24	3.94	3.40
Georgia	37	3.81	3.24
Hawaii	1	4.85	3.95
Idaho	44	3.88	3.20
Illinois	31	3.89	3.29
Indiana	48	3.88	3.27
Iowa	40	3.74	3.11
Kansas	38	3.76	3.00
Kentucky	50	3.86	3.28
Louisiana	32	3.69	3.11
Maine	13	3.97	3.47
Maryland	12	3.83	3.38
Massachusetts	9	3.91	3.43
Michigan	34	3.93	3.25
Minnesota	19	3.88	3.03
Mississippi	51	3.67	3.11
Missouri	35	3.62	2.94
Montana	23	3.82	3.04
Nebraska	46	3.80	3.10
Nevada	28	3.84	3.30
New Hampshire	11	3.83	3.35
New Jersey	6	3.72	3.25
New Mexico	39	3.78	3.05
New York	3	4.16	3.63
North Carolina	26	3.82	3.28
North Dakota	17	4.04	3.16
Ohio	41	3.86	3.23
Oklahoma	47	3.61	2.97
Oregon	14	3.86	3.29
Pennsylvania	20	3.92	3.40
Rhode Island	8	3.94	3.47
South Carolina	33	3.67	3.12
South Dakota	22	3.85	3.15
Tennessee	49	3.75	3.13
Texas	42	3.68	3.09
Utah	45	3.81	3.10
Vermont	10	4.03	3.50
Virginia	29	3.76	3.19
Washington	16	3.95	3.32
West Virginia	27	3.96	3.36
Wisconsin	25	3.87	3.14
Wyoming	30	3.89	3.20

State Individual Income Tax Collections: **D** - Rank, **E** - $ (per capita) / Local Individual Income Tax Collections: **F** - Rank, **G** - $ (per capita)	**Cost of Living Indicators**		
Income Tax Collections	**D**	**E**	**F**	**G**
Alabama	37	580	12	23
Alaska	44	0	14	0
Arizona	41	437	14	0
Arkansas	28	770	14	0
California	6	1,328	14	0
Colorado	21	875	14	0
Connecticut	2	1,802	14	0
Delaware	7	1,284	8	56
District of Columbia	44	0	1	2,073
Florida	44	0	14	0
Georgia	26	772	14	0
Hawaii	19	896	14	0
Idaho	31	733	14	0
Illinois	22	872	14	0
Indiana	32	701	6	248
Iowa	17	928	11	30
Kansas	15	932	13	1
Kentucky	25	780	7	247
Louisiana	39	522	14	0
Maine	12	1,069	14	0
Maryland	10	1,129	2	672
Massachusetts	3	1,745	14	0
Michigan	33	647	10	41
Minnesota	5	1,391	14	0
Mississippi	40	468	14	0
Missouri	30	753	9	50
Montana	23	808	14	0
Nebraska	16	928	14	0
Nevada	44	0	14	0
New Hampshire	42	63	14	0
New Jersey	8	1,198	14	0
New Mexico	38	526	14	0
New York	1	1,850	3	425
North Carolina	13	1,012	14	0
North Dakota	35	619	14	0
Ohio	29	764	4	370
Oklahoma	34	625	14	0
Oregon	4	1,409	14	0
Pennsylvania	27	770	5	321
Rhode Island	14	968	14	0
South Carolina	36	616	14	0
South Dakota	44	0	14	0
Tennessee	43	29	14	0
Texas	44	0	14	0
Utah	24	805	14	0
Vermont	20	888	14	0
Virginia	9	1,164	14	0
Washington	44	0	14	0
West Virginia	18	898	14	0
Wisconsin	11	1,123	14	0
Wyoming	44	0	14	0

State General Sales Tax Collections: **H** - Rank, **I** - $ (per capita) / Local General Sales Tax Collections: **J** - Rank, **K** - $ (per capita)	Cost of Living Indicators		
Sales Tax Collections	**H**	**I**	**J**	**K**
Alabama	43	451	8	373
Alaska	46	0	5	457
Arizona	16	896	9	358
Arkansas	12	928	15	310
California	20	815	18	239
Colorado	45	419	4	588
Connecticut	15	906	35	0
Delaware	46	0	35	0
District of Columbia	46	0	1	1,394
Florida	6	1,002	29	92
Georgia	41	512	10	349
Hawaii	1	1,793	35	0
Idaho	24	744	35	0
Illinois	38	576	26	130
Indiana	9	959	35	0
Iowa	26	726	19	218
Kansas	18	862	17	276
Kentucky	31	661	35	0
Louisiana	35	611	2	813
Maine	22	760	35	0
Maryland	30	662	35	0
Massachusetts	25	740	35	0
Michigan	10	959	35	0
Minnesota	17	866	33	20
Mississippi	7	995	35	0
Missouri	42	494	13	329
Montana	46	0	35	0
Nebraska	23	747	24	165
Nevada	5	1,063	28	111
New Hampshire	46	0	35	0
New Jersey	13	919	35	0
New Mexico	14	907	7	434
New York	36	592	3	635
North Carolina	34	634	20	215
North Dakota	4	1,110	23	181
Ohio	29	673	25	150
Oklahoma	39	571	6	457
Oregon	46	0	35	0
Pennsylvania	28	701	32	50
Rhode Island	21	785	35	0
South Carolina	37	591	30	75
South Dakota	8	970	11	347
Tennessee	11	958	16	303
Texas	19	836	21	209
Utah	33	646	22	209
Vermont	40	520	34	15
Virginia	44	423	27	124
Washington	2	1,534	12	338
West Virginia	32	652	35	0
Wisconsin	27	718	31	57
Wyoming	3	1,497	14	321

State Property Tax Collections: **L** - Rank, **M** - $ (per capita) / Local Property Tax Collections: **N** - Rank, **O** - $ (per capita)	Cost of Living Indicators		
Property Tax Collections	**L**	**M**	**N**	**O**
Alabama	15	66	50	471
Alaska	6	252	9	1,789
Arizona	13	116	35	968
Arkansas	3	326	51	289
California	14	84	21	1,322
Colorado	33	0	13	1,604
Connecticut	33	0	3	2,571
Delaware	33	0	45	726
District of Columbia	33	0	2	2,779
Florida	33	0	19	1,343
Georgia	22	8	30	1,036
Hawaii	33	0	37	951
Idaho	33	0	40	857
Illinois	25	5	8	1,873
Indiana	33	0	36	966
Iowa	33	0	16	1,421
Kansas	19	25	20	1,332
Kentucky	11	118	49	568
Louisiana	20	11	44	757
Maine	16	34	10	1,772
Maryland	10	135	23	1,297
Massachusetts	32	1	7	1,998
Michigan	8	192	25	1,181
Minnesota	9	144	17	1,377
Mississippi	21	8	41	845
Missouri	26	4	34	972
Montana	7	242	28	1,090
Nebraska	33	0	14	1,549
Nevada	12	116	33	975
New Hampshire	4	299	5	2,213
New Jersey	33	0	1	2,878
New Mexico	17	32	47	623
New York	33	0	4	2,321
North Carolina	33	0	39	886
North Dakota	28	3	29	1,040
Ohio	33	0	27	1,140
Oklahoma	33	0	48	583
Oregon	23	6	24	1,291
Pennsylvania	27	4	22	1,298
Rhode Island	30	2	6	2,163
South Carolina	31	2	31	1,015
South Dakota	33	0	26	1,177
Tennessee	33	0	42	790
Texas	33	0	15	1,519
Utah	33	0	38	893
Vermont	1	1,526	46	671
Virginia	24	5	18	1,352
Washington	5	269	32	988
West Virginia	29	3	43	767
Wisconsin	18	26	11	1,690
Wyoming	2	493	12	1,642

State Tax Collections: **P** - Rank, **Q** - $ (per capita) / Local Tax Collections: **R** - Rank, **S** - $ (per capita) / All - **T** - Rank, **U** - $ (per capita)	Cost of Living Indicators				
All Tax Collections	**P**	**Q**	**R**	**S**	**T**	**U**
Alabama	42	1,791	44	1,087	51	2,878
Alaska	1	7,571	5	2,399	1	9,969
Arizona	40	1,872	31	1,433	41	3,305
Arkansas	16	2,697	51	677	39	3,374
California	11	3,068	16	1,801	12	4,869
Colorado	41	1,825	6	2,376	21	4,201
Connecticut	5	3,735	4	2,605	6	6,340
Delaware	6	3,556	49	884	18	4,440
District of Columbia	51	0	1	8,491	2	8,491
Florida	45	1,685	23	1,693	38	3,378
Georgia	50	1,613	29	1,525	46	3,138
Hawaii	8	3,489	38	1,232	14	4,721
Idaho	36	2,044	48	908	49	2,953
Illinois	22	2,377	8	2,248	15	4,625
Indiana	30	2,281	36	1,261	33	3,542
Iowa	24	2,354	20	1,761	23	4,115
Kansas	23	2,355	22	1,718	24	4,074
Kentucky	26	2,328	45	995	40	3,323
Louisiana	38	1,926	24	1,683	32	3,610
Maine	14	2,765	19	1,789	16	4,555
Maryland	15	2,723	10	2,211	11	4,934
Massachusetts	10	3,323	12	2,069	8	5,393
Michigan	21	2,381	34	1,272	30	3,653
Minnesota	7	3,523	30	1,463	10	4,986
Mississippi	32	2,194	47	911	47	3,105
Missouri	46	1,679	27	1,583	42	3,262
Montana	29	2,292	42	1,125	37	3,417
Nebraska	31	2,238	13	1,966	20	4,204
Nevada	28	2,295	32	1,407	29	3,702
New Hampshire	43	1,773	7	2,249	25	4,022
New Jersey	12	3,066	3	2,929	7	5,996
New Mexico	25	2,342	41	1,134	35	3,476
New York	9	3,472	2	3,924	3	7,396
North Carolina	27	2,297	40	1,160	36	3,457
North Dakota	2	5,463	35	1,268	4	6,731
Ohio	33	2,167	21	1,742	27	3,909
Oklahoma	37	2,038	43	1,110	45	3,148
Oregon	35	2,082	28	1,537	31	3,619
Pennsylvania	19	2,535	14	1,835	19	4,370
Rhode Island	18	2,623	9	2,214	13	4,837
South Carolina	49	1,627	33	1,282	50	2,910
South Dakota	48	1,655	26	1,583	43	3,239
Tennessee	44	1,736	39	1,219	48	2,955
Texas	47	1,656	15	1,828	34	3,484
Utah	39	1,918	37	1,254	44	3,172
Vermont	3	4,294	50	722	9	5,016
Virginia	34	2,127	17	1,801	26	3,928
Washington	20	2,524	25	1,595	22	4,119
West Virginia	13	2,808	46	951	28	3,759
Wisconsin	17	2,680	18	1,791	17	4,471
Wyoming	4	4,271	11	2,102	5	6,373

A - Property Tax / **B** - Sales & Gross Receipts **C** - Motor Vehicle & Drivers License / Income Tax: **D** - Individual, **E** - Corporate / **F** - Other Taxes	State Tax Collections				
Total Revenue From: (Rank)	**A**	**B**	**C**	**D**	**E**	**F**
Alabama	12	17	34	28	31	26
Alaska	14	50	50	44	4	1
Arizona	8	9	49	37	26	47
Arkansas	4	23	40	33	28	34
California	15	42	15	6	7	28
Colorado	37	38	7	8	29	42
Connecticut	37	34	47	7	35	39
Delaware	37	49	46	17	6	4
District of Columbia	--	--	--	--	--	--
Florida	36	1	5	44	12	19
Georgia	21	31	38	5	39	50
Hawaii	37	7	13	35	45	46
Idaho	37	20	10	25	15	25
Illinois	26	40	8	11	3	40
Indiana	35	10	14	32	11	48
Iowa	37	27	2	20	19	30
Kansas	19	19	24	18	34	37
Kentucky	9	22	44	27	18	21
Louisiana	20	12	48	36	41	11
Maine	18	26	23	22	10	23
Maryland	10	36	25	15	24	31
Massachusetts	33	44	39	4	5	27
Michigan	7	11	11	34	44	43
Minnesota	11	28	17	19	23	29
Mississippi	22	8	33	40	14	17
Missouri	23	29	30	9	43	44
Montana	6	47	3	24	20	5
Nebraska	34	24	22	14	21	49
Nevada	13	4	28	44	47	8
New Hampshire	2	39	6	42	1	14
New Jersey	32	32	35	16	8	18
New Mexico	16	15	45	38	17	7
New York	37	45	37	3	9	24
North Carolina	37	37	20	10	22	33
North Dakota	31	46	43	41	37	2
Ohio	37	18	18	26	46	13
Oklahoma	37	35	1	30	25	9
Oregon	25	48	4	1	27	20
Pennsylvania	27	16	26	31	16	16
Rhode Island	30	13	41	23	33	41
South Carolina	29	14	36	21	42	35
South Dakota	37	3	9	44	36	10
Tennessee	37	6	32	43	2	15
Texas	37	5	12	44	47	6
Utah	37	25	21	12	32	38
Vermont	1	41	31	39	40	45
Virginia	24	43	27	2	30	32
Washington	5	2	19	44	47	22
West Virginia	28	21	42	29	38	12
Wisconsin	17	33	16	13	13	36
Wyoming	3	30	29	44	47	3

A - Property Tax / **B** - Sales & Gross Receipts **C** - Motor Vehicle & Drivers License / Income Tax: **D** - Individual, **E** - Corporate / **F** - Other Taxes						State Tax Collections	
Total Revenue From: (%)	**G**	**H**	**I**	**J**	**K**	**L**
Alabama	3.5913	51.10	2.47	33.33	4.56	4.94
Alaska	3.0557	3.52	0.83	0.00	9.41	83.19
Arizona	5.8153	62.17	1.36	23.85	4.99	1.81
Arkansas	12.1711	48.06	2.07	28.98	4.88	3.84
California	1.8509	34.37	3.41	48.97	7.07	4.32
Colorado	0	39.91	4.75	47.56	4.80	2.98
Connecticut	0	43.30	1.64	47.80	4.06	3.20
Delaware	0	14.61	1.64	39.03	7.81	36.91
District of Columbia	--	--	--	--	--	--
Florida	0.0004	82.64	5.02	0.00	6.07	6.28
Georgia	0.4159	43.76	2.14	49.12	3.56	1.00
Hawaii	0	64.93	3.75	27.93	1.45	1.94
Idaho	0	49.33	4.13	35.96	5.59	4.99
Illinois	0.1787	39.23	4.73	43.07	9.59	3.20
Indiana	0.0011	58.41	3.45	30.34	6.11	1.69
Iowa	0	45.11	6.75	38.68	5.44	4.02
Kansas	1.0031	49.68	2.78	38.98	4.28	3.28
Kentucky	5.0566	48.07	1.95	33.54	5.49	5.89
Louisiana	0.5663	54.36	1.60	27.51	3.23	12.73
Maine	1.0156	46.30	2.91	38.18	6.15	5.46
Maryland	4.4299	42.04	2.76	41.70	5.16	3.91
Massachusetts	0.0195	32.09	2.08	52.33	8.78	4.70
Michigan	7.4994	54.73	4.06	28.49	2.54	2.68
Minnesota	3.9284	44.45	3.29	38.85	5.18	4.29
Mississippi	0.3449	63.23	2.52	21.59	5.69	6.63
Missouri	0.2705	44.11	2.64	47.51	2.79	2.67
Montana	10.4577	22.15	6.17	36.60	5.38	19.23
Nebraska	0.0018	47.85	2.95	42.18	5.38	1.65
Nevada	3.4615	77.22	2.70	0.00	0.00	16.62
New Hampshire	17.2541	39.66	4.84	3.70	23.63	10.92
New Jersey	0.0206	43.74	2.40	40.53	7.03	6.28
New Mexico	1.1830	52.10	1.89	22.61	5.52	16.69
New York	0	31.96	2.17	54.19	6.38	5.29
North Carolina	0	42.00	3.05	45.72	5.37	3.86
North Dakota	0.0427	28.37	1.97	7.70	3.84	58.09
Ohio	0	50.61	3.07	34.83	0.45	11.04
Oklahoma	0	42.20	7.71	31.43	5.05	13.61
Oregon	0.1806	16.08	5.82	66.97	4.98	5.97
Pennsylvania	0.1167	52.05	2.73	30.66	5.58	8.86
Rhode Island	0.0746	52.57	2.05	37.94	4.36	3.00
South Carolina	0.1096	52.24	2.23	38.53	3.15	3.74
South Dakota	0	78.68	4.50	0.00	3.93	12.88
Tennessee	0	74.80	2.58	1.52	10.23	10.88
Texas	0	77.03	4.04	0.00	0.00	18.93
Utah	0	46.85	2.98	42.45	4.45	3.26
Vermont	34.4078	35.12	2.62	21.70	3.50	2.65
Virginia	0.1891	32.27	2.71	56.33	4.62	3.88
Washington	10.7638	80.41	3.07	0.00	0.00	5.76
West Virginia	0.1128	49.10	2.01	32.78	3.59	12.40
Wisconsin	1.0548	43.36	3.37	42.45	6.03	3.74
Wyoming	12.4161	43.91	2.66	0.00	0.00	41.01

Individual & Biz: **M** - Rank, **N** - $ (per capita) / Individual Only: **O** - Rank, **P** - $ (per capita)				State Tax Collections	
Total Tax Collections	**M**	**N**	**O**	**P**
Alabama	42	1,877	40	1,699
Alaska	1	9,638	50	714
Arizona	39	1,980	38	1,845
Arkansas	17	2,810	12	2,565
California	12	2,954	10	2,617
Colorado	40	1,976	39	1,822
Connecticut	5	4,295	2	4,032
Delaware	8	3,664	30	2,039
District of Columbia	--	--	--	--
Florida	47	1,708	47	1,497
Georgia	49	1,671	43	1,595
Hawaii	6	3,962	3	3,838
Idaho	37	2,115	35	1,891
Illinois	16	2,830	15	2,486
Indiana	28	2,402	24	2,242
Iowa	23	2,548	19	2,333
Kansas	21	2,571	18	2,377
Kentucky	29	2,391	27	2,128
Louisiana	41	1,954	42	1,643
Maine	15	2,842	13	2,546
Maryland	13	2,900	9	2,670
Massachusetts	10	3,431	7	3,013
Michigan	27	2,425	22	2,299
Minnesota	7	3,822	4	3,491
Mississippi	31	2,329	29	2,043
Missouri	46	1,794	41	1,697
Montana	25	2,447	26	2,152
Nebraska	30	2,349	25	2,193
Nevada	24	2,456	21	2,310
New Hampshire	50	1,671	49	1,157
New Jersey	11	3,097	8	2,757
New Mexico	26	2,440	34	1,898
New York	9	3,656	5	3,284
North Carolina	32	2,329	28	2,120
North Dakota	2	8,033	6	3,059
Ohio	34	2,246	33	1,993
Oklahoma	33	2,314	36	1,882
Oregon	35	2,231	32	2,013
Pennsylvania	19	2,582	23	2,272
Rhode Island	18	2,671	14	2,501
South Carolina	48	1,701	44	1,584
South Dakota	45	1,826	45	1,519
Tennessee	44	1,856	48	1,487
Texas	43	1,865	46	1,512
Utah	38	2,035	37	1,878
Vermont	4	4,405	1	4,155
Virginia	36	2,216	31	2,027
Washington	22	2,555	17	2,423
West Virginia	14	2,887	16	2,425
Wisconsin	20	2,575	20	2,324
Wyoming	3	4,426	11	2,611

State Revenue: **A** - Rank, **B** - $ State & Local Revenue: **C** - Rank, **D** - $			State Facts & Numbers	
Revenue - Per Capita	**A**	**B**	**C**	**D**
Alabama	49	5,277	51	8,432
Alaska	01	20,399	01	25,216
Arizona	45	5,803	45	8,961
Arkansas	24	7,726	37	9,440
California	12	8,788	06	13,653
Colorado	46	5,684	28	10,220
Connecticut	17	8,051	14	11,740
Delaware	07	10,195	08	12,214
District of Columbia	02	20,366	02	20,366
Florida	47	5,496	39	9,379
Georgia	50	5,272	50	8,576
Hawaii	09	9,288	17	11,462
Idaho	33	6,565	46	8,834
Illinois	40	6,267	27	10,379
Indiana	43	5,950	48	8,697
Iowa	22	7,836	20	11,236
Kansas	37	6,439	32	9,897
Kentucky	30	7,089	42	9,311
Louisiana	25	7,383	23	10,678
Maine	19	7,983	26	10,522
Maryland	29	7,093	22	10,679
Massachusetts	13	8,521	07	12,344
Michigan	34	6,519	36	9,451
Minnesota	14	8,493	13	11,828
Mississippi	21	7,853	24	10,524
Missouri	38	6,411	35	9,481
Montana	20	7,910	29	10,183
Nebraska	41	6,210	15	11,669
Nevada	39	6,378	38	9,393
New Hampshire	36	6,468	44	9,251
New Jersey	18	7,987	12	11,870
New Mexico	08	9,480	16	11,639
New York	05	10,503	04	16,544
North Carolina	35	6,480	34	9,567
North Dakota	04	11,157	05	13,786
Ohio	15	8,391	18	11,405
Oklahoma	31	6,877	43	9,274
Oregon	11	8,924	11	12,065
Pennsylvania	28	7,121	25	10,523
Rhode Island	10	8,939	09	13,132
South Carolina	32	6,718	33	9,691
South Dakota	27	7,220	30	10,156
Tennessee	48	5,367	40	9,344
Texas	51	5,114	49	8,614
Utah	44	5,949	47	8,821
Vermont	06	10,393	10	12,109
Virginia	42	6,204	41	9,328
Washington	26	7,310	19	11,286
West Virginia	16	8,299	31	10,099
Wisconsin	23	7,825	21	10,948
Wyoming	03	13,003	03	17,710

Personal Income (Per Capita): **E** - Rank, **F** - $ Median Household Income: **G** - Rank, **H** - $ Median House Value: **I** - Rank, **J** - $			State Facts & Numbers		
Income & House	**E**	**F**	**G**	**H**	**I**	**J**
Alabama	43	35,926	48	41,574	44	123,400
Alaska	09	49,436	03	67,712	12	241,400
Arizona	42	36,243	31	47,826	29	158,100
Arkansas	46	35,437	50	40,112	49	106,900
California	13	46,477	12	58,328	03	358,800
Colorado	17	45,775	15	56,765	15	235,000
Connecticut	02	59,687	04	67,276	08	278,600
Delaware	23	44,224	11	58,415	14	235,900
District of Columbia	01	74,773	05	66,583	02	436,000
Florida	28	41,012	41	45,040	30	154,900
Georgia	41	37,449	32	47,209	32	149,300
Hawaii	21	44,767	06	66,259	01	503,100
Idaho	50	34,481	37	45,489	27	160,000
Illinois	16	45,832	17	55,137	22	179,900
Indiana	39	38,119	33	46,974	45	122,600
Iowa	24	43,935	24	50,957	43	124,300
Kansas	25	43,015	27	50,241	40	128,500
Kentucky	45	35,643	47	41,724	46	120,800
Louisiana	31	40,057	44	42,944	33	138,800
Maine	30	40,087	36	46,709	23	173,900
Maryland	06	53,816	01	71,122	06	289,300
Massachusetts	03	55,976	07	65,339	04	328,300
Michigan	37	38,291	34	46,859	47	119,200
Minnesota	12	46,925	10	58,906	19	185,800
Mississippi	51	33,657	51	37,095	50	100,000
Missouri	34	39,133	38	45,321	35	137,100
Montana	36	38,555	40	45,076	20	183,600
Nebraska	20	45,012	26	50,723	42	127,800
Nevada	38	38,221	28	49,760	26	161,300
New Hampshire	10	49,129	08	63,280	13	239,100
New Jersey	04	54,987	02	69,667	05	325,800
New Mexico	44	35,682	46	42,558	28	159,300
New York	07	53,241	16	56,448	07	286,700
North Carolina	40	37,910	39	45,150	31	152,800
North Dakota	05	54,871	20	53,585	39	130,500
Ohio	32	40,057	35	46,829	38	130,600
Oklahoma	29	40,620	42	44,312	48	112,900
Oregon	33	39,166	29	49,161	16	233,900
Pennsylvania	19	45,083	22	51,230	25	164,700
Rhode Island	15	45,877	19	54,554	10	245,300
South Carolina	49	35,056	43	43,107	36	136,300
South Dakota	18	45,381	30	48,362	37	131,600
Tennessee	35	38,752	45	42,764	34	138,400
Texas	26	42,638	25	50,740	41	128,400
Utah	47	35,430	14	57,049	18	209,000
Vermont	22	44,545	21	52,977	17	215,700
Virginia	11	48,377	09	61,741	11	243,100
Washington	14	46,045	13	57,573	09	256,500
West Virginia	48	35,082	49	40,196	51	98,300
Wisconsin	27	42,121	23	51,059	24	167,200
Wyoming	08	50,567	18	54,901	21	183,200

Total Area - Square Miles: **K** - Rank, **L** - Count Land Area - Square Miles: **M** - Rank, **N** - Count Water Area - Square Miles: **O** - Rank, **P** - Count						**State Facts & Numbers**
Land & Water Area	**K**	**L**	**M**	**N**	**O**	**P**
Alabama	30	52,420	28	50,645	23	1,775
Alaska	01	665,384	01	570,641	01	94,743
Arizona	06	113,990	06	113,594	48	396
Arkansas	29	53,179	27	52,035	31	1,143
California	03	163,695	03	155,779	06	7,916
Colorado	08	104,094	08	103,642	44	452
Connecticut	48	5,543	48	4,842	38	701
Delaware	49	2,489	49	1,949	40	540
District of Columbia	51	68	51	61	51	7
Florida	22	65,758	26	53,625	03	12,133
Georgia	24	59,425	21	57,513	22	1,912
Hawaii	43	10,932	47	6,423	13	4,509
Idaho	14	83,569	11	82,643	33	926
Illinois	25	57,914	24	55,519	19	2,395
Indiana	38	36,420	38	35,826	39	593
Iowa	26	56,273	23	55,857	45	416
Kansas	15	82,278	13	81,759	42	520
Kentucky	37	40,408	37	39,486	24	921
Louisiana	31	52,378	33	43,204	05	9,174
Maine	39	35,380	39	30,843	12	4,537
Maryland	42	12,406	42	9,707	18	2,699
Massachusetts	44	10,554	45	7,800	16	2,754
Michigan	11	96,714	22	56,539	02	40,175
Minnesota	12	86,936	14	79,627	09	7,309
Mississippi	32	48,432	31	46,923	25	1,509
Missouri	21	69,707	18	68,742	32	965
Montana	04	147,040	04	145,546	26	1,494
Nebraska	16	77,348	15	76,824	41	524
Nevada	07	110,572	07	109,781	36	791
New Hampshire	46	9,349	44	8,953	47	397
New Jersey	47	8,723	46	7,354	27	1,368
New Mexico	05	121,590	05	121,298	49	292
New York	27	54,555	30	47,126	07	7,429
North Carolina	28	53,819	29	48,618	10	5,201
North Dakota	19	70,698	17	69,001	24	1,698
Ohio	34	44,826	35	40,861	14	3,965
Oklahoma	20	69,899	19	68,595	30	1,304
Oregon	09	98,379	10	95,988	20	2,391
Pennsylvania	33	46,054	32	44,743	28	1,312
Rhode Island	50	1,545	50	1,034	45	511
South Carolina	40	32,020	40	30,061	21	1,960
South Dakota	17	77,116	16	75,811	29	1,305
Tennessee	36	42,144	34	41,235	35	909
Texas	02	268,596	02	261,232	08	7,365
Utah	13	84,987	12	82,170	17	2,727
Vermont	45	9,616	43	9,217	46	400
Virginia	35	42,775	36	39,490	15	3,285
Washington	18	71,298	20	66,456	11	4,842
West Virginia	41	24,230	41	24,038	50	192
Wisconsin	23	65,496	25	54,158	04	11,399
Wyoming	10	97,813	09	97,093	37	720

Q - Number of Counties **R** - Name for Residents **S** - Capital City			**State Facts & Numbers**
People & Places	**Q**	**R**	**S**
Alabama	67	Alabamans	Montgomery
Alaska	27	Alaskans	Juneau
Arizona	15	Arizonans	Phoenix
Arkansas	75	Arkansans	Little Rock
California	58	Californians	Sacramento
Colorado	64	Coloradans	Denver
Connecticut	8	Connecticuters	Hartford
Delaware	3	Delawareans	Dover
District of Columbia	0	Washingtonians	Washington D.C.
Florida	67	Floridians	Tallahassee
Georgia	159	Georgians	Atlanta
Hawaii	5	Hawaiians	Honolulu
Idaho	44	Idahoans	Boise
Illinois	102	Illinoisan	Springfield
Indiana	92	Indianians	Indianapolis
Iowa	99	Iowans	Des Moines
Kansas	105	Kansans	Topeka
Kentucky	120	Kentuckians	Frankfort
Louisiana	64	Louisianans	Baton Rouge
Maine	16	Mainers	Augusta
Maryland	23	Marylanders	Annapolis
Massachusetts	14	Massachusettsans	Boston
Michigan	83	Michiganders	Lansing
Minnesota	87	Minnesotans	St. Paul
Mississippi	82	Mississippians	Jackson
Missouri	114	Missourians	Jefferson City
Montana	56	Montanans	Helena
Nebraska	93	Nebraskans	Lincoln
Nevada	16	Nevadans	Carson City
New Hampshire	10	New Hampshirites	Concord
New Jersey	21	New Jerseyites	Trenton
New Mexico	33	New Mexicans	Santa Fe
New York	62	New Yorkers	Albany
North Carolina	100	North Carolinians	Raleigh
North Dakota	53	North Dakotans	Bismarck
Ohio	88	Ohioans	Columbus
Oklahoma	77	Oklahomans	Oklahoma City
Oregon	36	Oregonians	Salem
Pennsylvania	66	Pennsylvanians	Harrisburg
Rhode Island	5	Rhode Islanders	Providence
South Carolina	46	South Carolinians	Columbia
South Dakota	64	South Dakotans	Pierre
Tennessee	95	Tennesseans	Nashville
Texas	254	Texans	Austin
Utah	29	Utahans	Salt Lake City
Vermont	14	Vermonters	Montpelier
Virginia	95	Virginians	Richmond
Washington	39	Washingtonians	Olympia
West Virginia	55	West Virginians	Charleston
Wisconsin	72	Wisconsinites	Madison
Wyoming	23	Wyomingites	Cheyenne

T - Nickname U - State Motto	**State Facts & Numbers**	
Nickname & Motto	**T**	**U**
Alabama	Heart of Dixie	We Dare Defend Our Rights
Alaska	The Last Frontier	North To The Future
Arizona	Grand Canyon State	God Enriches
Arkansas	The Natural State	The People Rule
California	The Golden State	Eureka (I have found it)
Colorado	Centennial State	Nothing Without Providence
Connecticut	Constitution State	He Who Transplanted Still Sustains
Delaware	First State / Diamond State	Liberty and Independence
District of Columbia	D.C.	Justice For All
Florida	The Sunshine State	In God We Trust
Georgia	Empire State of the South / Peach State	Wisdom, Justice, and Moderation
Hawaii	Aloha State	The Life Of The Land Is Perpetuated In Righteouness
Idaho	Gem State	It Is Perpetual
Illinois	Land of Lincoln	State Sovereignty, National Union
Indiana	Hoosier State	The Crossroads of America
Iowa	Hawkeye State	Our Liberties We Prize And Our Rights We Will Maintain
Kansas	Sunflower State	To The Stars Through Difficulties
Kentucky	Bluegrass State	United We Stand, Divided We Fall
Louisiana	Sportsman's Paradise	Union, Justice, and Confidence
Maine	Pine Tree State	I Direct
Maryland	Old Line State / Free State	Manly Deeds, Womanly Words
Massachusetts	Bay State / Old Colony State	By the Sword We Seek Peace, But Peace Only Under Liberty
Michigan	Great Lakes State	If You Are Seeking A Pleasant Peninsula, Look About You
Minnesota	North Star State	The Star Of The North
Mississippi	Magnolia State	By Valor And Arms
Missouri	Show Me State	The Welfare Of The People Shall Be The Supreme Law
Montana	Big Sky Country	Gold and Silver
Nebraska	Cornhusker State	Equality Before The Law
Nevada	The Silver State	All For Our Country
New Hampshire	Granite State	Live Free Or Die
New Jersey	Garden State	Liberty And Prosperity
New Mexico	Land Of Enchantment	It Grows As It Goes
New York	The Empire State	Ever Upward
North Carolina	Tar Heel State	To Be Rather Than To Seem
North Dakota	Peace Garden State	Liberty and Union, Now and Forever, One and Inseparable
Ohio	Buckeye State	With God, All Things Are Possible
Oklahoma	Sooner State	Labor Conquers All Things
Oregon	Beaver State	She Flies With Her Own Wings
Pennsylvania	Keystone State	Virtue, Liberty, and Independence
Rhode Island	The Ocean State	Hope
South Carolina	Palmetto State	Prepared In Mind And Resources
South Dakota	Mt. Rushmore State	Under God The People Rule
Tennessee	The Volunteer State	Agriculture and Commerce
Texas	The Lone Star State	Friendship
Utah	Beehive State	Industry
Vermont	Green Mountain State	Freedom and Unity
Virginia	Old Dominion	Thus Always To Tyrants
Washington	The Evergreen State	By and By
West Virginia	Mountain State	Mountaineers Are Always Free
Wisconsin	Badger State	Forward
Wyoming	Equality State / Cowboy State	Equal Rights

Bird, Flower & Tree	V	W	X
V - State Bird **W** - State Flower **X** - State Tree		**State Facts & Numbers**	
Alabama	Yellowhammer	Camellia	Southern Longleaf Pine
Alaska	Willow Ptarmigan	Forget-Me-Not	Sitka Spruce
Arizona	Cactus Wren	Saguaro Cactus Blossom	Palo Verde
Arkansas	Mockingbird	Apple Blossom	Pine Tree
California	California Valley Quail	California Poppy	California Redwood
Colorado	Lark Bunting	Rocky Mountain Columbine	Colorado Blue Spruce
Connecticut	American Robin	Mountain Laurel	White Oak
Delaware	Blue Hen Chicken	Peach Blossom	American Holly
District of Columbia	Wood Thrush	American Beauty Rose	Scarlet Oak
Florida	Mockingbird	Orange Blossom	Palmetto Palm
Georgia	Brown Thrasher	Cherokee Rose	Live Oak
Hawaii	Hawaiian Goose	Pua Aloalo (Hibiscus)	Kukui (Candlenut)
Idaho	Mountain Bluebird	Syringa	Western White Pine
Illinois	Cardinal	Native Violet	White Oak
Indiana	Cardinal	Peony	Tulip Tree
Iowa	Eastern Goldfinch	Wild Prairie Rose	Oak
Kansas	Western Meadowlark	Sunflower	Cottonwood
Kentucky	Cardinal	Goldenrod	Tulip Poplar
Louisiana	Eastern Brown Pelican	Magnolia Blossom	Bald Cypress
Maine	Black-Capped Chickadee	White Pine Cone and Tassel	Eastern White Pine
Maryland	Baltimore Oriole	Black-Eyed Susan	White Oak
Massachusetts	Black-Capped Chickadee	Mayflower	American Elm
Michigan	Robin	Apple Blossom	White Pine
Minnesota	Common Loon	Pink and White Lady's-Slipper	Red Pine
Mississippi	Mockingbird	Magnolia	Magnolia
Missouri	Bluebird	White Hawthorn	Flowering Dogwood
Montana	Western Meadowlark	Bitterroot	Ponderosa Pine
Nebraska	Western Meadowlark	Goldenrod	Cottonwood
Nevada	Mountain Bluebird	Sagebrush	Single Leaf Piñon and Bristlecone Pine
New Hampshire	Purple Finch	Purple Lilac	White Birch
New Jersey	Eastern Goldfinch	Purple Violet	Northern Red Oak
New Mexico	Roadrunner	Yucca Flower	Piñon
New York	Eastern Bluebird	Rose	Sugar Maple
North Carolina	Cardinal	Flowering Dogwood	Longleaf Pine
North Dakota	Western Meadowlark	Wild Prairie Rose	American Elm
Ohio	Cardinal	Scarlet Carnation	Buckeye
Oklahoma	Scissor-Tailed Flycatcher	Oklahoma Rose	Redbud
Oregon	Western Meadowlark	Oregon Grape	Douglas Fir
Pennsylvania	Ruffed Grouse	Mountain Laurel	Eastern Hemlock
Rhode Island	Rhode Island Red	Violet	Red Maple
South Carolina	Great Carolina Wren	Yellow Jessamine	Cabbage Palmetto
South Dakota	Ring-Necked Pheasant	American Pasqueflower	Black Hills Spruce
Tennessee	Mockingbird	Iris	Tulip Poplar
Texas	Mockingbird	Bluebonnet	Pecan
Utah	California Seagull	Sego Lily	Blue Spruce
Vermont	Hermit Thrush	Red Clover	Sugar Maple
Virginia	Cardinal	American Dogwood	American Dogwood
Washington	Willow Goldfinch	Coast Rhododendron	Western Hemlock
West Virginia	Cardinal	Big Rhododendron	Sugar Maple
Wisconsin	Robin	Wood Violet	Sugar Maple
Wyoming	Western Meadowlark	Indian Paintbrush	Plains Cottonwood

Y - State Song	**State Facts & Numbers**
State Song	**Y**
Alabama	Alabama
Alaska	Alaska's Flag
Arizona	Arizona March Song
Arkansas	Arkansas / Oh, Arkansas
California	I Love You, California
Colorado	Where The Columbines Grow
Connecticut	Yankee Doodle
Delaware	Our Delaware
District of Columbia	The Star-Spangled Banner
Florida	Swanee River
Georgia	Georgia On My Mind
Hawaii	Hawaii Ponoi (Hawaii's Own)
Idaho	Here We Have Idaho
Illinois	Illinois
Indiana	On The Banks Of The Wabash, Far Away
Iowa	The Song of Iowa
Kansas	Home On The Range
Kentucky	My Old Kentucky Home / Blue Moon of Kentucky
Louisiana	Give Me Louisiana
Maine	State Song of Maine
Maryland	Maryland, My Maryland
Massachusetts	All Hail To Massachusetts
Michigan	Michigan, My Michigan
Minnesota	Hail! Minnesota
Mississippi	Go Mis-sis-sip-pi
Missouri	Missouri Waltz
Montana	Montana
Nebraska	Beautiful Nebraska
Nevada	Home Means Nevada
New Hampshire	Old New Hampshire
New Jersey	None
New Mexico	O, Fair New Mexico
New York	I Love New York
North Carolina	The Old North Song
North Dakota	North Dakota Hymn
Ohio	Beautiful Ohio
Oklahoma	Oklahoma!
Oregon	Oregon, My Oregon
Pennsylvania	Pennsylvania
Rhode Island	Rhode Island, It's For Me
South Carolina	Carolina
South Dakota	Hail, South Dakota
Tennessee	The Tennessee Waltz
Texas	Texas, Our Texas
Utah	Utah, We Love Thee
Vermont	These Green Mountains
Virginia	Carry Me Back To Old Virginia
Washington	Washington, My Home
West Virginia	West Virginia, My Home Sweet Home
Wisconsin	On, Wisconsin!
Wyoming	Wyoming

Population: **A** - Count, **B** - Rank Population - Per Square Mile: **C** - Count, **D** - Rank	**Population**			
Population #'s	**A**	**B**	**C**	**D**
Alabama	4,822,023	23	92	26
Alaska	731,449	47	1	51
Arizona	6,553,255	15	57	34
Arkansas	2,949,131	32	55	35
California	38,041,430	1	232	12
Colorado	5,187,582	22	50	38
Connecticut	3,590,347	29	648	4
Delaware	917,092	45	368	7
District of Columbia	632,323	49	9,299	1
Florida	19,317,568	4	294	9
Georgia	9,919,945	8	167	17
Hawaii	1,392,313	40	127	21
Idaho	1,595,728	39	19	45
Illinois	12,875,255	5	222	13
Indiana	6,537,334	16	179	16
Iowa	3,074,186	30	55	36
Kansas	2,885,905	33	35	41
Kentucky	4,380,415	26	108	22
Louisiana	4,601,893	25	89	27
Maine	1,329,192	41	38	40
Maryland	5,884,563	19	474	6
Massachusetts	6,646,144	14	630	5
Michigan	9,883,360	9	102	23
Minnesota	5,379,139	21	62	32
Mississippi	2,984,926	31	62	33
Missouri	6,021,988	18	86	29
Montana	1,005,141	44	7	49
Nebraska	1,855,525	37	24	44
Nevada	2,758,931	35	25	43
New Hampshire	1,320,718	42	141	20
New Jersey	8,864,590	11	1,016	2
New Mexico	2,085,538	36	17	46
New York	19,570,261	3	359	8
North Carolina	9,752,073	10	181	15
North Dakota	699,628	48	10	48
Ohio	11,544,225	7	258	11
Oklahoma	3,814,820	28	55	37
Oregon	3,899,353	27	40	39
Pennsylvania	12,763,536	6	277	10
Rhode Island	1,050,292	43	680	3
South Carolina	4,723,723	24	148	19
South Dakota	833,354	46	11	47
Tennessee	6,456,243	17	153	18
Texas	26,059,203	2	97	24
Utah	2,855,287	34	34	42
Vermont	626,011	50	65	31
Virginia	8,185,867	12	191	14
Washington	6,897,012	13	97	25
West Virginia	1,855,413	38	77	30
Wisconsin	5,726,398	20	87	28
Wyoming	576,412	51	6	50

Male Population: **E** - Rank, **F** - % Female Population: **G** - Rank, **H** - %	**Population**			
Males & Females	**E**	**F**	**G**	**H**
Alabama	45	48.54	7	51.46
Alaska	1	52.04	51	47.96
Arizona	13	49.68	39	50.32
Arkansas	28	49.10	24	50.90
California	12	49.71	40	50.29
Colorado	7	50.12	45	49.88
Connecticut	42	48.67	10	51.33
Delaware	46	48.44	6	51.56
District of Columbia	51	47.23	1	52.77
Florida	35	48.88	17	51.12
Georgia	37	48.82	15	51.18
Hawaii	9	50.08	43	49.92
Idaho	8	50.10	44	49.90
Illinois	31	49.04	21	50.96
Indiana	27	49.20	25	50.80
Iowa	19	49.51	33	50.49
Kansas	17	49.61	35	50.39
Kentucky	26	49.20	26	50.80
Louisiana	33	48.95	19	51.05
Maine	34	48.94	18	51.06
Maryland	49	48.35	3	51.65
Massachusetts	48	48.36	4	51.64
Michigan	30	49.05	22	50.95
Minnesota	15	49.63	37	50.37
Mississippi	44	48.57	8	51.43
Missouri	32	48.98	20	51.02
Montana	6	50.20	46	49.80
Nebraska	16	49.62	36	50.38
Nevada	4	50.49	48	49.51
New Hampshire	23	49.33	29	50.67
New Jersey	41	48.68	11	51.32
New Mexico	22	49.41	30	50.59
New York	47	48.39	5	51.61
North Carolina	40	48.72	12	51.28
North Dakota	3	50.53	49	49.47
Ohio	36	48.82	16	51.18
Oklahoma	20	49.50	32	50.50
Oregon	21	49.49	31	50.51
Pennsylvania	39	48.73	13	51.27
Rhode Island	50	48.30	2	51.70
South Carolina	43	48.65	9	51.35
South Dakota	10	50.04	42	49.96
Tennessee	38	48.75	14	51.25
Texas	18	49.60	34	50.40
Utah	5	50.23	47	49.77
Vermont	25	49.25	27	50.75
Virginia	29	49.07	23	50.93
Washington	11	49.81	41	50.19
West Virginia	24	49.30	28	50.70
Wisconsin	14	49.63	38	50.37
Wyoming	2	51.00	50	49.00

I - Sex Ratio / **J** - Population Median Age Population By Age: **K** - Under 18, **L** - 18-44, **M** - 45-64, **N** - 65 +	**Population**				
Sex Ratio & Age	**I**	**J**	**K**	**L**	**M**	**N**
Alabama	94.3	37.9	23.7	35.7	26.8	13.8
Alaska	108.5	33.8	26.4	38.2	27.7	7.7
Arizona	98.7	35.9	25.5	36.2	24.5	13.8
Arkansas	96.5	37.4	24.4	35.2	26.0	14.4
California	98.8	35.2	25.0	38.7	24.9	11.4
Colorado	100.5	36.1	24.4	38.1	26.7	10.8
Connecticut	94.8	40.0	22.9	34.5	28.5	14.1
Delaware	93.9	38.8	22.9	35.5	27.2	14.4
District of Columbia	89.5	33.8	16.8	48.6	23.2	11.4
Florida	95.6	40.7	21.3	34.4	27.0	17.3
Georgia	95.4	35.3	25.7	38.2	25.4	10.7
Hawaii	100.3	38.6	22.3	36.2	27.2	14.3
Idaho	100.4	34.6	27.4	35.4	24.8	12.4
Illinois	96.2	36.6	24.4	37.0	26.1	12.5
Indiana	96.8	37.0	24.8	35.8	26.5	12.9
Iowa	98.1	38.1	23.9	34.6	26.7	14.8
Kansas	98.4	36.0	25.5	35.5	25.8	13.2
Kentucky	96.8	38.1	23.6	35.9	27.2	13.3
Louisiana	95.9	35.8	24.7	36.8	26.2	12.3
Maine	95.8	42.7	20.7	32.5	30.9	15.9
Maryland	93.6	38.0	23.4	36.6	27.7	12.3
Massachusetts	93.7	39.1	21.7	36.8	27.7	13.8
Michigan	96.3	38.9	23.7	34.6	27.9	13.8
Minnesota	98.5	37.4	24.2	35.8	27.1	12.9
Mississippi	94.4	36.0	25.5	36.0	25.8	12.7
Missouri	96.0	37.9	23.8	35.3	26.9	14.0
Montana	100.8	39.8	22.6	33.4	29.2	14.8
Nebraska	98.5	36.2	25.1	35.5	25.8	13.6
Nevada	102.0	36.3	24.6	37.7	25.6	12.1
New Hampshire	97.3	41.1	21.8	33.9	30.7	13.6
New Jersey	94.8	39.0	23.5	35.4	27.6	13.5
New Mexico	97.7	36.7	25.2	34.9	26.7	13.2
New York	93.8	38.0	22.3	37.4	26.7	13.6
North Carolina	95.0	37.4	23.9	36.8	26.3	13.0
North Dakota	102.1	37.0	22.3	36.7	26.5	14.5
Ohio	95.4	38.8	23.7	34.6	27.7	14.0
Oklahoma	98.0	36.2	24.8	36.0	25.8	13.4
Oregon	98.0	38.4	22.6	36.1	27.4	13.9
Pennsylvania	95.1	40.1	22.0	34.5	28.0	15.5
Rhode Island	93.4	39.4	21.3	36.5	27.8	14.4
South Carolina	94.7	37.9	23.4	36.1	26.9	13.6
South Dakota	100.1	36.9	24.9	34.4	26.4	14.3
Tennessee	95.1	38.0	23.6	36.0	27.0	13.4
Texas	98.4	33.6	27.3	38.4	24.0	10.3
Utah	100.9	29.2	31.5	39.7	19.8	9.0
Vermont	97.1	41.5	20.7	34.0	30.8	14.5
Virginia	96.3	37.5	23.2	37.5	27.1	12.2
Washington	99.3	37.3	23.5	37.1	27.1	12.3
West Virginia	97.3	41.3	20.9	33.8	29.2	16.1
Wisconsin	98.5	38.5	23.6	35.1	27.7	13.6
Wyoming	104.1	36.8	24.0	35.7	27.9	12.4

Made in the USA
San Bernardino, CA
10 August 2017